NON SANZ DROICT.

THE
Tragedie of King Richard the second.

*As it hath beene publikely acted
by the right Honourable the
Lorde Chamberlaine his Ser-
uants.*

LONDON
Printed by Valentine Simmes for Androw Wise, and
are to be sold at his shop in Paules church yard at
the signe of the Angel.
1597.

Title page of the earliest printed version (1597) of *Richard II*

William Shakespeare

The Tragedy of
King Richard the Second

With New and Updated
Critical Essays
and a Revised Bibliography

Edited by Kenneth Muir

THE SIGNET CLASSIC SHAKESPEARE
General Editor: Sylvan Barnet

$\mathcal{C}$

A SIGNET CLASSIC

SIGNET CLASSIC
Published by the Penguin Group
Penguin Putnam Inc., 375 Hudson Street, New York, New York 10014, U.S.A.
Penguin Books Ltd, 27 Wrights Lane, London W8 5TZ, England
Penguin Books Australia Ltd, Ringwood, Victoria, Australia
Penguin Books Canada Ltd, 10 Alcorn Avenue, Toronto, Ontario, Canada M4V 3B2
Penguin Books (N.Z.) Ltd, 182–190 Wairau Road, Auckland 10, New Zealand

Penguin Books Ltd, Registered Offices:
Harmondsworth, Middlesex, England

Published by Signet Classic, an imprint of Dutton NAL, a member of Penguin Putnam Inc.
The Signet Classic Edition of *The Tragedy of King Richard the Second* was first published
in 1963, and an updated edition was published in 1988.

First Signet Classic Printing (Second Revised Edition), January, 1999
10 9 8 7 6 5 4 3 2 1

 REGISTERED TRADEMARK—MARCA REGISTRADA

Library of Congress Catalog Card Number: 98–19257

Printed in the United States of America

BOOKS ARE AVAILABLE AT QUANTITY DISCOUNTS WHEN USED TO PROMOTE PRODUCTS OR
SERVICES. FOR INFORMATION PLEASE WRITE TO PREMIUM MARKETING DIVISION, PENGUIN
PUTNAM INC., 375 HUDSON STREET, NEW YORK, NEW YORK 10014.

Contents

Shakespeare: An Overview vii
  Biographical Sketch vii / *A Note on the Anti-Stratfordians, Especially Baconians and Oxfordians* xi / The Shakespeare Canon xv / Shakespeare's English xviii / Shakespeare's Theater xxvi / *A Note on the Use of Boy Actors in Female Roles* xxxiii / Shakespeare's Dramatic Language: Costumes, Gestures and Silences; Prose and Poetry xxxvi / The Play Text as a Collaboration xliii / Editing Texts xlix / Shakespeare on the Stage liv

Introduction lxiii
The Tragedy of King Richard the Second 1
Textual Note 110
The Sources of *Richard II* 113
  RAPHAEL HOLINSHED *From* Chronicles of England, Scotland, and Ireland 119

Commentaries
  WALTER PATER Shakespeare's English Kings 151
  RICHARD D. ALTICK Symphonic Imagery in *Richard II* 159
  DEREK TRAVERSI *From* Shakespeare from *Richard II* to *Henry V* 193
  S. SCHOENBAUM *Richard II* and the Realities of Power 206
  GRAHAM HOLDERNESS The Women 219
  KENNETH MUIR *Richard II* on Stage and Screen 232
Suggested References 243

Shakespeare: An Overview

Biographical Sketch

Between the record of his baptism in Stratford on 26 April 1564 and the record of his burial in Stratford on 25 April 1616, some forty official documents name Shakespeare, and many others name his parents, his children, and his grandchildren. Further, there are at least fifty literary references to him in the works of his contemporaries. More facts are known about William Shakespeare than about any other playwright of the period except Ben Jonson. The facts should, however, be distinguished from the legends. The latter, inevitably more engaging and better known, tell us that the Stratford boy killed a calf in high style, poached deer and rabbits, and was forced to flee to London, where he held horses outside a playhouse. These traditions are only traditions; they may be true, but no evidence supports them, and it is well to stick to the facts.

Mary Arden, the dramatist's mother, was the daughter of a substantial landowner; about 1557 she married John Shakespeare, a tanner, glove-maker, and trader in wool, grain, and other farm commodities. In 1557 John Shakespeare was a member of the council (the governing body of Stratford), in 1558 a constable of the borough, in 1561 one of the two town chamberlains, in 1565 an alderman (entitling him to the appellation of "Mr."), in 1568 high bailiff— the town's highest political office, equivalent to mayor. After 1577, for an unknown reason he drops out of local politics. What *is* known is that he had to mortgage his wife's property, and that he was involved in serious litigation.

The birthday of William Shakespeare, the third child and the eldest son of this locally prominent man, is unrecorded, but the Stratford parish register records that the infant was baptized on 26 April 1564. (It is quite possible that he was born on 23 April, but this date has probably been assigned by tradition because it is the date on which, fifty-two years later, he died, and perhaps because it is the feast day of St. George, patron saint of England.) The attendance records of the Stratford grammar school of the period are not extant, but it is reasonable to assume that the son of a prominent local official attended the free school—it had been established for the purpose of educating males precisely of his class—and received substantial training in Latin. The masters of the school from Shakespeare's seventh to fifteenth years held Oxford degrees; the Elizabethan curriculum excluded mathematics and the natural sciences but taught a good deal of Latin rhetoric, logic, and literature, including plays by Plautus, Terence, and Seneca.

On 27 November 1582 a marriage license was issued for the marriage of Shakespeare and Anne Hathaway, eight years his senior. The couple had a daughter, Susanna, in May 1583. Perhaps the marriage was necessary, but perhaps the couple had earlier engaged, in the presence of witnesses, in a formal "troth plight" which would render their children legitimate even if no further ceremony were performed. In February 1585, Anne Hathaway bore Shakespeare twins, Hamnet and Judith.

That Shakespeare was born is excellent; that he married and had children is pleasant; but that we know nothing about his departure from Stratford to London or about the beginning of his theatrical career is lamentable and must be admitted. We would gladly sacrifice details about his children's baptism for details about his earliest days in the theater. Perhaps the poaching episode is true (but it is first reported almost a century after Shakespeare's death), or perhaps he left Stratford to be a schoolmaster, as another tradition holds; perhaps he was moved (like Petruchio in *The Taming of the Shrew*) by

> Such wind as scatters young men through the world,
> To seek their fortunes farther than at home
> Where small experience grows.   (1.2.49–51)

In 1592, thanks to the cantankerousness of Robert Greene, we have our first reference, a snarling one, to Shakespeare as an actor and playwright. Greene, a graduate of St. John's College, Cambridge, had become a playwright and a pamphleteer in London, and in one of his pamphlets he warns three university-educated playwrights against an actor who has presumed to turn playwright:

> There is an upstart crow, beautified with our feathers, that with his *tiger's heart wrapped in a player's hide* supposes he is as well able to bombast out a blank verse as the best of you, and being an absolute Johannes-factotum [i.e., jack-of-all-trades] is in his own conceit the only Shake-scene in a country.

The reference to the player, as well as the allusion to Aesop's crow (who strutted in borrowed plumage, as an actor struts in fine words not his own), makes it clear that by this date Shakespeare had both acted and written. That Shakespeare is meant is indicated not only by *Shake-scene* but also by the parody of a line from one of Shakespeare's plays, *3 Henry VI*: "O, tiger's heart wrapped in a woman's hide" (1.4.137). If in 1592 Shakespeare was prominent enough to be attacked by an envious dramatist, he probably had served an apprenticeship in the theater for at least a few years.

In any case, although there are no extant references to Shakespeare between the record of the baptism of his twins in 1585 and Greene's hostile comment about "Shake-scene" in 1592, it is evident that during some of these "dark years" or "lost years" Shakespeare had acted and written. There are a number of subsequent references to him as an actor. Documents indicate that in 1598 he is a "principal comedian," in 1603 a "principal tragedian," in 1608 he is one of the "men players." (We do not have, however, any solid information about which roles he may have played; later traditions say he played Adam in *As You Like It* and the ghost in *Hamlet*, but nothing supports the assertions. Probably his role as dramatist came to supersede his role as actor.) The profession of actor was not for a gentleman, and it occasionally drew the scorn of university men like Greene who resented writing speeches for persons less educated than themselves, but it was respectable enough; players, if prosperous, were in effect members of the bourgeoisie, and there is nothing to suggest that Stratford considered William Shakespeare less than a solid citizen. When, in 1596, the Shakespeares were granted a coat of arms—i.e., the right to be considered gentlemen—the grant was made to Shakespeare's father, but probably William Shakespeare had arranged the matter on his own behalf. In subsequent transactions he is occasionally styled a gentleman.

Although in 1593 and 1594 Shakespeare published two narrative poems dedicated to the Earl of Southampton, *Venus and Adonis* and *The Rape of Lucrece*, and may well have written most or all of his sonnets in the middle nineties, Shakespeare's literary activity seems to have been almost entirely devoted to the theater. (It may be significant that the two narrative poems were written in years when the plague closed the theaters for several months.) In 1594 he was a charter member of a theatrical company called the Chamberlain's Men, which in 1603 became the royal company, the King's Men, making Shakespeare the king's playwright. Until he retired to Stratford (about 1611, apparently), he was with this remarkably stable company. From 1599 the company acted primarily at the Globe theater, in which Shakespeare held a one-tenth interest. Other Elizabethan dramatists are known to have acted, but no other is known also to have been entitled to a share of the profits.

Shakespeare's first eight published plays did not have his name on them, but this is not remarkable; the most popular play of the period, Thomas Kyd's *The Spanish Tragedy*, went through many editions without naming Kyd, and Kyd's authorship is known only because a book on the profession of acting happens to quote (and attribute to Kyd) some lines on the interest of Roman emperors in the drama. What is remarkable is that after 1598 Shakespeare's name commonly appears on printed plays—some of which are not his. Presumably his name was a drawing card, and publishers used it to attract potential buyers. Another indication of his popularity comes from Francis Meres, author of *Palladis Tamia: Wit's Treasury* (1598). In this anthology of snippets accompanied by an essay on literature, many playwrights are mentioned, but Shakespeare's name occurs

more often than any other, and Shakespeare is the only playwright whose plays are listed.

From his acting, his play writing, and his share in a
playhouse, Shakespeare seems to have made considerable
money. He put it to work, making substantial investments in
Stratford real estate. As early as 1597 he bought New Place,
the second-largest house in Stratford. His family moved in
soon afterward, and the house remained in the family until a
granddaughter died in 1670. When Shakespeare made his
will in 1616, less than a month before he died, he sought
to leave his property intact to his descendants. Of small
bequests to relatives and to friends (including three actors,
Richard Burbage, John Heminges, and Henry Condell), that
to his wife of the second-best bed has provoked the most
comment. It has sometimes been taken as a sign of an
unhappy marriage (other supposed signs are the apparently hasty marriage, his wife's seniority of eight years, and
his residence in London without his family). Perhaps the
second-best bed was the bed the couple had slept in, the best
bed being reserved for visitors. In any case, had Shakespeare
not excepted it, the bed would have gone (with the rest of his
household possessions) to his daughter and her husband.

On 25 April 1616 Shakespeare was buried within the
chancel of the church at Stratford. An unattractive monument to his memory, placed on a wall near the grave, says
that he died on 23 April. Over the grave itself are the lines,
perhaps by Shakespeare, that (more than his literary fame)
have kept his bones undisturbed in the crowded burial
ground where old bones were often dislodged to make way
for new:

> Good friend, for Jesus' sake forbear
> To dig the dust enclosed here.
> Blessed be the man that spares these stones
> And cursed be he that moves my bones.

A Note on the Anti-Stratfordians, Especially Baconians and Oxfordians

Not until 1769—more than a hundred and fifty years
after Shakespeare's death—is there any record of anyone

expressing doubt about Shakespeare's authorship of the plays and poems. In 1769, however, Herbert Lawrence nominated Francis Bacon (1561–1626) in *The Life and Adventures of Common Sense*. Since then, at least two dozen other nominees have been offered, including Christopher Marlowe, Sir Walter Raleigh, Queen Elizabeth I, and Edward de Vere, 17th earl of Oxford. The impulse behind all anti-Stratfordian movements is the scarcely concealed snobbish opinion that "the man from Stratford" simply could not have written the plays because he was a country fellow without a university education and without access to high society. Anyone, the argument goes, who used so many legal terms, medical terms, nautical terms, and so forth, and who showed some familiarity with classical writing, must have attended a university, and anyone who knew so much about courtly elegance and courtly deceit must himself have moved among courtiers. The plays do indeed reveal an author whose interests were exceptionally broad, but specialists in any given field—law, medicine, arms and armor, and so on—soon find that the plays do not reveal deep knowledge in specialized matters; indeed, the playwright often gets technical details wrong.

The claim on behalf of Bacon, forgotten almost as soon as it was put forth in 1769, was independently reasserted by Joseph C. Hart in 1848. In 1856 it was reaffirmed by W. H. Smith in a book, and also by Delia Bacon in an article; in 1857 Delia Bacon published a book, arguing that Francis Bacon had directed a group of intellectuals who wrote the plays.

Francis Bacon's claim has largely faded, perhaps because it was advanced with such evident craziness by Ignatius Donnelly, who in *The Great Cryptogram* (1888) claimed to break a code in the plays that proved Bacon had written not only the plays attributed to Shakespeare but also other Renaissance works, for instance the plays of Christopher Marlowe and the essays of Montaigne.

Consider the last two lines of the Epilogue in *The Tempest*:

As you from crimes would pardoned be,
Let your indulgence set me free.

What was Shakespeare—sorry, Francis Bacon, Baron Verulam—*really* saying in these two lines? According to Baconians, the lines are an anagram reading, "Tempest of Francis Bacon, Lord Verulam; do ye ne'er divulge me, ye words." Ingenious, and it is a pity that in the quotation the letter *a* appears only twice in the cryptogram, whereas in the deciphered message it appears three times. Oh, no problem; just alter "Verulam" to "Verul'm" and it works out very nicely.

Most people understand that with sufficient ingenuity one can torture any text and find in it what one wishes. For instance: Did Shakespeare have a hand in the King James Version of the Bible? It was nearing completion in 1610, when Shakespeare was forty-six years old. If you look at the 46th Psalm and count forward for forty-six words, you will find the word *shake*. Now if you go to the end of the psalm and count backward forty-six words, you will find the word *spear*. Clear evidence, according to some, that Shakespeare slyly left his mark in the book.

Bacon's candidacy has largely been replaced in the twentieth century by the candidacy of Edward de Vere (1550–1604), 17th earl of Oxford. The basic ideas behind the Oxford theory, advanced at greatest length by Dorothy and Charlton Ogburn in *This Star of England* (1952, rev. 1955), a book of 1297 pages, and by Charlton Ogburn in *The Mysterious William Shakespeare* (1984), a book of 892 pages, are these: (1) The man from Stratford could not possibly have had the mental equipment and the experience to have written the plays—only a courtier could have written them; (2) Oxford had the requisite background (social position, education, years at Queen Elizabeth's court); (3) Oxford did not wish his authorship to be known for two basic reasons: writing for the public theater was a vulgar pursuit, and the plays show so much courtly and royal disreputable behavior that they would have compromised Oxford's position at court. Oxfordians offer countless details to support the claim. For example, Hamlet's phrase "that ever I was born to set it right" (1.5.89) barely conceals "E. Ver, I was born to set it right," an unambiguous announcement of de Vere's authorship, according to *This Star of England* (p. 654). A second example: Consider Ben

Jonson's poem entitled "To the Memory of My Beloved Master William Shakespeare," prefixed to the first collected edition of Shakespeare's plays in 1623. According to Oxfordians, when Jonson in this poem speaks of the author of the plays as the "swan of Avon," he is alluding not to William Shakespeare, who was born and died in Stratford-on-Avon and who throughout his adult life owned property there; rather, he is alluding to Oxford, who, the Ogburns say, used "William Shakespeare" as his pen name, and whose manor at Bilton was on the Avon River. Oxfordians do not offer any evidence that Oxford took a pen name, and they do not mention that Oxford had sold the manor in 1581, forty-two years before Jonson wrote his poem. Surely a reference to the Shakespeare who was born in Stratford, who had returned to Stratford, and who had died there only seven years before Jonson wrote the poem is more plausible. And exactly why Jonson, who elsewhere also spoke of Shakespeare as a playwright, and why Heminges and Condell, who had acted with Shakespeare for about twenty years, should speak of Shakespeare as the author in their dedication in the 1623 volume of collected plays is never adequately explained by Oxfordians. Either Jonson, Heminges and Condell, and numerous others were in on the conspiracy, or they were all duped—equally unlikely alternatives. Another difficulty in the Oxford theory is that Oxford died in 1604, and some of the plays are clearly indebted to works and events later than 1604. Among the Oxfordian responses are: At his death Oxford left some plays, and in later years these were touched up by hacks, who added the material that points to later dates. *The Tempest*, almost universally regarded as one of Shakespeare's greatest plays and pretty clearly dated to 1611, does indeed date from a period after the death of Oxford, but it is a crude piece of work that should not be included in the canon of works by Oxford.

The anti-Stratfordians, in addition to assuming that the author must have been a man of rank and a university man, usually assume two conspiracies: (1) a conspiracy in Elizabethan and Jacobean times, in which a surprisingly large number of persons connected with the theater knew that the actor Shakespeare did not write the plays attributed to him but for some reason or other pretended that he did; (2) a conspiracy of today's Stratfordians, the professors who teach Shakespeare in the colleges and universities, who are said to have a vested interest in preserving Shakespeare as the author of the plays they teach. In fact, (1) it is inconceivable that the secret of Shakespeare's non-authorship could have been preserved by all of the people who supposedly were in on the conspiracy, and (2) academic fame awaits any scholar today who can disprove Shakespeare's authorship.

The Stratfordian case is convincing not only because hundreds or even thousands of anti-Stratford arguments—of the sort that say "ever I was born" has the secret double meaning "E. Ver, I was born"—add up to nothing at all but also because irrefutable evidence connects the man from Stratford with the London theater and with the authorship of particular plays. The anti-Stratfordians do not seem to understand that it is not enough to dismiss the Stratford case by saying that a fellow from the provinces simply couldn't have written the plays. Nor do they understand that it is not enough to dismiss all of the evidence connecting Shakespeare with the plays by asserting that it is perjured.

The Shakespeare Canon

We return to William Shakespeare. Thirty-seven plays as well as some nondramatic poems are generally held to constitute the Shakespeare canon, the body of authentic works. The exact dates of composition of most of the works are highly uncertain, but evidence of a starting point and/or of a final limiting point often provides a framework for informed guessing. For example, *Richard II* cannot be earlier than 1595, the publication date of some material to which it is indebted; *The Merchant of Venice* cannot be later than 1598, the year Francis Meres mentioned it. Sometimes arguments for a date hang on an alleged topical allusion, such as the lines about the unseasonable weather in *A Midsummer Night's Dream*, 2.1.81–117, but such an allusion, if indeed it is an allusion to an event in the real world, can be variously interpreted, and in any case there is always the possibility that a topical allusion was inserted years later, to bring the play up to date. (The issue of alterations in a text between the

time that Shakespeare drafted it and the time that it was
printed—alterations due to censorship or playhouse practice
or Shakespeare's own second thoughts—will be discussed
in "The Play Text as a Collaboration" later in this overview.) Dates are often attributed on the basis of style, and
although conjectures about style usually rest on other
conjectures (such as Shakespeare's development as a playwright, or the appropriateness of lines to character), sooner
or later one must rely on one's literary sense. There is no
documentary proof, for example, that *Othello* is not as early
as *Romeo and Juliet*, but one feels that *Othello* is a later,
more mature work, and because the first record of its performance is 1604, one is glad enough to set its composition at
that date and not push it back into Shakespeare's early years.
(*Romeo and Juliet* was first published in 1597, but evidence
suggests that it was written a little earlier.) The following
chronology, then, is indebted not only to facts but also to
informed guesswork and sensitivity. The dates, necessarily
imprecise for some works, indicate something like a scholarly consensus concerning the time of original composition.
Some plays show evidence of later revision.

Plays. The first collected edition of Shakespeare, published
in 1623, included thirty-six plays. These are all accepted as
Shakespeare's, though for one of them, *Henry VIII*, he is
thought to have had a collaborator. A thirty-seventh play,
Pericles, published in 1609 and attributed to Shakespeare on
the title page, is also widely accepted as being partly by
Shakespeare even though it is not included in the 1623
volume. Still another play not in the 1623 volume, *The Two
Noble Kinsmen*, was first published in 1634, with a title page
attributing it to John Fletcher and Shakespeare. Probably
most students of the subject now believe that Shakespeare
did indeed have a hand in it. Of the remaining plays
attributed at one time or another to Shakespeare, only
one, *Edward III*, anonymously published in 1596, is now
regarded by some scholars as a serious candidate. The
prevailing opinion, however, is that this rather simple-
minded play is not Shakespeare's; at most he may have
revised some passages, chiefly scenes with the Countess of

Salisbury. We include *The Two Noble Kinsmen* but do not include *Edward III* in the following list.

1588–94	*The Comedy of Errors*
1588–94	*Love's Labor's Lost*
1589–91	*2 Henry VI*
1590–91	*3 Henry VI*
1589–92	*1 Henry VI*
1592–93	*Richard III*
1589–94	*Titus Andronicus*
1593–94	*The Taming of the Shrew*
1592–94	*The Two Gentlemen of Verona*
1594–96	*Romeo and Juliet*
1595	*Richard II*
1595–96	*A Midsummer Night's Dream*
1596–97	*King John*
1594–96	*The Merchant of Venice*
1596–97	*1 Henry IV*
1597	*The Merry Wives of Windsor*
1597–98	*2 Henry IV*
1598–99	*Much Ado About Nothing*
1598–99	*Henry V*
1599	*Julius Caesar*
1599–1600	*As You Like It*
1599–1600	*Twelfth Night*
1600–1601	*Hamlet*
1601–1602	*Troilus and Cressida*
1602–1604	*All's Well That Ends Well*
1603–1604	*Othello*
1604	*Measure for Measure*
1605–1606	*King Lear*
1605–1606	*Macbeth*
1606–1607	*Antony and Cleopatra*
1605–1608	*Timon of Athens*
1607–1608	*Coriolanus*
1607–1608	*Pericles*
1609–10	*Cymbeline*
1610–11	*The Winter's Tale*
1611	*The Tempest*

1612–13	*Henry VIII*
1613	*The Two Noble Kinsmen*

Poems. In 1989 Donald W. Foster published a book in which he argued that "A Funeral Elegy for Master William Peter," published in 1612, ascribed only to the initials W.S., *may* be by Shakespeare. Foster later published an article in a scholarly journal, *PMLA* 111 (1996), in which he asserted the claim more positively. The evidence begins with the initials, and includes the fact that the publisher and the printer of the elegy had published Shakespeare's *Sonnets* in 1609. But such facts add up to rather little, especially because no one has found any connection between Shakespeare and William Peter (an Oxford graduate about whom little is known, who was murdered at the age of twenty-nine). The argument is based chiefly on statistical examinations of word patterns, which are said to correlate with Shakespeare's known work. Despite such correlations, however, many readers feel that the poem does not sound like Shakespeare. True, Shakespeare has a great range of styles, but his work is consistently imaginative and interesting. Many readers find neither of these qualities in "A Funeral Elegy."

1592–93	*Venus and Adonis*
1593–94	*The Rape of Lucrece*
1593–1600	*Sonnets*
1600–1601	*The Phoenix and the Turtle*

Shakespeare's English

1. Spelling and Pronunciation. From the philologist's point of view, Shakespeare's English is modern English. It requires footnotes, but the inexperienced reader can comprehend substantial passages with very little help, whereas for the same reader Chaucer's Middle English is a foreign language. By the beginning of the fifteenth century the chief grammatical changes in English had taken place, and the final unaccented *-e* of Middle English had been lost (though it survives even today in spelling, as in *name*); during the fifteenth century the dialect of London, the commercial and political center, gradually displaced the provincial dialects, at least in writing; by the end of the century, printing had helped to regularize and stabilize the language, especially spelling. Elizabethan spelling may seem erratic to us (there were dozens of spellings of *Shakespeare*, and a simple word like *been* was also spelled *beene* and *bin*), but it had much in common with our spelling. Elizabethan spelling was conservative in that for the most part it reflected an older pronunciation (Middle English) rather than the sound of the language as it was then spoken, just as our spelling continues to reflect medieval pronunciation—most obviously in the now silent but formerly pronounced letters in a word such as *knight*. Elizabethan pronunciation, though not identical with ours, was much closer to ours than to that of the Middle Ages. Incidentally, though no one can be certain about what Elizabethan English sounded like, specialists tend to believe it was rather like the speech of a modern stage Irishman (*time* apparently was pronounced *toime*, *old* pronounced *awld*, *day* pronounced *die*, and *join* pronounced *jine*) and not at all like the Oxford speech that most of us think it was.

An awareness of the difference between our pronunciation and Shakespeare's is crucial in three areas—in accent, or number of syllables (many metrically regular lines may look irregular to us); in rhymes (which may not look like rhymes); and in puns (which may not look like puns). Examples will be useful. Some words that were at least on occasion stressed differently from today are *aspèct*, *còmplete*, *fòrlorn*, *revènue*, and *sepùlcher*. Words that sometimes had an additional syllable are *emp[e]ress*, *Hen[e]ry*, *mon[e]th*, and *villain* (three syllables, *vil-lay-in*). An additional syllable is often found in possessives, like *moon*'s (pronounced *moones*) and in words ending in *-tion* or *-sion*. Words that had one less syllable than they now have are *needle* (pronounced *neel*) and *violet* (pronounced *vilet*). Among rhymes now lost are *one* with *loan*, *love* with *prove*, *beast* with *jest*, *eat* with *great*. (In reading, trust your sense of metrics and your ear, more than your eye.) An example of a pun that has become obliterated by a change in pronunciation is Falstaff's reply to Prince Hal's "Come, tell us your reason" in *1 Henry IV*: "Give you a reason on compulsion? If reasons were as plentiful as blackberries, I would give no man a reason upon compulsion, I" (2.4.237–40). The *ea* in *reason* was pronounced rather like a long *a,* like the *ai* in *raisin,* hence the comparison with blackberries.

Puns are not merely attempts to be funny; like metaphors they often involve bringing into a meaningful relationship areas of experience normally seen as remote. In *2 Henry IV,* when Feeble is conscripted, he stoically says, "I care not. A man can die but once. We owe God a death" (3.2.242–43), punning on *debt,* which was the way *death* was pronounced. Here an enormously significant fact of life is put into simple commercial imagery, suggesting its commonplace quality. Shakespeare used the same pun earlier in *1 Henry IV,* when Prince Hal says to Falstaff, "Why, thou owest God a death," and Falstaff replies, " 'Tis not due yet: I would be loath to pay him before his day. What need I be so forward with him that calls not on me?" (5.1.126–29).

Sometimes the puns reveal a delightful playfulness; sometimes they reveal aggressiveness, as when, replying to Claudius's "But now, my cousin Hamlet, and my son," Hamlet says, "A little more than kin, and less than kind!" (1.2.64–65). These are Hamlet's first words in the play, and we already hear him warring verbally against Claudius. Hamlet's "less than kind" probably means (1) Hamlet is not of Claudius's family or nature, *kind* having the sense it still has in our word *mankind*; (2) Hamlet is not kindly (affectionately) disposed toward Claudius; (3) Claudius is not naturally (but rather unnaturally, in a legal sense incestuously) Hamlet's father. The puns evidently were not put in as sops to the groundlings; they are an important way of communicating a complex meaning.

2. *Vocabulary.* A conspicuous difficulty in reading Shakespeare is rooted in the fact that some of his words are no longer in common use—for example, words concerned with armor, astrology, clothing, coinage, hawking, horsemanship, law, medicine, sailing, and war. Shakespeare had a large vocabulary—something near thirty thousand words—but it was not so much a vocabulary of big words as a vocabulary drawn from a wide range of life, and it is partly

his ability to call upon a great body of concrete language that gives his plays the sense of being in close contact with life. When the right word did not already exist, he made it up. Among words thought to be his coinages are *accommodation, all-knowing, amazement, bare-faced, countless, dexterously, dislocate, dwindle, fancy-free, frugal, indistinguishable, lackluster, laughable, overawe, premeditated, sea change, star-crossed.* Among those that have not survived are the verb *convive,* meaning to feast together, and *smilet,* a little smile.

Less overtly troublesome than the technical words but more treacherous are the words that seem readily intelligible to us but whose Elizabethan meanings differ from their modern ones. When Horatio describes the Ghost as an "erring spirit," he is saying not that the ghost has sinned or made an error but that it is wandering. Here is a short list of some of the most common words in Shakespeare's plays that often (but not always) have a meaning other than their most usual modern meaning:

'a	he
abuse	deceive
accident	occurrence
advertise	inform
an, and	if
annoy	harm
appeal	accuse
artificial	skillful
brave	fine, splendid
censure	opinion
cheer	(1) face (2) frame of mind
chorus	a single person who comments on the events
closet	small private room
competitor	partner
conceit	idea, imagination
cousin	kinsman
cunning	skillful
disaster	evil astrological influence
doom	judgment
entertain	receive into service

envy	malice
event	outcome
excrement	outgrowth (of hair)
fact	evil deed
fancy	(1) love (2) imagination
fell	cruel
fellow	(1) companion (2) low person (often an insulting term if addressed to someone of approximately equal rank)
fond	foolish
free	(1) innocent (2) generous
glass	mirror
hap, haply	chance, by chance
head	army
humor	(1) mood (2) bodily fluid thought to control one's psychology
imp	child
intelligence	news
kind	natural, acting according to nature
let	hinder
lewd	base
mere(ly)	utter(ly)
modern	commonplace
natural	a fool, an idiot
naughty	(1) wicked (2) worthless
next	nearest
nice	(1) trivial (2) fussy
noise	music
policy	(1) prudence (2) stratagem
presently	immediately
prevent	anticipate
proper	handsome
prove	test
quick	alive
sad	serious
saw	proverb
secure	without care, incautious
silly	innocent

sensible	capable of being perceived by the senses
shrewd	sharp
so	provided that
starve	die
still	always
success	that which follows
tall	brave
tell	count
tonight	last night
wanton	playful, careless
watch	keep awake
will	lust
wink	close both eyes
wit	mind, intelligence

All glosses, of course, are mere approximations; sometimes one of Shakespeare's words may hover between an older meaning and a modern one, and as we have seen, his words often have multiple meanings.

3. Grammar. A few matters of grammar may be surveyed, though it should be noted at the outset that Shakespeare sometimes made up his own grammar. As E.A. Abbott says in *A Shakespearian Grammar,* "Almost any part of speech can be used as any other part of speech": a noun as a verb ("he childed as I fathered"); a verb as a noun ("She hath made compare"); or an adverb as an adjective ("a seldom pleasure"). There are hundreds, perhaps thousands, of such instances in the plays, many of which at first glance would not seem at all irregular and would trouble only a pedant. Here are a few broad matters.

Nouns: The Elizabethans thought the *-s* genitive ending for nouns (as in *man's*) derived from *his*; thus the line " 'gainst the count his galleys I did some service," for "the count's galleys."

Adjectives: By Shakespeare's time adjectives had lost the endings that once indicated gender, number, and case. About the only difference between Shakespeare's adjectives and ours is the use of the now redundant *more* or *most* with the comparative ("some more fitter place") or superlative

("This was the most unkindest cut of all"). Like double comparatives and double superlatives, double negatives were acceptable; Mercutio "will not budge for no man's pleasure."

Pronouns: The greatest change was in pronouns. In Middle English *thou, thy,* and *thee* were used among familiars and in speaking to children and inferiors; *ye, your,* and *you* were used in speaking to superiors (servants to masters, nobles to the king) or to equals with whom the speaker was not familiar. Increasingly the "polite" forms were used in all direct address, regardless of rank, and the accusative *you* displaced the nominative *ye.* Shakespeare sometimes uses *ye* instead of *you,* but even in Shakespeare's day *ye* was archaic, and it occurs mostly in rhetorical appeals.

Thou, thy, and *thee* were not completely displaced, however, and Shakespeare occasionally makes significant use of them, sometimes to connote familiarity or intimacy and sometimes to connote contempt. In *Twelfth Night* Sir Toby advises Sir Andrew to insult Cesario by addressing him as *thou:* "If thou thou'st him some thrice, it shall not be amiss" (3.2.46–47). In *Othello* when Brabantio is addressing an unidentified voice in the dark he says, "What are you?" (1.1.91), but when the voice identifies itself as the foolish suitor Roderigo, Brabantio uses the contemptuous form, saying, "I have charged thee not to haunt about my doors" (93). He uses this form for a while, but later in the scene, when he comes to regard Roderigo as an ally, he shifts back to the polite *you,* beginning in line 163, "What said she to you?" and on to the end of the scene. For reasons not yet satisfactorily explained, Elizabethans used *thou* in addresses to God—"O God, thy arm was here," the king says in *Henry V* (4.8.108)—and to supernatural characters such as ghosts and witches. A subtle variation occurs in *Hamlet.* When Hamlet first talks with the Ghost in 1.5, he uses *thou,* but when he sees the Ghost in his mother's room, in 3.4, he uses *you,* presumably because he is now convinced that the Ghost is not a counterfeit but is his father.

Perhaps the most unusual use of pronouns, from our point of view, is the neuter singular. In place of our *its, his* was often used, as in "How far that little candle throws *his* beams." But the use of a masculine pronoun for a neuter noun came to seem unnatural, and so *it* was used for the possessive as well as the nominative: "The hedge-sparrow fed the cuckoo so long / That it had it head bit off by it young." In the late sixteenth century the possessive form *its* developed, apparently by analogy with the *-s* ending used to indicate a genitive noun, as in *book*'s, but *its* was not yet common usage in Shakespeare's day. He seems to have used *its* only ten times, mostly in his later plays. Other usages, such as "you have seen Cassio and she together" or the substitution of *who* for *whom,* cause little problem even when noticed.

Verbs, Adverbs, and Prepositions: Verbs cause almost no difficulty: The third person singular present form commonly ends in *-s,* as in modern English (e.g., "He blesses"), but sometimes in *-eth* (Portia explains to Shylock that mercy "blesseth him that gives and him that takes"). Broadly speaking, the *-eth* ending was old-fashioned or dignified or "literary" rather than colloquial, except for the words *doth, hath,* and *saith.* The *-eth* ending (regularly used in the King James Bible, 1611) is very rare in Shakespeare's dramatic prose, though not surprisingly it occurs twice in the rather formal prose summary of the narrative poem *Lucrece.* Sometimes a plural subject, especially if it has collective force, takes a verb ending in *-s,* as in "My old bones aches." Some of our strong or irregular preterites (such as *broke*) have a different form in Shakespeare (*brake*); some verbs that now have a weak or regular preterite (such as *helped*) in Shakespeare have a strong or irregular preterite (*holp*). Some adverbs that today end in *-ly* were not inflected: "grievous sick," "wondrous strange." Finally, prepositions often are not the ones we expect: "We are such stuff as dreams are made on," "I have a king here to my flatterer."

Again, none of the differences (except meanings that have substantially changed or been lost) will cause much difficulty. But it must be confessed that for some elliptical passages there is no widespread agreement on meaning. Wise editors resist saying more than they know, and when they are uncertain they add a question mark to their gloss.

Shakespeare's Theater

In Shakespeare's infancy, Elizabethan actors performed wherever they could—in great halls, at court, in the courtyards of inns. These venues implied not only different audiences but also different playing conditions. The innyards must have made rather unsatisfactory theaters: on some days they were unavailable because carters bringing goods to London used them as depots; when available, they had to be rented from the innkeeper. In 1567, presumably to avoid such difficulties, and also to avoid regulation by the Common Council of London, which was not well disposed toward theatricals, one John Brayne, brother-in-law of the carpenter turned actor James Burbage, built the Red Lion in an eastern suburb of London. We know nothing about its shape or its capacity; we can say only that it may have been the first building in Europe constructed for the purpose of giving plays since the end of antiquity, a thousand years earlier. Even after the building of the Red Lion theatrical activity continued in London in makeshift circumstances, in marketplaces and inns, and always uneasily. In 1574 the Common Council required that plays and playing places in London be licensed because

> sundry great disorders and inconveniences have been found to ensue to this city by the inordinate haunting of great multitudes of people, specially youth, to plays, interludes, and shows, namely occasion of frays and quarrels, evil practices of incontinency in great inns having chambers and secret places adjoining to their open stages and galleries.

The Common Council ordered that innkeepers who wished licenses to hold performance put up a bond and make contributions to the poor.

The requirement that plays and innyard theaters be licensed, along with the other drawbacks of playing at inns and presumably along with the success of the Red Lion, led James Burbage to rent a plot of land northeast of the city walls, on property outside the jurisdiction of the city. Here he built England's second playhouse, called simply the Theatre. About all that is known of its construction is that it was wood. It soon had imitators, the most famous being the Globe (1599), essentially an amphitheater built across the Thames (again outside the city's jurisdiction), constructed with timbers of the Theatre, which had been dismantled when Burbage's lease ran out.

Admission to the theater was one penny, which allowed spectators to stand at the sides and front of the stage that jutted into the yard. An additional penny bought a seat in a covered part of the theater, and a third penny bought a more comfortable seat and a better location. It is notoriously difficult to translate prices into today's money, since some things that are inexpensive today would have been expensive in the past and vice versa—a pipeful of tobacco (imported, of course) cost a lot of money, about three pennies, and an orange (also imported) cost two or three times what a chicken cost—but perhaps we can get some idea of the low cost of the penny admission when we realize that a penny could also buy a pot of ale. An unskilled laborer made about five or sixpence a day, an artisan about twelve pence a day, and the hired actors (as opposed to the sharers in the company, such as Shakespeare) made about ten pence a performance. A printed play cost five or sixpence. Of course a visit to the theater (like a visit to a baseball game today) usually cost more than the admission since the spectator probably would also buy food and drink. Still, the low entrance fee meant that the theater was available to all except the very poorest people, rather as movies and most athletic events are today. Evidence indicates that the audience ranged from apprentices who somehow managed to scrape together the minimum entrance fee and to escape from their masters for a few hours, to prosperous members of the middle class and aristocrats who paid the additional fee for admission to the galleries. The exact proportion of men to women cannot be determined, but women of all classes certainly were present. Theaters were open every afternoon but Sundays for much of the year, except in times of plague, when they were closed because of fear of infection. By the way, no evidence suggests the presence of toilet facilities. Presumably the patrons relieved themselves by making a quick trip to the fields surrounding the playhouses.

There are four important sources of information about the

structure of Elizabethan public playhouses—drawings, a contract, recent excavations, and stage directions in the plays. Of drawings, only the so-called de Witt drawing (c. 1596) of the Swan—really his friend Aernout van Buchell's copy of Johannes de Witt's drawing—is of much significance. The drawing, the only extant representation of the interior of an Elizabethan theater, shows an amphitheater of three tiers, with a stage jutting from a wall into the yard or

Johannes de Witt, a Continental visitor to London, made a drawing of the Swan theater in about the year 1596. The original drawing is lost; this is Aernout van Buchell's copy of it.

center of the building. The tiers are roofed, and part of the stage is covered by a roof that projects from the rear and is supported at its front on two posts, but the groundlings, who paid a penny to stand in front of the stage or at its sides, were exposed to the sky. (Performances in such a playhouse were held only in the daytime; artificial illumination was not used.) At the rear of the stage are two massive doors; above the stage is a gallery.

The second major source of information, the contract for the Fortune (built in 1600), specifies that although the Globe (built in 1599) is to be the model, the Fortune is to be square, eighty feet outside and fifty-five inside. The stage is to be forty-three feet broad, and is to extend into the middle of the yard, i.e., it is twenty-seven and a half feet deep.

The third source of information, the 1989 excavations of the Rose (built in 1587), indicate that the Rose was fourteen-sided, about seventy-two feet in diameter with an inner yard almost fifty feet in diameter. The stage at the Rose was about sixteen feet deep, thirty-seven feet wide at the rear, and twenty-seven feet wide downstage. The relatively small dimensions and the tapering stage, in contrast to the rectangular stage in the Swan drawing, surprised theater historians and have made them more cautious in generalizing about the Elizabethan theater. Excavations at the Globe have not yielded much information, though some historians believe that the fragmentary evidence suggests a larger theater, perhaps one hundred feet in diameter.

From the fourth chief source, stage directions in the plays, one learns that entrance to the stage was by the doors at the rear (*"Enter one citizen at one door, and another at the other"*). A curtain hanging across the doorway—or a curtain hanging between the two doorways—could provide a place where a character could conceal himself, as Polonius does, when he wishes to overhear the conversation between Hamlet and Gertrude. Similarly, withdrawing a curtain from the doorway could "discover" (reveal) a character or two. Such discovery scenes are very rare in Elizabethan drama, but a good example occurs in *The Tempest* (5.1.171), where a stage direction tells us, *"Here Prospero discovers Ferdinand and Miranda playing at chess."* There was also some sort of playing space "aloft" or "above" to represent, for instance, the top of a city's walls or a room above the street. Doubtless each theater had its own peculiarities, but perhaps we can talk about a "typical" Elizabethan theater if we realize that no theater need exactly fit the description, just as no mother is the average mother with 2.7 children.

This hypothetical theater is wooden, round, or polygonal (in *Henry V* Shakespeare calls it a "wooden *O*") capable of holding some eight hundred spectators who stood in the yard around the projecting elevated stage—these spectators were the "groundlings"—and some fifteen hundred additional spectators who sat in the three roofed galleries. The stage, protected by a "shadow" or "heavens" or roof, is entered from two doors; behind the doors is the "tiring house" (attiring house, i.e., dressing room), and above the stage is some sort of gallery that may sometimes hold spectators but can be used (for example) as the bedroom from which Romeo—according to a stage direction in one text—"goeth down." Some evidence suggests that a throne can be lowered onto the platform stage, perhaps from the "shadow"; certainly characters can descend from the stage through a trap or traps into the cellar or "hell." Sometimes this space beneath the stage accommodates a sound-effects man or musician (in *Antony and Cleopatra* "*music of the hautboys* [oboes] *is under the stage*") or an actor (in *Hamlet* the "*Ghost cries under the stage*"). Most characters simply walk on and off through the doors, but because there is no curtain in front of the platform, corpses will have to be carried off (Hamlet obligingly clears the stage of Polonius's corpse, when he says, "I'll lug the guts into the neighbor room"). Other characters may have fallen at the rear, where a curtain on a doorway could be drawn to conceal them.

Such may have been the "public theater," so called because its inexpensive admission made it available to a wide range of the populace. Another kind of theater has been called the "private theater" because its much greater admission charge (sixpence versus the penny for general admission at the public theater) limited its audience to the wealthy or the prodigal. The private theater was basically a large room, entirely roofed and therefore artificially illuminated, with a stage at one end. The theaters thus were distinct in two ways: One was essentially an amphitheater that catered to the general public; the other was a hall that catered to the wealthy. In 1576 a hall theater was established in Blackfriars, a Dominican priory in London that had been suppressed in 1538 and confiscated by the Crown and thus was not under the city's jurisdiction. All the actors in this Blackfriars theater were boys about eight to thirteen years old (in the public theaters similar boys played female parts; a boy Lady Macbeth played to a man Macbeth). Near the end of this section on Shakespeare's theater we will talk at some length about possible implications in this convention of using boys to play female roles, but for the moment we should say that it doubtless accounts for the relative lack of female roles in Elizabethan drama. Thus, in *A Midsummer Night's Dream*, out of twenty-one named roles, only four are female; in *Hamlet*, out of twenty-four, only two (Gertrude and Ophelia) are female. Many of Shakespeare's characters have fathers but no mothers—for instance, King Lear's daughters. We need not bring in Freud to explain the disparity; a dramatic company had only a few boys in it.

To return to the private theaters, in some of which all of the performers were children—the "eyrie of . . . little eyases" (nest of unfledged hawks—2.2.347–48) which Rosencrantz mentions when he and Guildenstern talk with Hamlet. The theater in Blackfriars had a precarious existence, and ceased operations in 1584. In 1596 James Burbage, who had already made theatrical history by building the Theatre, began to construct a second Blackfriars theater. He died in 1597, and for several years this second Blackfriars theater was used by a troupe of boys, but in 1608 two of Burbage's sons and five other actors (including Shakespeare) became joint operators of the theater, using it in the winter when the open-air Globe was unsuitable. Perhaps such a smaller theater, roofed, artificially illuminated, and with a tradition of a wealthy audience, exerted an influence in Shakespeare's late plays.

Performances in the private theaters may well have had intermissions during which music was played, but in the public theaters the action was probably uninterrupted, flowing from scene to scene almost without a break. Actors would enter, speak, exit, and others would immediately enter and establish (if necessary) the new locale by a few properties and by words and gestures. To indicate that the

scene took place at night, a player or two would carry a
torch. Here are some samples of Shakespeare establishing
the scene:

> This is Illyria, lady.   (*Twelfth Night,* 1.2.2)

> Well, this is the Forest of Arden.   (*As You Like It,* 2.4.14)

> This castle has a pleasant seat; the air
> Nimbly and sweetly recommends itself
> Unto our gentle senses.   (*Macbeth,* 1.6.1–3)

> The west yet glimmers with some streaks of day.
> (Macbeth, 3.3.5)

Sometimes a speech will go far beyond evoking the minimal
setting of place and time, and will, so to speak, evoke the
social world in which the characters move. For instance,
early in the first scene of *The Merchant of Venice* Salerio
suggests an explanation for Antonio's melancholy. (In the
following passage, *pageants* are decorated wagons, floats,
and *cursy* is the verb "to curtsy," or "to bow.")

> Your mind is tossing on the ocean,
> There where your argosies with portly sail—
> Like signiors and rich burghers on the flood,
> Or as it were the pageants of the sea—
> Do overpeer the petty traffickers
> That cursy to them, do them reverence,
> As they fly by them with their woven wings.   (1.1.8–14)

Late in the nineteenth century, when Henry Irving produced the play with elaborate illusionistic sets, the first
scene showed a ship moored in the harbor, with fruit vendors
and dock laborers, in an effort to evoke the bustling and
exotic life of Venice. But Shakespeare's words give us this
exotic, rich world of commerce in his highly descriptive language when Salerio speaks of "argosies with portly sail" that
fly with "woven wings"; equally important, through Salerio
Shakespeare conveys a sense of the orderly, hierarchical

society in which the lesser ships, "the petty traffickers," curtsy and thereby "do . . . reverence" to their superiors, the merchant prince's ships, which are "Like signiors and rich burghers."

On the other hand, it is a mistake to think that except for verbal pictures the Elizabethan stage was bare. Although Shakespeare's Chorus in *Henry V* calls the stage an "unworthy scaffold" (Prologue 1.10) and urges the spectators to "eke out our performance with your mind" (Prologue 3.35), there was considerable spectacle. The last act of *Macbeth*, for instance, has five stage directions calling for *"drum and colors,"* and another sort of appeal to the eye is indicated by the stage direction *"Enter Macduff, with Macbeth's head."* Some scenery and properties may have been substantial; doubtless a throne was used, but the pillars supporting the roof would have served for the trees on which Orlando pins his poems in *As You Like It*.

Having talked about the public theater—"this wooden *O*"—at some length, we should mention again that Shakespeare's plays were performed also in other locales. Alvin Kernan, in *Shakespeare, the King's Playwright: Theater in the Stuart Court 1603–1613* (1995) points out that "several of [Shakespeare's] plays contain brief theatrical performances, set always in a court or some noble house. When Shakespeare portrayed a theater, he did not, except for the choruses in *Henry V*, imagine a public theater" (p. 195). (Examples include episodes in *The Taming of the Shrew*, *A Midsummer Night's Dream*, *Hamlet*, and *The Tempest*.)

A Note on the Use of Boy Actors in Female Roles

Until fairly recently, scholars were content to mention that the convention existed; they sometimes also mentioned that it continued the medieval practice of using males in female roles, and that other theaters, notably in ancient Greece and in China and Japan, also used males in female roles. (In classical Noh drama in Japan, males still play the female roles.) Prudery may have been at the root of the academic failure to talk much about the use of boy actors, or maybe there really is not much more to say than that it was a convention of a male-centered culture (Stephen Greenblatt's view, in *Shakespearean Negotiations* [1988]). Further, the very nature of a convention is that it is not thought about: Hamlet is a Dane and Julius Caesar is a Roman, but in Shakespeare's plays they speak English, and we in the audience never give this odd fact a thought. Similarly, a character may speak in the presence of others and we understand, again without thinking about it, that he or she is not heard by the figures on the stage (the aside); a character alone on the stage may speak (the soliloquy), and we do not take the character to be unhinged; in a realistic (box) set, the fourth wall, which allows us to see what is going on, is miraculously missing. The no-nonsense view, then, is that the boy actor was an accepted convention, accepted unthinkingly—just as today we know that Kenneth Branagh is not Hamlet, Al Pacino is not Richard III, and Denzel Washington is not the Prince of Aragon. In this view, the audience takes the performer for the role, and that is that; such is the argument we now make for race-free casting, in which African-Americans and Asians can play roles of persons who lived in medieval Denmark and ancient Rome. But gender perhaps is different, at least today. It is a matter of abundant academic study: The Elizabethan theater is now sometimes called a transvestite theater, and we hear much about cross-dressing.

Shakespeare himself in a very few passages calls attention to the use of boys in female roles. At the end of *As You Like It* the boy who played Rosalind addresses the audience, and says, "O men, . . . if I were a woman, I would kiss as many of you as had beards that pleased me." But this is in the Epilogue; the plot is over, and the actor is stepping out of the play and into the audience's everyday world. A second reference to the practice of boys playing female roles occurs in *Antony and Cleopatra*, when Cleopatra imagines that she and Antony will be the subject of crude plays, her role being performed by a boy:

> The quick comedians
> Extemporally will stage us, and present
> Our Alexandrian revels: Antony
> Shall be brought drunken forth, and I shall see
> Some squeaking Cleopatra boy my greatness.   (5.2.216–20)

In a few other passages, Shakespeare is more indirect. For instance, in *Twelfth Night* Viola, played of course by a boy, disguises herself as a young man and seeks service in the house of a lord. She enlists the help of a Captain, and (by way of explaining away her voice and her beardlessness) says,

> I'll serve this duke
> Thou shalt present me as an eunuch to him.   (1.2.55–56)

In *Hamlet*, when the players arrive in 2.2, Hamlet jokes with the boy who plays a female role. The boy has grown since Hamlet last saw him: "By'r Lady, your ladyship is nearer to heaven than when I saw you last by the altitude of a chopine" (a lady's thick-soled shoe). He goes on: "Pray God your voice . . . be not cracked" (434–38).

Exactly how sexual, how erotic, this material was and is, is now much disputed. Again, the use of boys may have been unnoticed, or rather not thought about—an unexamined convention—by most or all spectators most of the time, perhaps *all* of the time, except when Shakespeare calls the convention to the attention of the audience, as in the passages just quoted. Still, an occasional bit seems to invite erotic thoughts. The clearest example is the name that Rosalind takes in *As You Like It*, Ganymede—the beautiful youth whom Zeus abducted. Did boys dressed to play female roles carry homoerotic appeal for straight men (Lisa Jardine's view, in *Still Harping on Daughters* [1983]), or for gay men, or for some or all women in the audience? Further, when the boy actor played a woman who (for the purposes of the plot) disguised herself as a male, as Rosalind, Viola, and Portia do—so we get a boy playing a woman playing a man—what sort of appeal was generated, and for what sort of spectator?

Some scholars have argued that the convention empowered women by letting female characters display a freedom unavailable in Renaissance patriarchal society; the convention, it is said, undermined rigid gender distinctions. In this view, the convention (along with plots in which female characters for a while disguised themselves as young men) allowed Shakespeare to say what some modern gender critics say: Gender is a constructed role rather than a biological given, something we make, rather than a fixed binary opposition of male and female (see Juliet Dusinberre, in *Shakespeare and the Nature of Women* [1975]). On the other hand, some scholars have maintained that the male disguise assumed by some female characters serves only to reaffirm traditional social distinctions since female characters who don male garb (notably Portia in *The Merchant of Venice* and Rosalind in *As You Like It*) return to their female garb and at least implicitly (these critics say) reaffirm the status quo. (For this last view, see Clara Claiborne Park, in an essay in *The Woman's Part*, ed. Carolyn Ruth Swift Lenz et al. [1980].) Perhaps no one answer is right for all plays; in *As You Like It* cross-dressing empowers Rosalind, but in *Twelfth Night* cross-dressing comically traps Viola.

Shakespeare's Dramatic Language: Costumes, Gestures and Silences; Prose and Poetry

Because Shakespeare was a dramatist, not merely a poet, he worked not only with language but also with costume, sound effects, gestures, and even silences. We have already discussed some kinds of spectacle in the preceding section, and now we will begin with other aspects of visual language; a theater, after all, is literally a "place for seeing." Consider the opening stage direction in *The Tempest*, the first play in the first published collection of Shakespeare's plays: *"A tempestuous noise of thunder and Lightning heard: Enter a Ship-master, and a Boteswain."*

Costumes: What did that shipmaster and that boatswain wear? Doubtless they wore something that identified them as men of the sea. Not much is known about the costumes that Elizabethan actors wore, but at least three points are clear: (1) many of the costumes were splendid versions of contemporary Elizabethan dress; (2) some attempts were made to approximate the dress of certain occupations and of antique or exotic characters such as Romans, Turks, and Jews; (3) some costumes indicated that the wearer was supernatural. Evidence for elaborate Elizabethan clothing can be found in the plays themselves and in contemporary comments about the "sumptuous" players who wore the discarded clothing of noblemen, as well as in account books that itemize such things as "a scarlet cloak with two broad gold laces, with gold buttons down the sides."

The attempts at approximation of the dress of certain occupations and nationalities also can be documented from the plays themselves, and it derives additional confirmation from a drawing of the first scene of Shakespeare's *Titus Andronicus*—the only extant Elizabethan picture of an identifiable episode in a play. (See pp. xxxviii–xxxix.) The drawing, probably done in 1594 or 1595, shows Queen Tamora pleading for mercy. She wears a somewhat medieval-looking robe and a crown; Titus wears a toga and a wreath, but two soldiers behind him wear costumes fairly close to Elizabethan dress. We do not know, however, if the drawing represents an actual stage production in the public theater, or perhaps a private production, or maybe only a reader's visualization of an episode. Further, there is some conflicting evidence: In *Julius Caesar* a reference is made to Caesar's doublet (a close-fitting jacket), which, if taken literally, suggests that even the protagonist did not wear Roman clothing; and certainly the lesser characters, who are said to wear hats, did not wear Roman garb.

It should be mentioned, too, that even ordinary clothing can be symbolic: Hamlet's "inky cloak," for example, sets him apart from the brightly dressed members of Claudius's court and symbolizes his mourning; the fresh clothes that are put on King Lear partly symbolize his return to sanity. Consider, too, the removal of disguises near the end of some plays. For instance, Rosalind in *As You Like It* and Portia and Nerissa in *The Merchant of Venice* remove their male attire, thus again becoming fully themselves.

Gestures and Silences: Gestures are an important part of a dramatist's language. King Lear kneels before his daughter Cordelia for a benediction (4.7.57–59), an act of humility that contrasts with his earlier speeches banishing her and that contrasts also with a comparable gesture, his ironic

kneeling before Regan (2.4.153–55). Northumberland's failure to kneel before King Richard II (3.3.71–72) speaks volumes. As for silences, consider a moment in *Coriolanus*: Before the protagonist yields to his mother's entreaties (5.3.182), there is this stage direction: *"Holds her by the hand, silent."* Another example of "speech in dumbness" occurs in *Macbeth*, when Macduff learns that his wife and children have been murdered. He is silent at first, as Malcolm's speech indicates: "What, man! Ne'er pull your hat upon your brows. Give sorrow words" (4.3.208–09). (For a discussion of such moments, see Philip C. McGuire's *Speechless Dialect: Shakespeare's Open Silences* [1985].)

Of course when we think of Shakespeare's work, we think primarily of his language, both the poetry and the prose.

Prose: Although two of his plays (*Richard II* and *King John*) have no prose at all, about half the others have at least one quarter of the dialogue in prose, and some have notably more: *1 Henry IV* and *2 Henry IV*, about half; *As You Like It*

and *Twelfth Night*, a little more than half; *Much Ado About Nothing*, more than three quarters; and *The Merry Wives of Windsor*, a little more than five sixths. We should remember that despite Molière's joke about M. Jourdain, who was amazed to learn that he spoke prose, most of us do not speak prose. Rather, we normally utter repetitive, shapeless, and often ungrammatical torrents; prose is something very different—a sort of literary imitation of speech at its most coherent.

Today we may think of prose as "natural" for drama; or even if we think that poetry is appropriate for high tragedy we may still think that prose is the right medium for comedy. Greek, Roman, and early English comedies, however, were written in verse. In fact, prose was not generally considered a literary medium in England until the late fifteenth century; Chaucer tells even his bawdy stories in verse. By the end of the 1580s, however, prose had established itself on the English comic stage. In tragedy, Marlowe made some use of prose, not simply in the speeches of clownish servants but even in the speech of a tragic hero, Doctor Faustus. Still, before Shakespeare, prose normally was used in the theater only for special circumstances: (1) letters and proclamations, to set them off from the poetic dialogue; (2) mad characters, to indicate that normal thinking has become disordered; and (3) low comedy, or speeches uttered by clowns even when they are not being comic. Shakespeare made use of these conventions, but he also went far beyond them. Sometimes he begins a scene in prose and then shifts into verse as the emotion is heightened; or conversely, he may shift from verse to prose when a speaker is lowering the emotional level, as when Brutus speaks in the Forum.

Shakespeare's prose usually is not prosaic. Hamlet's prose includes not only small talk with Rosencrantz and Guildenstern but also princely reflections on "What a piece of work is a man" (2.2.312). In conversation with Ophelia, he shifts from light talk in verse to a passionate prose denunciation of women (3.1.103), though the shift to prose here is perhaps also intended to suggest the possibility of madness. (Consult Brian Vickers, *The Artistry of Shakespeare's Prose* [1968].)

Poetry: Drama in rhyme in England goes back to the Middle Ages, but by Shakespeare's day rhyme no longer dominated poetic drama; a finer medium, blank verse (strictly speaking, unrhymed lines of ten syllables, with the stress on every second syllable) had been adopted. But before looking at unrhymed poetry, a few things should be said about the chief uses of rhyme in Shakespeare's plays. (1) A couplet (a pair of rhyming lines) is sometimes used to convey emotional heightening at the end of a blank verse speech; (2) characters sometimes speak a couplet as they leave the stage, suggesting closure; (3) except in the latest plays, scenes fairly often conclude with a couplet, and sometimes, as in *Richard II*, 2.1.145–46, the entrance of a new character within a scene is preceded by a couplet, which wraps up the earlier portion of that scene; (4) speeches of two characters occasionally are linked by rhyme, most notably in *Romeo and Juliet*, 1.5.95–108, where the lovers speak a sonnet between them; elsewhere a taunting reply occasionally rhymes with the previous speaker's last line; (5) speeches with sententious or gnomic remarks are sometimes in rhyme, as in the duke's speech in *Othello* (1.3.199–206); (6) speeches of sardonic mockery are sometimes in rhyme—for example, Iago's speech on women in *Othello* (2.1.146–58)—and they sometimes conclude with an emphatic couplet, as in Bolingbroke's speech on comforting words in *Richard II* (1.3.301–2); (7) some characters are associated with rhyme, such as the fairies in *A Midsummer Night's Dream*; (8) in the early plays, especially *The Comedy of Errors* and *The Taming of the Shrew*, comic scenes that in later plays would be in prose are in jingling rhymes; (9) prologues, choruses, plays-within-the-play, inscriptions, vows, epilogues, and so on are often in rhyme, and the songs in the plays are rhymed.

Neither prose nor rhyme immediately comes to mind when we first think of Shakespeare's medium: It is blank verse, unrhymed iambic pentameter. (In a mechanically exact line there are five iambic feet. An iambic foot consists of two syllables, the second accented, as in *away*; five feet make a pentameter line. Thus, a strict line of iambic pentameter contains ten syllables, the even syllables being stressed more heavily than the odd syllables. Fortunately, Shakespeare usually varies the line somewhat.) The first speech in *A Midsummer Night's Dream*, spoken by Duke Theseus to his betrothed, is an example of blank verse:

> Now, fair Hippolyta, our nuptial hour
> Draws on apace. Four happy days bring in
> Another moon; but, O, methinks, how slow
> This old moon wanes! She lingers my desires,
> Like to a stepdame, or a dowager,
> Long withering out a young man's revenue.   (1.1.1–6)

As this passage shows, Shakespeare's blank verse is not mechanically unvarying. Though the predominant foot is the iamb (as in *apace* or *desires*), there are numerous variations. In the first line the stress can be placed on "fair," as the regular metrical pattern suggests, but it is likely that "Now" gets almost as much emphasis; probably in the second line "Draws" is more heavily emphasized than "on," giving us a trochee (a stressed syllable followed by an unstressed one); and in the fourth line each word in the phrase "This old moon wanes" is probably stressed fairly heavily, conveying by two spondees (two feet, each of two stresses) the oppressive tedium that Theseus feels.

In Shakespeare's early plays much of the blank verse is end-stopped (that is, it has a heavy pause at the end of each line), but he later developed the ability to write iambic pentameter verse paragraphs (rather than lines) that give the illusion of speech. His chief techniques are (1) enjambing, i.e., running the thought beyond the single line, as in the first three lines of the speech just quoted; (2) occasionally replacing an iamb with another foot; (3) varying the position of the chief pause (the caesura) within a line; (4) adding an occasional unstressed syllable at the end of a line, traditionally called a feminine ending; (5) and beginning or ending a speech with a half line.

Shakespeare's mature blank verse has much of the rhythmic flexibility of his prose; both the language, though richly figurative and sometimes dense, and the syntax seem natural. It is also often highly appropriate to a particular character. Consider, for instance, this speech from *Hamlet*, in which Claudius, King of Denmark ("the Dane"), speaks to Laertes:

> And now, Laertes, what's the news with you?
> You told us of some suit. What is't, Laertes?
> You cannot speak of reason to the Dane
> And lose your voice. What wouldst thou beg, Laertes,
> That shall not be my offer, not thy asking?   (1.2.42–46)

Notice the short sentences and the repetition of the name "Laertes," to whom the speech is addressed. Notice, too, the shift from the royal "us" in the second line to the more intimate "my" in the last line, and from "you" in the first three lines to the more intimate "thou" and "thy" in the last two lines. Claudius knows how to ingratiate himself with Laertes.

For a second example of the flexibility of Shakespeare's blank verse, consider a passage from *Macbeth*. Distressed by the doctor's inability to cure Lady Macbeth and by the imminent battle, Macbeth addresses some of his remarks to the doctor and others to the servant who is arming him. The entire speech, with its pauses, interruptions, and irresolution (in "Pull't off, I say," Macbeth orders the servant to remove the armor that the servant has been putting on him), catches Macbeth's disintegration. (In the first line, *physic* means "medicine," and in the fourth and fifth lines, *cast the water* means "analyze the urine.")

> Throw physic to the dogs, I'll none of it.
> Come, put mine armor on. Give me my staff.
> Seyton, send out.—Doctor, the thanes fly from me.—
> Come, sir, dispatch. If thou couldst, doctor, cast
> The water of my land, find her disease
> And purge it to a sound and pristine health,
> I would applaud thee to the very echo,
> That should applaud again.—Pull't off, I say.—
> What rhubarb, senna, or what purgative drug,
> Would scour these English hence? Hear'st thou of them?
>
> (5.3.47–56)

Blank verse, then, can be much more than unrhymed iambic pentameter, and even within a single play Shakespeare's blank verse often consists of several styles, depending on the speaker and on the speaker's emotion at the moment.

The Play Text as a Collaboration

Shakespeare's fellow dramatist Ben Jonson reported that the actors said of Shakespeare, "In his writing, whatsoever he penned, he never blotted out line," i.e., never crossed out material and revised his work while composing. None of Shakespeare's plays survives in manuscript (with the possible exception of a scene in *Sir Thomas More*), so we cannot fully evaluate the comment, but in a few instances the published work clearly shows that he revised his manuscript. Consider the following passage (shown here in facsimile) from the best early text of *Romeo and Juliet*, the Second Quarto (1599):

Ro. Would I were fleepe and peace fo fweet to reſt
The grey eyde morne ſmiles on the frowning night,
Checkring the Eaſterne Clouds with ſtreaks of light,
And darkneſſe fleckted like a drunkard reeles,
From forth daies pathway, made by *Tytans* wheeles.
Hence will I to my ghoſtly Friers cloſe cell,
His helpe to craue, and my deare hap to tell.

          Exit.

 Enter Frier alone with a basket.   (night,
Fri. The grey-eyed morne ſmiles on the frowning
Checking the Eaſterne clowdes with ſtreaks of light:
And fleckeld darkneſſe like a drunkard reeles,
From forth daies path, and *Titans* burning wheeles:
Now erethe ſun aduance his burning eie,

Romeo rather elaborately tells us that the sun at dawn is
dispelling the night (morning is smiling, the eastern clouds
are checked with light, and the sun's chariot—Titan's
wheels—advances), and he will seek out his spiritual father,
the Friar. He exits and, oddly, the Friar enters and says pretty
much the same thing about the sun. Both speakers say that
"the gray-eyed morn smiles on the frowning night," but there
are small differences, perhaps having more to do with the
business of printing the book than with the author's
composition: For Romeo's "checkring," "fleckted," and
"pathway," we get the Friar's "checking," "fleckeld," and
"path." (Notice, by the way, the inconsistency in Elizabethan
spelling: Romeo's "clouds" become the Friar's "clowdes.")
 Both versions must have been in the printer's copy, and it
seems safe to assume that both were in Shakespeare's manuscript. He must have written one version—let's say he first
wrote Romeo's closing lines for this scene—and then he
decided, no, it's better to give this lyrical passage to the
Friar, as the opening of a new scene, but he neglected to
delete the first version. Editors must make a choice, and they
may feel that the reasonable thing to do is to print the text as
Shakespeare intended it. But how can we know what he
intended? Almost all modern editors delete the lines from

Romeo's speech, and retain the Friar's lines. They don't do this because they know Shakespeare's intention, however. They give the lines to the Friar because the first published version (1597) of *Romeo and Juliet* gives only the Friar's version, and this text (though in many ways inferior to the 1599 text) is thought to derive from the memory of some actors, that is, it is thought to represent a performance, not just a script. Maybe during the course of rehearsals Shakespeare—an actor as well as an author—unilaterally decided that the Friar should speak the lines; if so (remember that we don't know this to be a fact) his final intention was to give the speech to the Friar. Maybe, however, the actors talked it over and settled on the Friar, with or without Shakespeare's approval. On the other hand, despite the 1597 version, one might argue (if only weakly) on behalf of giving the lines to Romeo rather than to the Friar, thus: (1) Romeo's comment on the coming of the daylight emphasizes his separation from Juliet, and (2) the figurative language seems more appropriate to Romeo than to the Friar. Having said this, in the Signet edition we have decided in this instance to draw on the evidence provided by earlier text and to give the lines to the Friar, on the grounds that since Q1 reflects a production, in the theater (at least on one occasion) the lines were spoken by the Friar.

A playwright sold a script to a theatrical company. The script thus belonged to the company, not the author, and author and company alike must have regarded this script not as a literary work but as the basis for a play that the actors would create on the stage. We speak of Shakespeare as the author of the plays, but readers should bear in mind that the texts they read, even when derived from a single text, such as the First Folio (1623), are inevitably the collaborative work not simply of Shakespeare with his company—doubtless during rehearsals the actors would suggest alterations—but also with other forces of the age. One force was governmental censorship. In 1606 parliament passed "an Act to restrain abuses of players," prohibiting the utterance of oaths and the name of God. So where the earliest text of *Othello* gives us "By heaven" (3.3.106), the first Folio gives "Alas," presumably reflecting the compliance of stage practice with the law. Similarly, the 1623 version of *King Lear* omits the oath "Fut" (probably from "By God's foot") at 1.2.142, again presumably reflecting the line as it was spoken on the stage. Editors who seek to give the reader the play that Shakespeare initially conceived—the "authentic" play conceived by the solitary Shakespeare—probably will restore the missing oaths and references to God. Other editors, who see the play as a collaborative work, a construction made not only by Shakespeare but also by actors and compositors and even government censors, may claim that what counts is the play as it was actually performed. Such editors regard the censored text as legitimate, since it is the play that was (presumably) finally put on. A performed text, they argue, has more historical reality than a text produced by an editor who has sought to get at what Shakespeare initially wrote. In this view, the text of a play is rather like the script of a film; the script is not the film, and the play text is not the performed play. Even if we want to talk about the play that Shakespeare "intended," we will find ourselves talking about a script that he handed over to a company with the intention that it be implemented by actors. The "intended" play is the one that the actors—we might almost say "society"—would help to construct.

Further, it is now widely held that a play is also the work of readers and spectators, who do not simply receive meaning, but who create it when they respond to the play. This idea is fully in accord with contemporary post-structuralist critical thinking, notably Roland Barthes's "The Death of the Author," in *Image-Music-Text* (1977) and Michel Foucault's "What Is an Author?," in *The Foucault Reader* (1984). The gist of the idea is that an author is not an isolated genius; rather, authors are subject to the politics and other social structures of their age. A dramatist especially is a worker in a collaborative project, working most obviously with actors—parts may be written for particular actors—but working also with the audience. Consider the words of Samuel Johnson, written to be spoken by the actor David Garrick at the opening of a theater in 1747:

> The stage but echoes back the public voice;
> The drama's laws, the drama's patrons give,
> For we that live to please, must please to live.

The audience—the public taste as understood by the playwright—helps to determine what the play is. Moreover, even members of the public who are not part of the playwright's immediate audience may exert an influence through censorship. We have already glanced at governmental censorship, but there are also other kinds. Take one of Shakespeare's most beloved characters, Falstaff, who appears in three of Shakespeare's plays, the two parts of *Henry IV* and *The Merry Wives of Windsor*. He appears with this name in the earliest printed version of the first of these plays, *1 Henry IV*, but we know that Shakespeare originally called him (after an historical figure) Sir John Oldcastle. Oldcastle appears in Shakespeare's source (partly reprinted in the Signet edition of *1 Henry IV*), and a trace of the name survives in Shakespeare's play, 1.2.43–44, where Prince Hal punningly addresses Falstaff as "my old lad of the castle." But for some reason—perhaps because the family of the historical Oldcastle complained—Shakespeare had to change the name. In short, the play as we have it was (at least in this detail) subject to some sort of censorship. If we think that a text should present what we take to be the author's intention, we probably will want to replace *Falstaff* with *Oldcastle*. But if we recognize that a play is a collaboration, we may welcome the change, even if it was forced on Shakespeare. Somehow *Falstaff*, with its hint of *false-staff*, i.e., inadequate prop, seems just right for this fat knight who, to our delight, entertains the young prince with untruths. We can go as far as saying that, at least so far as a play is concerned, an insistence on the author's original intention (even if we could know it) can sometimes impoverish the text.

The tiny example of Falstaff's name illustrates the point that the text we read is inevitably only a version—something in effect produced by the collaboration of the playwright with his actors, audiences, compositors, and editors—of a fluid text that Shakespeare once wrote, just as the *Hamlet* that we see on the screen starring Kenneth Branagh is not the *Hamlet* that Shakespeare saw in an open-air playhouse starring Richard Burbage. *Hamlet* itself, as we shall note in a moment, also exists in several versions. It is not surprising that there is now much talk about the *instability* of Shakespeare's texts.

Because he was not only a playwright but was also an actor and a shareholder in a theatrical company, Shakespeare probably was much involved with the translation of the play from a manuscript to a stage production. He may or may not have done some rewriting during rehearsals, and he may or may not have been happy with cuts that were made. Some plays, notably *Hamlet* and *King Lear*, are so long that it is most unlikely that the texts we read were acted in their entirety. Further, for both of these plays we have more than one early text that demands consideration. In *Hamlet*, the Second Quarto (1604) includes some two hundred lines not found in the Folio (1623). Among the passages missing from the Folio are two of Hamlet's reflective speeches, the "dram of evil" speech (1.4.13–38) and "How all occasions do inform against me" (4.4.32–66). Since the Folio has more numerous and often fuller stage directions, it certainly looks as though in the Folio we get a theatrical version of the play, a text whose cuts were probably made—this is only a hunch, of course—not because Shakespeare was changing his conception of Hamlet but because the playhouse demanded a modified play. (The problem is complicated, since the Folio not only cuts some of the Quarto but adds some material. Various explanations have been offered.)

Or take an example from *King Lear*. In the First and Second Quarto (1608, 1619), the final speech of the play is given to Albany, Lear's surviving son-in-law, but in the First Folio version (1623), the speech is given to Edgar. The Quarto version is in accord with tradition—usually the highest-ranking character in a tragedy speaks the final words. Why does the Folio give the speech to Edgar? One possible answer is this: The Folio version omits some of Albany's speeches in earlier scenes, so perhaps it was decided (by Shakespeare? by the players?) not to give the final lines to so pale a character. In fact, the discrepancies are so many between the two texts, that some scholars argue we do not simply have texts showing different theatrical productions. Rather, these scholars say, Shakespeare substantially revised the play, and we really have two versions of *King Lear* (and of *Othello* also, say some)—two different plays—not simply two texts, each of which is in some ways imperfect.

In this view, the 1608 version of *Lear* may derive from Shakespeare's manuscript, and the 1623 version may derive from his later revision. The Quartos have almost three hundred lines not in the Folio, and the Folio has about a hundred lines not in the Quartos. It used to be held that all the texts were imperfect in various ways and from various causes— some passages in the Quartos were thought to have been set from a manuscript that was not entirely legible, other passages were thought to have been set by a compositor who was new to setting plays, and still other passages were thought to have been provided by an actor who misremembered some of the lines. This traditional view held that an editor must draw on the Quartos and the Folio in order to get Shakespeare's "real" play. The new argument holds (although not without considerable strain) that we have two authentic plays, Shakespeare's early version (in the Quarto) and Shakespeare's—or his theatrical company's—revised version (in the Folio). Not only theatrical demands but also Shakespeare's own artistic sense, it is argued, called for extensive revisions. Even the titles vary: Q1 is called *True Chronicle Historie of the life and death of King Lear and his three Daughters*, whereas the Folio text is called *The Tragedie of King Lear*. To combine the two texts in order to produce what the editor thinks is the play that Shakespeare intended to write is, according to this view, to produce a text that is false to the history of the play. If the new view is correct, and we do have texts of two distinct versions of *Lear* rather than two imperfect versions of one play, it supports in a textual way the poststructuralist view that we cannot possibly have an unmediated vision of (in this case) a play by Shakespeare; we can only recognize a plurality of visions.

Editing Texts

Though eighteen of his plays were published during his lifetime, Shakespeare seems never to have supervised their publication. There is nothing unusual here; when a playwright sold a play to a theatrical company he surrendered his ownership to it. Normally a company would not publish the play, because to publish it meant to allow competitors to acquire the piece. Some plays did get published: Apparently hard-up actors sometimes pieced together a play for a publisher; sometimes a company in need of money sold a play; and sometimes a company allowed publication of a play that no longer drew audiences. That Shakespeare did not concern himself with publication is not remarkable; of his contemporaries, only Ben Jonson carefully supervised the publication of his own plays.

In 1623, seven years after Shakespeare's death, John Heminges and Henry Condell (two senior members of Shakespeare's company, who had worked with him for about twenty years) collected his plays—published and unpublished—into a large volume, of a kind called a folio. (A folio is a volume consisting of large sheets that have been folded once, each sheet thus making two leaves, or four pages. The size of the page of course depends on the size of the sheet—a folio can range in height from twelve to sixteen inches, and in width from eight to eleven; the pages in the 1623 edition of Shakespeare, commonly called the First Folio, are approximately thirteen inches tall and eight inches wide.) The eighteen plays published during Shakespeare's lifetime had been issued one play per volume in small formats called quartos. (Each sheet in a quarto has been folded twice, making four leaves, or eight pages, each page being about nine inches tall and seven inches wide, roughly the size of a large paperback.)

Heminges and Condell suggest in an address "To the great variety of readers" that the republished plays are presented in better form than in the quartos:

Before you were abused with diverse stolen and surreptitious copies, maimed and deformed by the frauds and stealths of injurious impostors that exposed them; even those, are now offered to your view cured and perfect of their limbs, and all the rest absolute in their numbers, as he [i.e., Shakespeare] conceived them.

There is a good deal of truth to this statement, but some of the quarto versions are better than others; some are in fact preferable to the Folio text.

Whoever was assigned to prepare the texts for publication

in the first Folio seems to have taken the job seriously and yet not to have performed it with uniform care. The sources of the texts seem to have been, in general, good unpublished copies or the best published copies. The first play in the collection, *The Tempest*, is divided into acts and scenes, has unusually full stage directions and descriptions of spectacle, and concludes with a list of the characters, but the editor was not able (or willing) to present all of the succeeding texts so fully dressed. Later texts occasionally show signs of carelessness: in one scene of *Much Ado About Nothing* the names of actors, instead of characters, appear as speech prefixes, as they had in the Quarto, which the Folio reprints; proofreading throughout the Folio is spotty and apparently was done without reference to the printer's copy; the pagination of *Hamlet* jumps from 156 to 257. Further, the proofreading was done while the presses continued to print, so that each play in each volume contains a mix of corrected and uncorrected pages.

Modern editors of Shakespeare must first select their copy; no problem if the play exists only in the Folio, but a considerable problem if the relationship between a Quarto and the Folio—or an early Quarto and a later one—is unclear. In the case of *Romeo and Juliet*, the First Quarto (Q1), published in 1597, is vastly inferior to the Second (Q2), published in 1599. The basis of Q1 apparently is a version put together from memory by some actors. Not surprisingly, it garbles many passages and is much shorter than Q2. On the other hand, occasionally Q1 makes better sense than Q2. For instance, near the end of the play, when the parents have assembled and learned of the deaths of Romeo and Juliet, in Q2 the Prince says (5.3.208–9),

Come, *Montague;* for thou art early vp
To see thy sonne and heire, now earling downe.

The last three words of this speech surely do not make sense, and many editors turn to Q1, which instead of "now earling downe" has "more early downe." Some modern editors take only "early" from Q1, and print "now early down"; others take "more early," and print "more early down." Further, Q1 (though, again, quite clearly a garbled and abbreviated text) includes some stage directions that are not found in Q2, and today many editors who base their text on Q2 are glad to add these stage directions, because the directions help to give us a sense of what the play looked like on Shakespeare's stage. Thus, in 4.3.58, after Juliet drinks the potion, Q1 gives us this stage direction, not in Q2: *"She falls upon her bed within the curtains."*

In short, an editor's decisions do not end with the choice of a single copy text. First of all, editors must reckon with Elizabethan spelling. If they are not producing a facsimile, they probably modernize the spelling, but ought they to preserve the old forms of words that apparently were pronounced quite unlike their modern forms—*lanthorn, alablaster*? If they preserve these forms are they really preserving Shakespeare's forms or perhaps those of a compositor in the printing house? What is one to do when one finds *lanthorn* and *lantern* in adjacent lines? (The editors of this series in general, but not invariably, assume that words should be spelled in their modern form, unless, for instance, a rhyme is involved.) Elizabethan punctuation, too, presents problems. For example, in the First Folio, the only text for the play, Macbeth rejects his wife's idea that he can wash the blood from his hand (2.2.60–62):

> No: this my Hand will rather
> The multitudinous Seas incarnardine,
> Making the Greene one, Red.

Obviously an editor will remove the superfluous capitals, and will probably alter the spelling to "incarnadine," but what about the comma before "Red"? If we retain the comma, Macbeth is calling the sea "the green one." If we drop the comma, Macbeth is saying that his bloody hand will make the sea ("the Green") *uniformly* red.

An editor will sometimes have to change more than spelling and punctuation. Macbeth says to his wife (1.7.46–47):

> I dare do all that may become a man,
> Who dares no more, is none.

For two centuries editors have agreed that the second line is unsatisfactory, and have emended "no" to "do": "Who dares do more is none." But when in the same play (4.2.21–22) Ross says that fearful persons

> Floate vpon a wilde and violent Sea
> Each way, and moue,

need we emend the passage? On the assumption that the compositor misread the manuscript, some editors emend "each way, and move" to "and move each way"; others emend "move" to "none" (i.e., "Each way and none"). Other editors, however, let the passage stand as in the original. The editors of the Signet Classic Shakespeare have restrained themselves from making abundant emendations. In their minds they hear Samuel Johnson on the dangers of emendation: "I have adopted the Roman sentiment, that it is more honorable to save a citizen than to kill an enemy." Some departures (in addition to spelling, punctuation, and lineation) from the copy text have of course been made, but the original readings are listed in a note following the play, so that readers can evaluate the changes for themselves.

Following tradition, the editors of the Signet Classic Shakespeare have prefaced each play with a list of characters, and throughout the play have regularized the names of the speakers. Thus, in our text of *Romeo and Juliet*, all speeches by Juliet's mother are prefixed "Lady Capulet," although the 1599 Quarto of the play, which provides our copy text, uses at various points seven speech tags for this one character: *Capu. Wi.* (i.e., Capulet's wife), *Ca. Wi., Wi., Wife, Old La.* (i.e., Old Lady), *La.,* and *Mo.* (i.e., Mother). Similarly, in *All's Well That Ends Well*, the character whom we regularly call "Countess" is in the Folio (the copy text) variously identified as *Mother, Countess, Old Countess, Lady,* and *Old Lady.* Admittedly there is some loss in regularizing, since the various prefixes may give us a hint of the way Shakespeare (or a scribe who copied Shakespeare's manuscript) was thinking of the character in a particular scene—for instance, as a mother, or as an old lady. But too much can be made of these differing prefixes, since the social relationships implied are *not* always relevant to the given scene.

We have also added line numbers and in many cases act and scene divisions as well as indications of locale at the beginning of scenes. The Folio divided most of the plays into acts and some into scenes. Early eighteenth-century editors increased the divisions. These divisions, which provide a convenient way of referring to passages in the plays, have been retained, but when not in the text chosen as the basis for the Signet Classic text they are enclosed within square brackets, [ ], to indicate that they are editorial additions. Similarly, though no play of Shakespeare's was equipped with indications of the locale at the heads of scene divisions, locales have here been added in square brackets for the convenience of readers, who lack the information that costumes, properties, gestures, and scenery afford to spectators. Spectators can tell at a glance they are in the throne room, but without an editorial indication the reader may be puzzled for a while. It should be mentioned, incidentally, that there are a few authentic stage directions—perhaps Shakespeare's, perhaps a prompter's—that suggest locales, such as *"Enter Brutus in his orchard,"* and *"They go up into the Senate house."* It is hoped that the bracketed additions in the Signet text will provide readers with the sort of help provided by these two authentic directions, but it is equally hoped that the reader will remember that the stage was not loaded with scenery.

Shakespeare on the Stage

Each volume in the Signet Classic Shakespeare includes a brief stage (and sometimes film) history of the play. When we read about earlier productions, we are likely to find them eccentric, obviously wrongheaded—for instance, Nahum Tate's version of *King Lear*, with a happy ending, which held the stage for about a century and a half, from the late seventeenth century until the end of the first quarter of the nineteenth. We see engravings of David Garrick, the greatest actor of the eighteenth century, in eighteenth-century garb as King Lear, and we smile, thinking how absurd the production must have been. If we are more thoughtful, we say, with the English novelist L. P. Hartley, "The past is a foreign country: they do things differently there." But if the eighteenth-century staging is a foreign country, what of the plays of the late sixteenth and seventeenth centuries? A foreign language, a foreign theater, a foreign audience.

Probably all viewers of Shakespeare's plays, beginning with Shakespeare himself, at times have been unhappy with the plays on the stage. Consider three comments about production that we find in the plays themselves, which suggest Shakespeare's concerns. The Chorus in *Henry V* complains that the heroic story cannot possibly be adequately staged:

> But pardon, gentles all,
> The flat unraisèd spirits that hath dared
> On this unworthy scaffold to bring forth
> So great an object. Can this cockpit hold
> The vasty fields of France? Or may we cram
> Within this wooden *O* the very casques
> That did affright the air at Agincourt?
>
> . . . .
> Piece out our imperfections with your thoughts.
>
> (Prologue 1.8–14,23)

Second, here are a few sentences (which may or may not represent Shakespeare's own views) from Hamlet's longish lecture to the players:

> Speak the speech, I pray you, as I pronounced it to you, trippingly on the tongue. But if you mouth it, as many of our players do, I had as lief the town crier spoke my lines. . . . O, it offends me to the soul to hear a robustious periwig-pated fellow tear a passion to tatters, to very rags, to split the ears of the groundlings. . . . And let those that play your clowns speak no more than is set down for them, for there be of them that will themselves laugh, to set on some quantity of barren spectators to laugh too, though in the meantime some necessary question of the play be then to be considered. That's villainous and shows a most pitiful ambition in the fool that uses it. (3.2.1–47)

Finally, we can quote again from the passage cited earlier in this introduction, concerning the boy actors who played the female roles. Cleopatra imagines with horror a theatrical version of her activities with Antony:

> The quick comedians
> Extemporally will stage us, and present
> Our Alexandrian revels: Antony
> Shall be brought drunken forth, and I shall see
> Some squeaking Cleopatra boy my greatness
> I' th' posture of a whore.   (5.2.216–21)

It is impossible to know how much weight to put on such passages—perhaps Shakespeare was just being modest about his theater's abilities—but it is easy enough to think that he was unhappy with some aspects of Elizabethan production. Probably no production can fully satisfy a playwright, and for that matter, few productions can fully satisfy *us;* we regret this or that cut, this or that way of costuming the play, this or that bit of business.

One's first thought may be this: Why don't they just do "authentic" Shakespeare, "straight" Shakespeare, the play as Shakespeare wrote it? But as we read the plays—words written to be performed—it sometimes becomes clear that we do not know *how* to perform them. For instance, in *Antony and Cleopatra* Antony, the Roman general who has succumbed to Cleopatra and to Egyptian ways, says, "The nobleness of life / Is to do thus" (1.1.36–37). But what is "thus"? Does Antony at this point embrace Cleopatra? Does he embrace and kiss her? (There are, by the way, very few scenes of kissing on Shakespeare's stage, possibly because boys played the female roles.) Or does he make a sweeping gesture, indicating the Egyptian way of life?

This is not an isolated example; the plays are filled with lines that call for gestures, but we are not sure what the gestures should be. *Interpretation* is inevitable. Consider a passage in *Hamlet*. In 3.1, Polonius persuades his daughter, Ophelia, to talk to Hamlet while Polonius and Claudius eavesdrop. The two men conceal themselves, and Hamlet encounters Ophelia. At 3.1.131 Hamlet suddenly says to her, "Where's your father?" Why does Hamlet, apparently out of nowhere—they have not been talking about Polonius—ask this question? Is this an example of the "antic disposition" (fantastic behavior) that Hamlet earlier (1.5.172) had told Horatio and others—including us—he would display? That is, is the question about the whereabouts of her father a seemingly irrational one, like his earlier question (3.1.103) to Ophelia, "Ha, ha! Are you honest?" Or, on the other hand, has Hamlet (as in many productions) suddenly glimpsed Polonius's foot protruding from beneath a drapery at the rear? That is, does Hamlet ask the question because he has suddenly seen something suspicious and now is testing Ophelia? (By the way, in productions that do give Hamlet a physical cue, it is almost always Polonius rather than Claudius who provides the clue. This itself is an act of interpretation on the part of the director.) Or (a third possibility) does Hamlet get a clue from Ophelia, who inadvertently betrays the spies by nervously glancing at their place of hiding? This is the interpretation used in the BBC television version, where Ophelia glances in fear toward the hiding place just after Hamlet says "Why wouldst thou be a breeder of sinners?" (121–22). Hamlet, realizing that he is being observed, glances here and there *before* he asks "Where's your father?" The question thus is a climax to what he has been doing while speaking the preceding lines. Or (a fourth interpretation) does Hamlet suddenly, without the aid of any clue whatsoever, intuitively (insightfully, mysteriously, wonderfully) sense that someone is spying? Directors must decide, of course—and so must readers.

Recall, too, the preceding discussion of the texts of the plays, which argued that the texts—though they seem to be before us in permanent black on white—are unstable. The Signet text of *Hamlet*, which draws on the Second Quarto (1604) and the First Folio (1623) is considerably longer than any version staged in Shakespeare's time. Our version, even if spoken very briskly and played without any intermission, would take close to four hours, far beyond "the two hours' traffic of our stage" mentioned in the Prologue to *Romeo and Juliet*. (There are a few contemporary references to the duration of a play, but none mentions more than three hours.) Of Shakespeare's plays, only *The Comedy of Errors*, *Macbeth*, and *The Tempest* can be done in less than three hours without cutting. And even if we take a play that exists only in a short text, *Macbeth*, we cannot claim that we are experiencing the very play that Shakespeare conceived, partly because some of the Witches' songs almost surely are non-Shakespearean additions, and partly because we are not willing to watch the play performed without an intermission and with boys in the female roles.

Further, as the earlier discussion of costumes mentioned, the plays apparently were given chiefly in contemporary, that is, in Elizabethan dress. If today we give them in the costumes that Shakespeare probably saw, the plays seem not contemporary but curiously dated. Yet if we use our own dress, we find lines of dialogue that are at odds with what we see; we may feel that the language, so clearly not our own, is inappropriate coming out of people in today's dress. A common solution, incidentally, has been to set the plays in the nineteenth century, on the grounds that this attractively distances the plays (gives them a degree of foreignness, allowing for interesting costumes) and yet doesn't put them into a museum world of Elizabethan England.

Inevitably our productions are adaptations, *our* adaptations, and inevitably they will look dated, not in a century but in twenty years, or perhaps even in a decade. Still, we cannot escape from our own conceptions. As the director Peter Brook has said, in *The Empty Space* (1968):

> It is not only the hair-styles, costumes and make-ups that look dated. All the different elements of staging—the shorthands of behavior that stand for emotions; gestures, gesticulations and tones of voice—are all fluctuating on an invisible stock exchange all the time. . . . A living theatre that thinks it can stand aloof from anything as trivial as fashion will wilt. (p. 16)

As Brook indicates, it is through today's hairstyles, costumes, makeup, gestures, gesticulations, tones of voice—this includes our *conception* of earlier hairstyles, costumes, and so forth if we stage the play in a period other than our own—that we inevitably stage the plays.

It is a truism that every age invents its own Shakespeare, just as, for instance, every age has invented its own classical world. Our view of ancient Greece, a slave-holding society

in which even free Athenian women were severely circum-
scribed, does not much resemble the Victorians' view of
ancient Greece as a glorious democracy, just as, perhaps, our
view of Victorianism itself does not much resemble theirs.
We cannot claim that the Shakespeare on our stage is the
true Shakespeare, but in our stage productions we find a
Shakespeare that speaks to us, a Shakespeare that our ancestors doubtless did not know but one that seems to us to be the
true Shakespeare—at least for a while.

Our age is remarkable for the wide variety of kinds of
staging that it uses for Shakespeare, but one development
deserves special mention. This is the now common practice
of race-blind or color-blind or nontraditional casting, which
allows persons who are not white to play in Shakespeare.
Previously blacks performing in Shakespeare were limited
to a mere three roles, Othello, Aaron (in *Titus Andronicus*),
and the Prince of Morocco (in *The Merchant of Venice*),
and there were no roles at all for Asians. Indeed, African-
Americans rarely could play even one of these three roles,
since they were not welcome in white companies. Ira
Aldridge (c.1806–1867), a black actor of undoubted talent,
was forced to make his living by performing Shakespeare
in England and in Europe, where he could play not only
Othello but also—in whiteface—other tragic roles such as
King Lear. Paul Robeson (1898–1976) made theatrical history when he played Othello in London in 1930, and there
was some talk about bringing the production to the United
States, but there was more talk about whether American
audiences would tolerate the sight of a black man—a real
black man, not a white man in blackface—kissing and then
killing a white woman. The idea was tried out in summer
stock in 1942, the reviews were enthusiastic, and in the following year Robeson opened on Broadway in a production
that ran an astounding 296 performances. An occasional all-
black company sometimes performed Shakespeare's plays,
but otherwise blacks (and other minority members) were in
effect shut out from performing Shakespeare. Only since
about 1970 has it been common for nonwhites to play major
roles along with whites. Thus, in a 1996–97 production of
Antony and Cleopatra, a white Cleopatra, Vanessa Redgrave, played opposite a black Antony, David Harewood.

Multiracial casting is now especially common at the New York Shakespeare Festival, founded in 1954 by Joseph Papp, and in England, where even siblings such as Claudio and Isabella in *Measure for Measure* or Lear's three daughters may be of different races. Probably most viewers today soon stop worrying about the lack of realism, and move beyond the color of the performers' skin to the quality of the performance.

Nontraditional casting is not only a matter of color or race; it includes sex. In the past, occasionally a distinguished woman of the theater has taken on a male role—Sarah Bernhardt (1844–1923) as Hamlet is perhaps the most famous example—but such performances were widely regarded as eccentric. Although today there have been some performances involving cross-dressing (a drag *As You Like It* staged by the National Theatre in England in 1966 and in the United States in 1974 has achieved considerable fame in the annals of stage history), what is more interesting is the casting of women in roles that traditionally are male but that need not be. Thus, a 1993–94 English production of *Henry V* used a woman—*not* cross-dressed—in the role of the governor of Harfleur. According to Peter Holland, who reviewed the production in *Shakespeare Survey* 48 (1995), "having a female Governor of Harfleur feminized the city and provided a direct response to the horrendous threat of rape and murder that Henry had offered, his language and her body in direct connection and opposition" (p. 210). Ten years from now the device may not play so effectively, but today it speaks to us. Shakespeare, born in the Elizabethan Age, has been dead nearly four hundred years, yet he is, as Ben Jonson said, "not of an age but for all time." We must understand, however, that he is "for all time" precisely because each age finds in his abundance something for itself and something of itself.

And here we come back to two issues discussed earlier in this introduction—the instability of the text and, curiously, the Bacon/Oxford heresy concerning the authorship of the plays. *Of course* Shakespeare wrote the plays, and we should daily fall on our knees to thank him for them—and yet there is something to the idea that he is not their only author. Every editor, every director and actor, and every reader to some degree shapes them, too, for when we edit, direct, act, or read, we inevitably become Shakespeare's collaborator and re-create the plays. The plays, one might say, are so cunningly contrived that they guide our responses, tell us how we ought to feel, and make a mark on us, but (for better or for worse) we also make a mark on them.

—SYLVAN BARNET
Tufts University

Introduction

Richard II, at least in its present form, was written and performed in 1595, after the publication of Samuel Daniel's *Civil Wars* (which was registered in October 1594) and before December 9, when there was a private performance before Sir Edward Hoby and his friends. The play was a popular one. According to Elizabeth I, by 1601 it had been played "forty" times; but when the Essex conspirators asked Shakespeare's company to put on a special performance on the eve of the rebellion, because they thought that the deposition of Richard would be good propaganda, the players protested that it was "so old and so long out of use" that it would attract only a small audience. The conspirators therefore subsidized the performance.

Shakespeare had already dealt with the remote effects of Bolingbroke's usurpation in *Henry VI* and *Richard III*, and his obvious model in the present play was *Edward II*, a play in which Christopher Marlowe had brilliantly dramatized the deposition and murder of Richard of Bordeaux's great-grandfather. There were already at least two plays on the reign of Richard II, *Jack Straw* and *Woodstock*, and it has been argued by Professor John Dover Wilson (in his edition of *Richard II*) that Shakespeare's tragedy was based on a lost play by the author of *The Troublesome Reign of King John*, the source of Shakespeare's *King John*. The main arguments that have been advanced in support of this theory are (1) the presence of various details in the play that presuppose knowledge on the part of the audience; (2) the presence of "fossil" rhymes in blank verse speeches, which seem to indicate that the speeches were originally in rhymed verse; (3) the badness of certain scenes (e.g., 5.3) which, it is supposed, Shakespeare borrowed from the source play;

(4) the use by Shakespeare, either directly or indirectly, of facts available only in two or three French chronicles that were still in manuscript. The last of these points is discussed in the appendix on sources. On the other three, I agree with most scholars that the existence of the source play has not been proved. I can see no resemblance between the style of *The Troublesome Reign* and that of the suspected scenes of *Richard II*; Shakespeare himself may have revised his own play, turning some rhymed verse into blank verse; the obscurities, which in any case are unnoticed in performance, may be explained by sheer carelessness in introducing facts that Shakespeare remembered from his reading; and it is not positively necessary to find a scapegoat for the feeble passages of rhymed verse in Act 5. It will be remembered that in the other plays written about this time—*A Midsummer Night's Dream* and *Romeo and Juliet*—there is a considerable amount of rhyme, more than there had been in previous plays. These three plays have another characteristic in common— they are the first in which Shakespeare uses patterns of imagery for dramatic purposes.[1] The reasons for the rhymed verse are not far to seek. Shakespeare completed his second narrative poem in 1594, and he was still writing sonnets in 1595. Blank verse, moreover, was still a comparatively new medium for drama. Marlowe had led his audiences away from "jigging veins of rhyming mother wits" only seven years previously. The academic dramatists—Daniel and Greville—still used rhyme in their plays. Peele had used it in some scenes of *The Arraignment of Paris* and Kyd, though he had used blank verse for *The Spanish Tragedy*, reverted to rhyme in his *Cornelia*. The Countess of Pembroke was known to favor it. Apart from Marlowe's, very little good blank verse had been written, and the best nondramatic poets—Spenser, Sidney, Daniel, Drayton—all stuck to rhyme. Looking back, we can see that Wilton, where the Countess lived, was the home of lost causes; but to Shakespeare, to whom rhyme came easily, the matter was not so obvious. After all, his early blank verse was comparatively

---

[1] See Richard D. Altick's analysis (printed below) of the play from this point of view. The imagery of the play has also been discussed by Mark Van Doren, W. H. Clemen, and Brents Stirling in the works listed in the Suggested References.

artificial and certainly rhetorical. He did not suffer from Mr. Eliot's fear that the audience would realize that it was listening to poetry. The acting, too, in these early years, had a strong element of formality: the delivery of the verse was more important than the realistic portrayal of character. Shakespeare was only just beginning to portray character by varying the verse. He did this brilliantly with Juliet's Nurse and in the contrast between Richard and Bolingbroke in the abdication scene. But his touch was still uncertain. The Gardener scene (3.4) was admirably conceived as a commentary by the common man on the state of England, and as a parabolic statement, which links up with Gaunt's description of England as "this other Eden." But the execution of the scene falls far short of the conception. The Gardener, speaking in formal blank verse, indistinguishable from that uséd by royal and aristocratic characters, never really emerges from his role as a chorus. It would have been better, perhaps, to have written the scene in prose; but, for some reason, Shakespeare avoided prose altogether. Perhaps he was trying to please his new aristocratic friends.

Whatever the reasons, Shakespeare introduced a considerable amount of rhymed verse into *Richard II*. Some of it is successful, as in Bolingbroke's couplets in the third scene of the play (144–47). But one scene (5.3.73–134) is so bad that critics would like to believe that Shakespeare did not write it; or that, if he wrote it at all, it must belong to a much earlier version of the play, left inadvertently or ill-advisedly unrevised. As we have seen, however, Shakespeare hardly used rhyme at all in some of his early plays, so that the scene was probably written at the same period as the rest of the play. Swinburne, in *A Study of Shakespeare*, called the scene "the last hysterical struggle of rhyme to maintain its place in tragedy." The situation is farcical, with York, the Duchess, and Aumerle on their knees at once, and York actually urging the execution of his son. Shakespeare must have been aware of the absurdity, but he seems to have miscalculated the effect of the scene.

Richard II can be regarded either as a history play, the first of the tetralogy that includes the two parts of *Henry IV* and *Henry V*, or as a tragedy complete in itself. There are several indications in the play that Shakespeare had already planned to continue the story—e.g., the Bishop of Carlisle's prophecy, Richard's own prophecy about Northumberland, the references to Prince Hal and Glendower, and the introduction of Hotspur—but when the play was first printed it was entitled *The Tragedy of Richard II*. Although it is a political tragedy, since we are as much concerned with the fate of England as with the fate of the hero, Richard has a more central role than Henry VI in three earlier histories or Henry IV in the next two histories.

The critics have been very much divided on the amount of sympathy we should extend to Richard. Some find him wholly admirable, and others regard him as wholly contemptible. To Kreyssig,

> he affords us the shocking spectacle of an absolute bankruptcy, mental and spiritual no less than in the world of outward affairs, caused by one condition only: that nature has given him the character of a Dilettante, and called him to a position which, more than any other, demands the Artist.[2]

To Walter Pater, writing a few years later, Richard seemed to be "an exquisite poet." Swinburne, in *Three Plays of Shakespeare*, declared that the third scene

> reveals the protagonist of the play as so pitifully mean and cruel a weakling that no future action or suffering can lift him above the level which divides and purifies pity from contempt.

Later in his essay, Swinburne accused Richard of "callous cruelty" and "heartless hypocrisy," remarking that "the histrionic young tyrant" was removed

> once for all beyond reach of manly sympathy or compassion unqualified by scorn. If we can ever be sorry for anything that befalls so vile a sample of royalty, our sorrow must be so diluted and adulterated by recollection of his wickedness and

---

[2]Quoted by A. P. Rossiter, *Angel with Horns and Other Shakespeare Lectures*, ed. Graham Storey. New York: Theatre Arts Books; London: Longmans, Green & Company, Ltd., 1961, p. 39.

baseness that the tribute could hardly be acceptable to any but the most pitiable example or exception of mankind.

Walter Raleigh, however, remarked in *Shakespeare* that "It is difficult to condemn Richard without taking sides against poetry"; and two recent poets have sprung to Richard's defense, as they would have defended a minor poet of our own day, whose life had been a failure in the eyes of the world. W. B. Yeats, in *Ideas of Good and Evil*, passed lightly over the King's faults and declared that Shakespeare

> made his king fail, a little because he lacked some qualities that were doubtless common among his scullions, but more because he had certain qualities that are uncommon in all ages. To suppose that Shakespeare preferred the man who deposed his king is to suppose that Shakespeare judged men with the eyes of a Municipal Councilor weighing the merits of a Town Clerk; and that had he been by when Verlaine cried out from his bed, "Sir, you have been made by the stroke of a pen, but I have been made by the breath of God," he would have thought the Hospital Superintendent the better man.

John Masefield, obviously much influenced by Yeats's essay, declares in *William Shakespeare* that Richard fails because he is not common:

> The tragedy of the sensitive soul, always acute, becomes terrible when that soul is made king here by one of the accidents of life.

John Bailey, irritated by Yeats and Masefield, retorted tartly in *The Continuity of Letters*:

> Fools such critics are. . . . For their own choice Mr. Yeats and Mr. Masefield are free. Only they must not father it upon Shakespeare. No man has ever known the theater better than he; and if he had meant us to admire Richard and despise Henry [Henry V, not Henry IV] we should most assuredly not have escaped doing it; but there is no audience from his day to ours which has not instantly and instinctively worshiped Henry and pitied Richard.

We may note in passing that many good critics have had reservations about Henry V, and modern audiences (except in time of war) have been less enthusiastic about him than Bailey appears to be, and more sympathetic to Richard, especially when the part was played by Sir John Gielgud. But the debate continues. A. P. Rossiter, to give a last example, unkindly suggests that there is "something in Richard which calls out the latent homosexuality of critics"; and to Pater's claim that Richard's nature is "that of a poet," he replies: "If so, surely a very *bad* poet."

Some of Richard's sympathetic critics seem to forget that he is depicted as a murderer; and those who find no redeeming features in his character ignore or misinterpret the changes brought about by suffering. Shakespeare's model for his play (as we have seen) was *Edward II*. Marlowe's method was to concentrate on Edward's misgovernment in the opening acts of the play and to arouse sympathy for him after his deposition, partly by stressing the unscrupulousness of his opponents, partly by showing that Edward was beloved by his favorites, and partly by a detailed presentation of his sufferings. Shakespeare's method is similar. In the first two acts he gives a vivid portrayal of Richard's misgovernment, which is brought home to us particularly by the patriotic indignation of Gaunt's dying speeches. In the later acts, although we are shown again and again Richard's weaknesses of character, Shakespeare arouses sympathy for him by the poetic beauty of his long arias, by his tragic isolation, by the pathos of his leave-taking from his Queen, by the account of his entry into London, and by the episode of the loyal groom. Yet Shakespeare's method differs in several respects from Marlowe's. Richard's initial guilt is greater than Edward's, his suffering is mental rather than physical, and his character is purged by it. Although some critics believe that his scene with the Queen and his soliloquy in prison reveal that he is still an incorrigible sentimentalist, turning everything, like Ophelia, to favor and to prettiness, there are signs that he has acquired a greater self-awareness and a recognition of his faults:

I wasted time, and now doth Time waste me: (5.5.49)

But the greatest difference between the attitudes of the two dramatists is that Marlowe never mentions, while Shakespeare continually stresses, the divine right of kings. We are warned over and over again that Richard's deposition is a sin which will be punished by the horrors of civil war. It was to stress this point that Shakespeare deviated from his sources in giving the Bishop of Carlisle his eloquent prophecy just before the deposition scene.

Professor J. Dover Wilson has called *Richard II* "a Tudor passion play," a description which fits in with the frequent references to Scripture by which Shakespeare achieves its particular tone and atmosphere. Some of Richard's speeches are lamentations on the fall of princes, a recognition of the mortality of man and of the peculiar vulnerability of those called to high estate, which read like transmutations of Lydgate's *Fall of Princes* or of *The Mirror for Magistrates*. These link up with the medieval conception of tragedy as a fall from greatness into misery. But the Scriptural references are mainly designed to emphasize the sin of rebellion against an anointed king, and they show that Shakespeare was steeped in the teaching of the Homilies, with whatever reservations he may have had about it. Richard compares his treacherous friends to Judas and those who show an outward pity at his fall to Pilate. He imagines that Bolingbroke will tremble at his sin; he boasts that the deputy elected by the Lord cannot be deposed by the breath of worldly men, that angels will fight on his side, and that the unborn children of the rebels will be struck by pestilence. Bolingbroke, for having broken his oath of allegiance, is damned in the book of heaven. England, rent by civil war, will be called Golgotha. The Bishop of Carlisle warns Bolingbroke not to set house against house; and Bolingbroke himself compares Richard's murderer to Cain. In prison Richard meditates on two Gospel texts.

Richard's own Biblical references are an appeal for Christian compassion. It is possible, indeed, that Shakespeare had in mind the whole problem of charity and pity; but Professor Peter Alexander, who makes this suggestion in *Shakespeare's Life and Art*, goes on to complain that the fallen king's insistence on his own position . . . is incompatible with the self-forgetfulness which is as essential to the tragic as to the Christian hero. For this is not the waking as from a dream of some disinterested heart to the self-seeking of society, but the long lament of one who gave short shrift to a dying Gaunt; and this contrast between Richard's indifference to others and exquisite sensibility for himself makes tragedy impossible.

Even if we could believe in the self-forgetfulness of Hamlet, Lear, or Othello, we may well feel that Professor Alexander does not make allowances for the development of Richard's character in the course of the play, nor for the Elizabethan convention by which a character comments on his own situation. When Lear talks of his own pitiful state, or when Othello or Antony makes his final apologia, these characters are not meant to be indulging in self-pity or vanity: they are used by the dramatist to guide the feelings of the audience. In the mature tragedies, it is true, we do not get the self-comparison of a character to Christ; but the method is largely justified in Richard's case by the central importance in the play of the concept of Divine Right. The same consideration justifies the strong element of ritual in the play.

We are presented throughout the play with the contrast between Richard and his successor. Richard, the anointed King, is unfit to rule, in spite of his good qualities, and in spite of his belated acquisition of self-knowledge. Henry Bolingbroke is a born ruler, but his reign is doomed to misery because he is a usurper. The contrast is brought out in other ways. Richard is frivolous, witty, eloquent, and poetic, a man of words who wears his heart upon his sleeve, one who is continually playing a part, to whom, as John Palmer says in *Political Characters*, "nothing has interest or significance but what concerns himself." He loses his crown not because he stops the duel at Coventry—an action which he takes with the approval of his council, and which can hardly be regarded as an example of his love of play acting—but because of his murder of Gloucester before the beginning of the play, because of his confiscation of Gaunt's estates, because his return from Ireland is delayed by contrary winds, and because he despairs on his arrival in England. This last point, which is usually taken as a prime example of his refusal to face realities, could as plausibly be used to prove that he was more realistic than his supporters. He is brought to his ruin, as all Shakespeare's tragic heroes are, by a combination of fate and faults of character.

Henry is a contrast in every respect. He is generally taciturn, although he can turn on his charm like a tap, as is apparent from the way even Northumberland is captivated by it. The account given in 1.4 of his triumphant journey into exile, although put into the mouth of an enemy, is corroborated by what he himself admits in *I Henry IV*:

> And then I stole all courtesy from heaven,
> And dressed myself in such humility
> That I did pluck allegiance from men's hearts,
> Loud shouts and salutations from their mouths,
> Even in the presence of the crownèd King. (3.2.50–54)

The same calculated behavior is described in Hotspur's account of their first meeting. Bolingbroke, like Claudius, is a "king of smiles," a "fawning greyhound" who proffered Hotspur "a candy deal of courtesy." We do not see Henry in any personal relationship, except with his father in the first act, and in his complaints about his son in the last. We see him as a politician (in the Elizabethan sense of the term, "unscrupulous self-seeker") who subordinates everything to his ambition. He obtains the crown, as he confesses on his deathbed, by "bypaths and indirect crook'd ways." Shakespeare presents the character with a masterly ambiguity. As John Palmer points out:

> Bolingbroke gives no sign of his purpose—and for an excellent reason. He is that most dangerous of climbing politicians, the man who will go further than his rivals because he never allows himself to know where he is going. Every step in his progress toward the throne is dictated by circumstances, and he never permits himself to have a purpose till it is more than half fulfilled.

The same point is made by Brents Stirling:

> Three times—at the end of 3.3, at the end of the deposition scene, and in the Exton scenes at the end of the play—Henry has taken, if it may be so called, a decisive step. Each time the move he has made has been embodied in a terse statement, and each time someone else has either evoked it from him or stated its implications for him.

The characterization, apart from that of Richard and Boling-broke, is less effective than that of the minor characters in *Richard III*. But it is not so bad as is sometimes pretended. Swinburne, with customary exaggeration, attacked what he regarded as Shakespeare's incompetence:

> The poet was not yet dramatist enough to feel for each of his characters an equal or proportionate regard; to divide and disperse his interest among the various crowd of figures which claim each in its place . . . a fair and adequate share of their creator's attention and sympathy. His present interest was wholly concentrated on the single figure of Richard; . . . the subordinate figures became to him but heavy and vexatious encumbrances, to be shifted on and off the stage with as much haste and as little of labor as might be possible to an impatient and uncertain hand. . . . Even after a lifelong study of this as of all other plays of Shakespeare, it is for me at least impossible to determine what I doubt the poet could himself have clearly defined—the main principle, the motive and the meaning of such characters as York, Norfolk, and Aumerle. The Gaveston and the Mortimer of Marlowe are far more solid and definite figures than these; yet none after Richard is more important to the scheme of Shakespeare. They are fitful, shifting, vaporous; their outlines change, withdraw, dissolve, and leave not a rack behind.

Swinburne's views were influenced by his assumption that the play was one of Shakespeare's earliest. If he had realized that the poet was not a novice when he wrote it, but the author of nine or ten other plays, he might have been less anxious to complain of its immaturity. Even in Shakespeare's greatest plays, the minor characters are little more than sketches; and it must be said that York, Mowbray, and Aumerle are not really as important to the scheme of the play as Gaveston and Mortimer are in *Edward II*. The three characters, moreover, are not really as indeterminate and vague as Swinburne pretends. York, for example, whom Swinburne described as

> an incomparable, an incredible, an unintelligible and a monstrous nullity . . . a living and driveling picture of hysterical impotence on the downward grade to dotage and distraction,

is, in fact, a perfectly credible portrait of a man torn between conflicting loyalties. He deplores Richard's behavior but he is chosen to be Lord Governor because the King realizes that his criticisms were disinterested:

> For he is just, and always loved us well.   (2.1.221)

York tries to be faithful to his trust; but it is clear from 2.2 that he is muddled, incompetent, and powerless. Both here, and in later scenes, Shakespeare extracts some humor from York's bumbling inefficiency. In 2.3 his loyalty to the King, his sympathy with Bolingbroke's wrongs, and his shortage of troops combine to paralyze him. He begins by calling Bolingbroke a traitor; before long he admits:

> I have had feeling of my cousin's wrongs.   (140)

He confesses that his forces are too weak for him to arrest the traitor, and follows a declaration of neutrality by extending an invitation to the rebels to spend the night in the castle. Before the end of the scene he has half agreed to go with the rebels to Bristol, where Bolingbroke intends to execute the King's favorites. York has become a traitor almost without knowing it. Far from being incredible, the character is very shrewdly drawn.

Once Richard's downfall is assured, York becomes a wholehearted supporter of the new regime. Characteristically, York is full of pity for Richard; he remonstrates with

Northumberland for leaving out his title (3.3.7–8), and, although he is chosen to escort the King to his deposition, he movingly describes the entrance of Bolingbroke and Richard into London. His new loyalty is soon tested. When he finds that Aumerle has plotted to kill Bolingbroke, it never enters his head to be ashamed of his own coat-turning: he rushes off to Windsor to beg for his son's death. This is partly prudence—he has agreed to be pledge for Aumerle's "lasting fealty to the new-made king"—but partly the genuine zeal of a convert. The scene in which he goes on his knees to Bolingbroke, absurd as it is, is not out of character.

A similar defense could be made of Aumerle, who is deeply attached to Richard and loyal to him after his fall. He submits to Bolingbroke only when his carelessness has put his life in danger. Shakespeare tells us enough about him for the purposes of the play—his dislike of Bolingbroke revealed in his account of his leave-taking and in the accusations leveled against him in 4.1, his love for Richard shown by his tears in 3.3, and by his conspiracy against the usurper. There are some indications of irresponsibility in his character, but Shakespeare deliberately leaves unsettled whether or not he was implicated in Gloucester's murder. The scene at the beginning of Act 4 where he is accused was described by Swinburne as "a morally chaotic introduction of incongruous causes, inexplicable plaintiffs, and incomprehensible defendants." But the question of which side is telling the truth is irrelevant to the effect which Shakespeare wished to give. Aumerle has to be attacked, not because of his guilt, but because he is an opponent of the usurper.

The third character of whom Swinburne complains, Thomas Mowbray, Duke of Norfolk, appears only in two scenes of the first act. Shakespeare could rely on most of his audience knowing that Richard himself was ultimately responsible for Gloucester's murder—and those who did not know were plainly informed by Gaunt in the second scene—and they would therefore appreciate that Bolingbroke's attack on Mowbray was aimed at the King, or at least at his favorites. Richard can only banish Bolingbroke if he consents to the perpetual banishment of Mowbray. If these facts are understood, Mowbray's conduct becomes intelligible. He tries to defend himself without betraying Richard, and he is bitterly surprised at his sentence of banishment. Some critics have thought that a character with such a doubtful past should not have been given the sympathetic lines in which he expresses his patriotism, and that he should not have been given so fine an epitaph as Carlisle's speech (4.1.91ff.). But there are no black and no white characters in *Richard II*. We need be no more surprised at Mowbray fighting

> For Jesu Christ in glorious Christian field,   (93)

than that Bolingbroke should intend to expiate his responsibility for Richard's death by making a pilgrimage to the Holy Land.

Sometimes, it must be admitted, Shakespeare does not fully succeed in making his characters live. In the second scene of the play, for example, he tries to give reality to the portrait of the Duchess of Gloucester by making her forget what she was going to say:

> Commend me to thy brother, Edmund York.
> Lo! this is all: nay, yet depart not so;
> Though this be all, do not so quickly go.
> I shall remember more. Bid him . . . Ah! what?
> With all good speed at Plashy visit me.   (62–66)

Here the effect is blurred by the rigidity of the verse and the intrusive rhyme.

It has been necessary to defend the reality of the minor characters in the play because the conflict between Richard and Bolingbroke does not take place in a dramatic and political vacuum. The background is filled in economically and well: and the patriotism of Gaunt, the loyalty of Aumerle, the oscillation of York, the prophetic fervor of the Bishop of Carlisle are all essential to the effect of the tragedy.

In *Titus Andronicus* and *Richard III* Shakespeare had submerged tragedy in melodrama; in *Romeo and Juliet* the tragedy is brought about by accident rather than by defect of character; in *Richard II* the tragedy is firmly based on character and, as in *King Lear*, the character of the hero acquires greater depth as his fortunes decline. It may therefore be said that, in spite of its obvious weaknesses, and in spite of its inferiority in some respects to *Richard III*—it contains finer poetry and greater complexity but is usually less effective in the theater—it is closer to mature Shakespearean tragedy than any of the previous plays had been.

—KENNETH MUIR
University of Liverpool

The Tragedy of
King Richard the Second

The Tragedy of
King Richard the Second

[ACT 1

Scene 1. *Windsor Castle.*]

Enter King Richard, John of Gaunt, with other
Nobles and Attendants.

Richard. Old John of Gaunt, time-honored Lancaster,
  Hast thou according to thy oath and band° [1]
  Brought hither Henry Hereford,° thy bold son,
  Here to make good the boist'rous late appeal,°
  Which then our° leisure would not let us hear,   5
  Against the Duke of Norfolk, Thomas Mowbray?

Gaunt. I have, my liege.

Richard. Tell me, moreover, hast thou sounded him,
  If he appeal° the Duke on ancient malice,
  Or worthily,° as a good subject should,   10
  On some known ground of treachery in him?

Gaunt. As near as I could sift° him on that
    argument,°
  On some apparent° danger seen in him
  Aimed at your Highness, no inveterate malice.

---

[1] The degree sign (°) indicates a footnote, which is keyed to the text
by line number. Text references are printed in **boldface** type; the annota-
tion follows in roman type.

1.1. 2 **band** bond   3 **Hereford** (pronounced "Herford")   4 **appeal** accusation of treason   5 **our** (the royal plural)   9 **appeal** accuse   10 **worthily**
according to desert   12 **sift** examine thoroughly   12 **argument** subject
13 **apparent** obvious

15 *Richard.* Then call them to our presence: face to face,
And frowning brow to brow, ourselves will hear
The accuser and the accusèd freely speak.
High-stomached° are they both, and full of ire,
In rage, deaf as the sea, hasty as fire.

Enter Bolingbroke and Mowbray.

20 *Bolingbroke.*° Many years of happy days befall
My gracious sovereign, my most loving liege!

Mowbray. Each day still better other's happiness,
Until the heavens envying earth's good hap,
Add an immortal title to your crown!

25 *Richard.* We thank you both; yet one but flatters us,
As well appeareth by the cause you come,
Namely to appeal each other of high treason.
Cousin of Hereford, what dost thou object
Against the Duke of Norfolk, Thomas Mowbray?

Bolingbroke. First—heaven be the record to my
30 speech!—
In the devotion of a subject's love,
Tend'ring° the precious safety of my prince,
And free from other misbegotten hate,
Come I appellant° to this princely presence.
35 Now, Thomas Mowbray, do I turn to thee,
And mark my greeting° well: for what I speak,
My body shall make good upon this earth,
Or my divine soul answer it in heaven.
Thou art a traitor and a miscreant,°
40 Too good to be so, and too bad to live;
Since the more fair and crystal is the sky,
The uglier seem the clouds that in it fly.
Once more, the more to aggravate the note,°
With a foul traitor's name stuff I thy throat,
45 And wish—so please my sovereign—ere I move,

---

18 **High-stomached** high-spirited   20 **Bolingbroke** (pronounced and spelled "Bullingbrooke" in Shakespeare's time)   32 **Tend'ring** cherishing   34 **appellant** accuser   36 **greeting** address   39 **miscreant** unbeliever, villain   43 **note** reproach

What my tongue speaks my right-drawn° sword
   may prove.

Mowbray. Let not my cold words here accuse my
   zeal:°
'Tis not the trial of a woman's war,
The bitter clamor of two eager° tongues,
Can arbitrate this cause betwixt us twain;   *50*
The blood is hot that must be cooled for this.
Yet can I not of such tame patience boast,
As to be hushed, and naught at all to say.
First, the fair reverence of° your Highness
   curbs me
From giving reins and spurs to my free speech,   *55*
Which else would post° until it had returned
These terms of treason doubled down his throat.
Setting aside his high blood's royalty,
And let him be° no kinsman to my liege,
I do defy him, and I spit at him,   *60*
Call him a slanderous coward and a villain;
Which to maintain, I would allow him odds,
And meet him were I tied° to run afoot
Even to the frozen ridges of the Alps,
Or any other ground inhabitable,°   *65*
Where ever Englishman durst set his foot.
Meantime, let this° defend my loyalty:
By all my hopes° most falsely doth he lie.

Bolingbroke. Pale trembling coward, there I throw
   my gage,
Disclaiming here the kindred of the King,°   *70*
And lay aside my high blood's royalty,
Which fear, not reverence, makes thee to except.°
If guilty dread have left thee so much strength
As to take up mine honor's pawn,° then stoop.

46 **right-drawn** drawn to defend the right   47 **accuse my zeal** make me
seem unzealous   49 **eager** sharp   54 **fair reverence of** respect due to
56 **post** speed   59 **let him be** suppose him to be   63 **tied** obliged
65 **inhabitable** uninhabitable   67 **this** (his sword)   68 **hopes** i.e., of
heaven   70 **Disclaiming . . . King** (referring to Mowbray's words, lines
58–59)   72 **except** use as excuse   74 **pawn** pledge (his glove or hood,
which he throws down)

75 By that, and all the rites of knighthood else,
    Will I make good against thee, arm to arm,
    What I have spoke, or thou canst worse devise.

Mowbray. I take it up; and by that sword I swear,
    Which gently laid my knighthood on my shoulder,
80 I'll answer thee in any fair degree°
    Or chivalrous design of knightly trial;
    And when I mount, alive may I not light,°
    If I be traitor or unjustly fight.

Richard. What doth our cousin lay to Mowbray's
        charge?
85 It must be great that can inherit us°
    So much as of a thought of ill in him.

Bolingbroke. Look what I speak, my life shall prove
        it true:
    That Mowbray hath received eight thousand nobles°
    In name of lendings° for your Highness' soldiers,
90 The which he hath detained for lewd° employments,
    Like a false traitor and injurious villain.
    Besides, I say, and will in battle prove,
    Or° here, or elsewhere to the furthest verge
    That ever was surveyed by English eye,
95 That all the treasons for these eighteen years
    Complotted and contrivèd in this land
    Fetch° from false Mowbray, their first head and
        spring.
    Further, I say and further will maintain
    Upon his bad life to make all this good,
100 That he did plot the Duke of Gloucester's° death,
    Suggest° his soon-believing adversaries,
    And, consequently,° like a traitor coward,
    Sluiced out his innocent soul through streams of
        blood;
    Which blood, like sacrificing Abel's, cries

80 **degree** manner   82 **light** dismount   85 **inherit us** make us have
88 **nobles** gold coins   89 **lendings** money on trust   90 **lewd** base
93 **Or** either   97 **Fetch** derive   100 **Gloucester** Thomas of Woodstock,
who had been murdered at Richard's orders   101 **Suggest** incite   102
consequently afterward

Even from the tongueless caverns of the earth   *105*
To me for justice and rough chastisement:
And, by the glorious worth of my descent,
This arm shall do it, or° this life be spent.

Richard. How high a pitch° his resolution soars!
Thomas of Norfolk, what say'st thou to this?   *110*

Mowbray. O! let my sovereign turn away his face,
And bid his ears a little while be deaf,
Till I have told this slander of his blood
How God and good men hate so foul a liar.

Richard. Mowbray, impartial are our eyes and ears.   *115*
Were he my brother, nay, my kingdom's heir,
As he is but my father's brother's son,
Now by my scepter's awe I make a vow,
Such neighbor nearness to our sacred blood
Should nothing privilege him, nor partialize°   *120*
The unstooping firmness of my upright soul.
He is our subject, Mowbray, so art thou:
Free speech and fearless I to thee allow.

Mowbray. Then, Bolingbroke, as low as to thy heart,
Through the false passage of thy throat, thou
    liest.   *125*
Three parts of that receipt I had° for Calais
Disbursed I duly to his Highness' soldiers;
The other part reserved I by consent,
For that my sovereign liege was in my debt
Upon remainder of a dear account,°   *130*
Since last I went to France to fetch his Queen.
Now swallow down that lie. For Gloucester's death,
I slew him not; but, to my own disgrace,
Neglected my sworn duty° in that case.
For you, my noble Lord of Lancaster,   ·   *135*
The honorable father to my foe,
Once did I lay an ambush for your life,

108 **or** before   109 **pitch** peak of a falcon's flight (the King is uneasy that his own guilt will come to light)   120 **partialize** make partial 126 **that receipt I had** what I received   130 **dear account** private or expensive debt   134 **duty** (either to kill Gloucester, or to reveal the murder)

A trespass that doth vex my grievèd soul;
But, ere I last received the sacrament,
140   I did confess it, and exactly begged
Your grace's pardon, and I hope I had it.
This is my fault: as for the rest appealed,
It issues from the rancor of a villain,
A recreant° and most degenerate traitor;
145   Which in myself I boldly will defend,
And interchangeably° hurl down my gage
Upon this overweening traitor's foot,
To prove myself a loyal gentleman
Even in the best blood chambered in his bosom.
150   In haste whereof, most heartily I pray
Your Highness to assign our trial day.

Richard. Wrath-kindled gentlemen, be ruled by me.
Let's purge this choler° without letting blood:°
This we prescribe, though no physician;
155   Deep malice makes too deep incision;
Forget, forgive, conclude, and be agreed;
Our doctors say this is no month to bleed.
Good uncle, let this end where it begun:
We'll calm the Duke of Norfolk, you your son.

160   *Gaunt.* To be a make-peace shall become my age:
Throw down, my son, the Duke of Norfolk's gage.

Richard. And Norfolk, throw down his.

Gaunt.   When,° Harry, when?
Obedience bids I should not bid again.

Richard. Norfolk, throw down; we bid—there is no
        boot.°

Mowbray. Myself I throw, dread sovereign, at thy
165   foot.
My life thou shalt command, but not my shame:
The one my duty owes; but my fair name

144 **recreant** renegade   146 **interchangeably** in exchange   153 **choler**
anger   153 **letting blood** (pun on bleeding medicinally and bloodshed)
162 **When** (exclamation of impatience)   164 **boot** remedy

Despite of death that lives upon my grave,
To dark dishonor's use thou shalt not have.
I am disgraced, impeached,° and baffled° here,   *170*
Pierced to the soul with slander's venomed spear,
The which no balm can cure but his heart-blood
Which breathed this poison.

Richard.   Rage must be withstood.
Give me his gage; lions make leopards° tame.

Mowbray. Yea, but not change his spots.° Take but
    my shame,   *175*
And I resign my gage. My dear dear lord,
The purest treasure mortal times afford
Is spotless reputation—that away,
Men are but gilded loam, or painted clay.
A jewel in a ten-times-barred-up chest   *180*
Is a bold spirit in a loyal breast;
Mine honor is my life, both grow in one;
Take honor from me, and my life is done;
Then, dear my liege, mine honor let me try;
In that I live, and for that will I die.   *185*

Richard. Cousin, throw up° your gage; do you begin.

Bolingbroke. O, God defend my soul from such deep
    sin!
Shall I seem crestfallen in my father's sight?
Or with pale beggar-fear° impeach my height°
Before this out-dared dastard? Ere my tongue   *190*
Shall wound my honor with such feeble wrong,°
Or sound so base a parle,° my teeth shall tear
The slavish motive° of recanting fear,
And spit it bleeding in his high disgrace,

---

170 **impeached** accused   170 **baffled** treated with infamy   174 **lions make leopards tame** (alluding to the rampant lion in the King's royal arms and the standing beast in Mowbray's)   175 **spots** (alluding to the proverb and punning on spots, meaning stains)   186 **throw up** (perhaps to the upper stage on which Richard sits)   189 **beggar-**fear appropriate to a beggar   189 **height** rank   191 **feeble wrong** a wrong so grave that the man who submits to it exhibits himself as feeble   192 **parle** parley, truce   193 **motive** moving organ, i.e., tongue

195   Where shame doth harbor, even in Mowbray's face.

                                        [Exit Gaunt.°]

        Richard. We were not born to sue, but to command:
            Which since we cannot do to make you friends,
            Be ready, as your lives shall answer it,
            At Coventry upon Saint Lambert's day.°
200   There shall your swords and lances arbitrate
            The swelling difference of your settled hate:
            Since we cannot atone° you, we shall see
            Justice design the victor's chivalry.°
            Lord Marshal, command our officers-at-arms
205   Be ready to direct these home alarms.

                                Exit [Richard with others].

        [Scene 2. *London. Gaunt's house.*]

        *Enter John of Gaunt with the Duchess of
                    Gloucester.*

        Gaunt. Alas, the part I had in Woodstock's° blood
            Doth more solicit me than your exclaims°
            To stir against the butchers of his life;
            But since correction lieth in those hands°
5   Which made the fault that we cannot correct,
            Put we our quarrel to the will of heaven,
            Who, when they° see the hours° ripe on earth,
            Will rain hot vengeance on offenders' heads.

        Duchess. Finds brotherhood in thee no sharper spur?
10   Hath love in thy old blood no living fire?

195s.d. **Exit Gaunt** (Gaunt begins Scene 2, and therefore according
to stage convention must leave the stage before the end of Scene 1)
199 **Saint Lambert's day** (Sept. 17)   202 **atone** reconcile   203 **design
the victor's chivalry** indicate whose prowess will win the victory (i.e.,
the victor will be vindicated)   1.2. 1 **Woodstock** Gloucester, Gaunt's
brother   2 **exclaims** outcries   4 **those hands** i.e., the King's   7 **they**
God and his angels   7 **hours** (two syllables)

Edward's seven sons, whereof thyself art one,
Were as seven vials of his sacred blood,
Or seven fair branches springing from one root.
Some of those seven are dried by nature's course,
Some of those branches by the destinies cut: *15*
But Thomas, my dear lord, my life, my Gloucester,
One vial full of Edward's sacred blood,
One flourishing branch of his most royal root,
Is cracked, and all the precious liquor spilt,
Is hacked down, and his summer leaves all faded   *20*
By Envy's hand and Murder's bloody ax.
Ah! Gaunt, his blood was thine; that bed,
    that womb,
That metal,° that self° mold that fashioned thee,
Made him a man: and though thou livest and
    breathest,
Yet art thou slain in him; thou dost consent   *25*
In some large measure to thy father's death,
In that thou seest thy wretched brother die,
Who was the model° of thy father's life.
Call it not patience, Gaunt, it is despair:
In suff'ring° thus thy brother to be slaught'red,   *30*
Thou showest the naked pathway° to thy life,
Teaching stern Murder how to butcher thee.
That which in mean men we entitle patience
Is pale cold cowardice in noble breasts.
What shall I say? To safeguard thine own life,   *35*
The best way is to venge my Gloucester's death.

Gaunt. God's is the quarrel; for God's substitute,
His deputy° anointed in His sight,
Hath caused his death, the which if wrongfully,
Let heaven revenge, for I may never lift   *40*
An angry arm against His minister.

Duchess. Where, then, alas, may I complain myself?°

___

23 **metal** stuff   23 **self** same   28 **model** copy   30 **suff'ring** allowing
31 **naked pathway** open road (for his murderers)   38 **deputy** (the idea
that the King, however unworthy, is God's deputy is stressed throughout
the play)   42 **Where . . . myself** to whom shall I complain

Gaunt. To God, the widow's champion and defense.

Duchess. Why, then, I will. Farewell, old Gaunt,
45   Thou goest to Coventry, there to behold
        Our cousin° Hereford and fell° Mowbray fight.
        O! sit my husband's wrongs on Hereford's spear,
        That it may enter butcher Mowbray's breast;
        Or if misfortune° miss the first career,°
50   Be Mowbray's sins so heavy in his bosom,
        That they may break his foaming courser's back,
        And throw the rider headlong in the lists,
        A caitiff recreant° to my cousin Hereford.
        Farewell, old Gaunt; thy sometimes° brother's wife
55   With her companion, Grief, must end her life.

Gaunt. Sister, farewell, I must to Coventry:
        As much good stay with thee, as go with me.

Duchess. Yet one word more: grief boundeth where it
            falls,
        Not with the empty hollowness, but weight.°
60   I take my leave before I have begun,
        For sorrow ends not when it seemeth done.
        Commend me to thy brother, Edmund York.°
        Lo! this is all: nay, yet depart not so;
        Though this be all, do not so quickly go.
65   I shall remember more. Bid him . . . Ah! what?
        With all good speed at Plashy° visit me.
        Alack! and what shall good old York there see
        But empty lodgings and unfurnished walls,
        Unpeopled offices,° untrodden stones,
70   And what hear there for welcome but my groans?
        Therefore commend me, let him not come there,
        To seek out sorrow that dwells everywhere.
        Desolate, desolate will I hence and die!
        The last leave of thee takes my weeping eye.

                                            Exeunt.

46 **cousin** kinsman   46 **fell** ruthless   49 **misfortune** disaster (to Mowbray)   49 **career** encounter   53 **caitiff recreant** captive coward   54 **sometimes** sometime, former   58–59 **grief . . . weight** i.e., my grief returns because it is heavy, not like a ball   62 **York** Duke of York   66 **Plashy** (in Essex)   69 **offices** kitchens, servants' quarters, etc.

[Scene 3. *The lists at Coventry.*]

Enter Lord Marshal and the Duke of Aumerle.

Marshal. My Lord Aumerle, is Harry Hereford armed?

Aumerle. Yea, at all points, and longs to enter in.

Marshal. The Duke of Norfolk, sprightfully° and bold,
Stays but the summons of the appellant's trumpet.

Aumerle. Why, then, the champions are prepared, and
    stay   5
For nothing but his Majesty's approach.

*The trumpets sound, and the King enters with his
nobles, [including Gaunt, Bushy, Bagot, Green].
When they are set, enter [Mowbray,] the Duke
of Norfolk, in arms, defendant, [and a Herald].*

Richard. Marshal, demand of yonder champion
The cause of his arrival here in arms;
Ask him his name; and orderly proceed
To swear him in the justice of his cause.   10

Marshal. In God's name and the King's, say who thou
    art
And why thou comest thus knightly clad in arms,
Against what man thou com'st, and what thy
    quarrel.
Speak truly on thy knighthood and thy oath,
As so defend thee heaven and thy valor.   15

Mowbray. My name is Thomas Mowbray, Duke of
    Norfolk,

1.3. 3 **sprightfully** full of spirit

Who hither come engagèd by my oath—
Which God defend° a knight should violate!
Both to defend my loyalty and truth
20   To God, my king, and my succeeding issue,
Against the Duke of Hereford that appeals° me;
And by the grace of God, and this mine arm,
To prove him in defending of myself
A traitor to my God, my king, and me;
25   And as I truly° fight, defend me, heaven!

The trumpets sound. Enter [Bolingbroke,] Duke
of Hereford, appellant, in armor.

Richard. Marshal, demand of yonder knight in arms,
Both who he is, and why he cometh hither
Thus plated° in habiliments of war,
And formally, according to our law,
30   Depose° him in the justice of his cause.

Marshal. What is thy name? And wherefore com'st
thou hither
Before King Richard in his royal lists?
Against whom comest thou? And what's thy
quarrel?
Speak like a true knight, so defend thee heaven.

35   *Bolingbroke.* Harry of Hereford, Lancaster and Derby
Am I, who ready here do stand in arms
To prove by God's grace, and my body's valor
In lists, on Thomas Mowbray, Duke of Norfolk,
That he is a traitor, foul and dangerous,
40   To God of heaven, King Richard and to me:
And as I truly fight, defend me, heaven!

Marshal. On pain of death, no person be so bold
Or daring-hardy° as to touch the lists,
Except the Marshal and such officers
45   Appointed to direct these fair designs.

18 **defend** forbid   21 **appeals** accuses   25 **truly** with truth on my side
28 **plated** in plate armor   30 **Depose** examine on oath   43 **daring-hardy**
reckless

Bolingbroke. Lord Marshal, let me kiss my Sovereign's
   hand,
  And bow my knee before his Majesty;
  For Mowbray and myself are like two men
  That vow a long and weary pilgrimage:
  Then let us take a ceremonious leave   *50*
  And loving farewell of our several friends.

Marshal. The appellant in all duty greets your
   Highness,
  And craves to kiss your hand and take his leave.

Richard. We will descend and fold him in our arms.
  Cousin of Hereford, as thy cause is right,   *55*
  So be thy fortune in this royal fight:
  Farewell, my blood, which if today thou shed,
  Lament we may, but not revenge thee dead.

Bolingbroke. O, let no noble eye profane a tear
  For me, if I be gored with Mowbray's spear: *60*
  As confident as is the falcon's flight
  Against a bird, do I with Mowbray fight.
  My loving lord, I take my leave of you;
  Of you, my noble cousin, Lord Aumerle,
  Not sick, although I have to do with death,   *65*
  But lusty, young, and cheerly° drawing breath.
  Lo! as at English feasts, so I regreet°
  The daintiest last, to make the end most sweet.
  O thou, the earthly author of my blood,
  Whose youthful spirit in me regenerate°   *70*
  Doth with a twofold vigor lift me up
  To reach at victory above my head,
  Add proof° unto mine armor with thy prayers,
  And with thy blessings steel my lance's point,
  That it may enter Mowbray's waxen° coat   *75*
  And furbish new the name of John a° Gaunt
  Even in the lusty havior° of his son.

Gaunt. God in thy good cause make thee prosperous;

66 **cheerly** cheerfully   67 **regreet** greet again   70 **regenerate** reborn
73 **proof** invulnerability   75 **waxen** i.e., soft   76 **a** o', of   77 **havior**
behavior

Be swift like lightning in the execution,
80 And let thy blows doubly redoubled
Fall like amazing° thunder on the casque
Of thy adverse° pernicious enemy:
Rouse up thy youthful blood, be valiant and live.

Bolingbroke. Mine innocency and St. George to
thrive!

85 *Mowbray.* However God or fortune cast my lot,
There lives or dies, true to King Richard's throne,
A loyal, just and upright gentleman.
Never did captive with a freer heart
Cast off his chains of bondage, and embrace
90 His golden, uncontrolled enfranchisement°
More than my dancing soul doth celebrate
This feast of battle with mine adversary.
Most mighty liege, and my companion peers,
Take from my mouth the wish of happy years;
95 As gentle and as jocund as to jest°
Go I to fight: truth hath a quiet breast.

Richard. Farewell, my lord; securely° I espy
Virtue with valor couchèd° in thine eye.
Order the trial, Marshal, and begin.

100 *Marshal.* Harry of Hereford, Lancaster and Derby,
Receive thy lance, and God defend the right.

Bolingbroke. Strong as a tower in hope,° I cry Amen.

Marshal. Go bear this lance to Thomas, Duke of
Norfolk.

First Herald. Harry of Hereford, Lancaster and Derby,
105 Stands here for God, his Sovereign and himself,
On pain to be° found false and recreant,
To prove the Duke of Norfolk, Thomas Mowbray,
A traitor to his God, his king, and him,

---

81 **amazing** stupefying 82 **adverse** placed opposite 90 **enfranchise-
ment** liberation 95 **jest** sport 97 **securely** confidently 98 **couchèd**
lying hidden 102 **Strong as a tower in hope** (cf. Psalms 61:3) 106 **On
pain to be** at the risk of being

   And dares him to set forward to the fight.

Second Herald. Here standeth Thomas Mowbray,
      Duke of Norfolk,   *110*
   On pain to be found false and recreant,
   Both to defend himself, and to approve°
   Henry of Hereford, Lancaster and Derby,
   To God, his sovereign, and to him disloyal,
   Courageously and with a free desire   *115*
   Attending but the signal to begin.

Marshal. Sound trumpets; and set forward
      combatants!
               [*A charge sounded.*]
   Stay, the King hath thrown his warder° down.

Richard. Let them lay by their helmets and their spears
   And both return back to their chairs° again.   *120*
   Withdraw with us, and let the trumpets sound,
   While we return these dukes what we decree.
               [*A long flourish.*°]
   Draw near,
   And list° what with our council we have done.
   For that our kingdom's earth should not be soiled   *125*
   With that dear blood which it hath fosterèd;
   And for our eyes do hate the dire aspect
   Of civil wounds plowed up with neighbor's sword,
   And for we think the eagle-wingèd pride
   Of sky-aspiring and ambitious thoughts   *130*
   With rival-hating envy set on you
   To wake our peace, which in our country's cradle
   Draws the sweet infant breath of gentle sleep,
   Which so roused up with boist'rous untuned
      drums,
   With harsh resounding trumpets' dreadful bray,   *135*
   And grating shock of wrathful iron arms,
   Might from our quiet confines fright fair Peace,
   And make us wade even in our kindred's blood;

112 **approve** prove   118 **warder** truncheon (a signal to stop the combat)
120 **chairs** (on which the combatants sat before mounting)   122s.d. **flourish** trumpet call   124 **list** hear

Therefore we banish you our territories:
140   You, cousin Hereford, upon pain of life,
Till twice five summers have enriched our fields,
Shall not regreet our fair dominions,
But tread the stranger° paths of banishment.

Bolingbroke. Your will be done: this must my
     comfort be,
145   That sun that warms you here shall shine on me,
And those his golden beams to you here lent
Shall point on me, and gild my banishment.

Richard. Norfolk, for thee remains a heavier doom
Which I with some unwillingness pronounce:
150   The sly slow hours shall not determinate°
The dateless° limit of thy dear° exile;
The hopeless word° of "Never to return"
Breathe I against thee, upon pain of life.

Mowbray. A heavy sentence,° my most sovereign
     liege,
155   And all unlooked for from your Highness' mouth:
A dearer merit,° not so deep a maim
As to be cast forth in the common air
Have I deservèd at your Highness' hands!
The language I have learnt these forty years,
160   My native English, now I must forgo,
And now my tongue's use is to me no more
Than an unstringèd viol or a harp,
Or like a cunning° instrument cased up,
Or being open, put into his hands
165   That knows no touch to tune the harmony.
Within my mouth you have enjailed my tongue,
Doubly portcullised° with my teeth and lips,
And dull unfeeling barren ignorance

---

143 **stranger** foreign   150 **determinate** put a limit to   151 **dateless** endless   151 **dear** severe   152 **word** utterance   154 **sentence** (punning on "word")   156 **dearer merit** better reward   163 **cunning** ingenious and requiring skill in the playing   167 **portcullised** (a portcullis was a grating which could be let down in the gateway of a castle to block it)

Is made my jailer to attend on me.
I am too old to fawn upon a nurse,   *170*
Too far in years to be a pupil now;
What is thy sentence then but speechless death,
Which robs my tongue from breathing native
    breath?

Richard. It boots° thee not to be compassionate:°
After our sentence, plaining comes too late.   *175*

Mowbray. Then thus I turn me from my country's
    light,
To dwell in solemn shades of endless night.

                    [*Turns to go.*]

Richard. Return again, and take an oath with thee.
Lay on our royal sword your banished hands;
Swear by the duty that you owe to God—   *180*
Our part therein we banish with yourselves—°
To keep the oath that we administer:
You never shall—so help you truth and God!—
Embrace each other's love in banishment,
Nor never look upon each other's face,   *185*
Nor never write, regreet, nor reconcile
This louring tempest of your home-bred hate,
Nor never by advisèd° purpose meet
To plot, contrive, or complot° any ill
'Gainst us, our state, our subjects, or our land.   *190*

Bolingbroke. I swear.

Mowbray.   And I, to keep all this.

Bolingbroke. Norfolk, so far as to mine enemy—
By this time, had the King permitted us,
One of our souls had wandered in the air,
Banished this frail sepulcher° of our flesh,   *195*
As now our flesh is banished from this land:

---

174 **boots** avails   174 **compassionate** expressing passionate feeling
181 **Our ... yourselves** i.e., we absolve you from allegiance to us
188 **advisèd** deliberate   189 **complot** plot with others   195 **sepulcher**
(here accented on second syllable)

Confess thy treasons ere thou fly the realm;
Since thou hast far to go, bear not along
The clogging burden of a guilty soul.

200 *Mowbray.* No, Bolingbroke, if ever I were traitor,
My name be blotted from the book of life,
And I from heaven banished as from hence!
But what thou art, God, thou, and I, do know,
And all too soon, I fear, the King shall rue.
205 Farewell, my liege, now no way can I stray:
Save back to England all the world's my way.

                                        Exit.

Richard. Uncle, even in the glasses° of thine eyes
I see thy grievèd heart: thy sad aspect°
Hath from the number of his banished years
Plucked four away. [*To Bolingbroke*] Six frozen
210   winters spent,
Return with welcome home from banishment.

Bolingbroke. How long a time lies in one little word.
Four lagging winters and four wanton° springs
End in a word—such is the breath of kings.

215 *Gaunt.* I thank my liege that in regard of me
He shortens four years of my son's exile,
But little vantage° shall I reap thereby:
For ere the six years that he hath to spend
Can change their moons and bring their times°
        about,
220 My oil-dried lamp and time-bewasted light
Shall be extinct with age and endless night;
My inch of taper will be burnt and done,
And blindfold Death° not let me see my son.

Richard. Why! uncle, thou hast many years to live.

225 *Gaunt.* But not a minute, King, that thou canst give;

207 **glasses** (eyes were thought to reflect the heart)   208 **aspect** (accent on second syllable)   213 **wanton** luxuriant   217 **vantage** advantage   219 **times** seasons   223 **blindfold Death** (Death is thought of as eyeless, like a skull, and also as Atropos, Milton's "blind fury with the abhorred shears," cutting short human lives)

Shorten my days thou canst with sullen sorrow
And pluck nights from me, but not lend a morrow;
Thou canst help time to furrow me with age,
But stop no wrinkle in his pilgrimage:
Thy word is current° with him for my death,   230
But dead, thy kingdom cannot buy my breath.

Richard. Thy son is banished upon good advice,
   Whereto thy tongue a party-verdict° gave:
   Why at our justice seem'st thou then to lour?

Gaunt. Things sweet to taste prove in digestion sour.   235
   You urged me as a judge, but I had rather
   You would have bid me argue like a father.
   O, had it been a stranger, not my child,
   To smooth his fault I should have been more mild:
   A partial slander° sought I to avoid,   240
   And in the sentence my own life destroyed.
   Alas! I looked when some of you should say
   I was too strict to make mine own away;
   But you gave leave to my unwilling tongue
   Against my will to do myself this wrong.   245

Richard. Cousin, farewell, and uncle, bid him so;
   Six years we banish him, and he shall go.

         [*Flourish.*] *Exit* [*King Richard with his train*].

Aumerle. Cousin, farewell; what presence must not
      know,°
   From where you do remain let paper show.

Marshal. My lord, no leave take I, for I will ride   250
   As far as land will let me by your side.

Gaunt. O, to what purpose dost thou hoard thy words,
   That thou returnest no greeting to thy friends?

Bolingbroke. I have too few to take my leave of you,
   When the tongue's office should be prodigal°   255

230 **current** valid   233 **party-verdict** one person's share of a joint ver-
dict   240 **partial slander** imputation of partiality   248 **what presence
must not know** (perhaps "as I cannot have your news from you in person," or "what you cannot say in present company." Aumerle is anxious
to know Bolingbroke's intentions)   255 **prodigal** lavish

To breathe the abundant dolor of the heart.

Gaunt. Thy grief° is but thy absence for a time.

Bolingbroke. Joy absent, grief is present for that time.

Gaunt. What is six winters? They are quickly gone.

Bolingbroke. To men in joy; but grief makes one hour
260   ten.

Gaunt. Call it a travel that thou tak'st for pleasure.

Bolingbroke. My heart will sigh when I miscall it so,
    Which finds it an enforcèd pilgrimage.

Gaunt. The sullen passage of thy weary steps
265   Esteem as foil° wherein thou art to set
    The precious jewel of thy home return.

Bolingbroke. Nay, rather, every tedious stride I make
    Will but remember° me what a deal of world
    I wander from the jewels that I love.
270   Must I not serve a long apprenticehood
    To foreign passages,° and in the end,
    Having my freedom,° boast of nothing else
    But that I was a journeyman° to grief?°

Gaunt. All places that the eye of heaven° visits
275   Are to a wise man ports and happy havens.
    Teach thy necessity to reason thus:
    There is no virtue° like necessity.
    Think not the King did banish thee,
    But thou the King. Woe doth the heavier sit
280   Where it perceives it is but faintly° borne.
    Go, say I sent thee forth to purchase honor,
    And not the King exiled thee; or suppose
    Devouring pestilence hangs in our air,
    And thou art flying to a fresher clime.

257 **grief** (1) grievance (2) sorrow 265 **foil** setting (metal leaf serv-
ing as a background) 268 **remember** remind 271 **passages** experiences
272 **Having my freedom** at the end of his apprenticeship and of his exile
273 **a journeyman to grief** an employee of Grief (instead of his own master) 273 **journeyman** (1) artisan (2) traveler 274 **eye of heaven** sun (as
in Ovid) 277 **virtue** efficacy 280 **faintly** faintheartedly

Look what° thy soul holds dear, imagine it   285
To lie that way thou goest, not whence thou com'st.
Suppose the singing birds musicians,
The grass whereon thou tread'st the presence
    strewed,°
The flowers fair ladies, and thy steps no more
Than a delightful measure or a dance;   290
For gnarling° sorrow hath less power to bite
The man that mocks at it and sets it light.

Bolingbroke. O, who can hold a fire in his hand
By thinking on the frosty Caucasus?
Or clóy the hungry edge of appetite   295
By bare imagination of a feast?
Or wallow naked in December snow
By thinking on fantastic° summer's heat?
O, no! the apprehension of the good
Gives but the greater feeling to the worse.   300
Fell° Sorrow's tooth doth never rankle° more
Than when he bites, but lanceth° not the sore.

Gaunt. Come, come, my son, I'll bring thee on thy way.
Had I thy youth and cause, I would not stay.°

Bolingbroke. Then England's ground, farewell; sweet
    soil, adieu;   305
My mother and my nurse that bears° me yet!
Where'er I wander, boast of this I can:
Though banished, yet a true-born Englishman.

                                            Exeunt.

285 **Look what** whatever   288 **presence strewed** royal presence chamber
strewn with rushes   291 **gnarling** snarling (with perhaps a suggestion of
the twisting effects of sorrow)   298 **fantastic** imaginary   301 **Fell** fierce
301 **rankle** fester   302 **lanceth** cuts with a surgeon's knife   304 **I would
not stay** i.e., away from England   306 **bears** (1) gives birth to (2) supports
me (for a discussion of these speeches see K. Muir, *Review of English Studies* X, 1959: 283–86.)

[Scene 4. *The Court.*]

Enter the King, with Bagot, [Green], etc.
at one door, and the Lord Aumerle at another.

Richard. We did observe.° Cousin Aumerle,
    How far brought you high Hereford on his way?

Aumerle. I brought high Hereford, if you call him so,
    But to the next high way, and there I left him.

Richard. And say, what store of parting tears were
5   shed?

Aumerle. Faith, none for me,° except the northeast
    wind,
    Which then blew bitterly against our faces,
    Awaked the sleeping rheum, and so by chance
    Did grace our hollow parting with a tear.

Richard. What said our cousin when you parted with
10   him?

Aumerle. "Farewell."
    And for my heart disdainèd that my tongue
    Should so profane the word, that taught me craft
    To counterfeit oppression of such grief
15   That words seemed buried in my sorrow's grave.
    Marry, would the word "Farewell" have length'ned
    hours
    And added years to his short banishment,
    He should have had a volume of farewells;
    But since it would not, he had none of me.

20 *Richard.* He is our cousin,° cousin, but 'tis doubt,
    When time shall call him home from banishment,

1.4. 1 **We did observe** (continuing a conversation) 6 **for me** for my
part   20 **cousin** (Richard, Aumerle, and Bolingbroke were cousins)

Whether our kinsman come to see his friends.
Ourself and Bushy, Bagot here and Green,
Observed his courtship to the common people,
How he did seem to dive into their hearts   25
With humble and familiar courtesy,
What reverence he did throw away on slaves,
Wooing poor craftsmen with the craft of smiles
And patient underbearing of his fortune,
As 'twere to banish their affects with him.   30
Off goes his bonnet to an oyster-wench;
A brace of draymen bid God speed him well,
And had the tribute of his supple knee,
With "Thanks, my countrymen, my loving
    friends";
As were our England in reversion his,   35
And he our subjects' next degree in hope.

Green. Well, he is gone, and with him go these
    thoughts.
Now for the rebels which stand out in Ireland;
Expedient manage° must be made, my liege,
Ere further leisure yield them further means   40
For their advantage and your Highness' loss.

Richard. We will ourself in person to this war,
And for our coffers with too great a court
And liberal largess are grown somewhat light,
We are enforced to farm° our royal realm,   45
The revenue whereof shall furnish us
For our affairs in hand. If that come short,
Our substitutes at home shall have blank charters;°
Whereto, when they shall know what men are rich,
They shall subscribe them for large sums of gold,   50
And send them after to supply our wants,
For we will make for Ireland presently.
                  Enter Bushy.
Bushy, what news?

39 **manage** management   45 **farm** lease (Richard leased the crown
lands and customs dues to his favorites for £7000 a month)   48 **blank
charters** (documents given to Richard's agents, with power to insert
what sums they pleased for the rich to pay)

Bushy. Old John of Gaunt is grievous sick, my Lord,
55　　Suddenly taken, and hath sent posthaste
　　To intreat your Majesty to visit him.

Richard. Where lies he?

Bushy. At Ely House.

Richard. Now put it, God, in the physician's mind
60　　To help him to his grave immediately!
　　The lining° of his coffers shall make coats
　　To deck our soldiers for these Irish wars.
　　Come, gentlemen, let's all go visit him;
　　Pray God we may make haste and come too late!

65　*All.* Amen!　　　　　　　　　　　　　*Exeunt.*

61 **lining** contents (with pun on *coats*)

[ACT 2

Scene 1. *London. Ely House.*]

Enter John of Gaunt, sick, with the Duke of York,
[the Earl of Northumberland, Attendants], etc.

Gaunt. Will the King come, that I may breathe my last
  In wholesome counsel to his unstaid° youth?

York. Vex not yourself, nor strive not with your
    breath,
  For all in vain comes counsel to his ear.

Gaunt. O, but they say the tongues of dying men   *5*
  Enforce attention like deep harmony:
  Where words are scarce they are seldom spent
    in vain,
  For they breathe truth that breathe their words
    in pain;
  He that no more must say is listened more
  Than they whom youth and ease have taught to
    glose;°   *10*
  More are men's ends marked than their lives before;
  The setting sun, and music at the close,°
  As the last taste of sweets is sweetest last,°
  Writ in remembrance more than things long
    past:

2.1. 2 **unstaid** unrestrained   10 **glose** utter pleasing words   12 **close** conclusion of a musical phrase   13 **last** (because it comes last)

27

15   Though Richard my life's counsel would not hear,
     My death's sad tale° may yet undeaf his ear.

York. No, it is stopped with other flattering sounds:
     As praises—of whose taste the wise° are fond—
     Lascivious meters, to whose venom° sound
20   The open ear of youth doth always listen;
     Report of fashions in proud Italy
     Whose manners still° our tardy-apish° nation
     Limps after in base imitation.°
     Where doth the world thrust forth a vanity—
25   So it be new, there's no respect how vile—
     That is not quickly buzzed into his ears?
     Then all too late comes counsel to be heard,
     Where will° doth mutiny with wit's regard.°
     Direct not him whose way himself will choose:
     'Tis breath thou lack'st, and that breath wilt
30   thou lose.

Gaunt. Methinks I am a prophet new inspired,
     And thus expiring° do foretell of him:
     His rash fierce blaze of riot° cannot last,
     For violent fires soon burn out themselves.
     Small showers last long, but sudden storms are
35   short;
     He tires betimes that spurs too fast betimes;°
     With eager feeding, food doth choke the feeder.
     Light vanity, insatiate cormorant,°
     Consuming means, soon preys upon itself.
40   This royal throne of kings, this scept'red isle,
     This earth of majesty, this seat of Mars,
     This other Eden, demi-paradise,
     This fortress built by Nature for herself

---

16 **My death's sad tale** my solemn dying words   18 **the wise** even
the wise (see Textual Note)   19 **venom** venomous   22 **still** always
22 **tardy-apish** imitative, but behind the fashion   23 **imitation** (five
syllables. Complaints of the aping of foreign fashions were common in
Elizabethan England. For this speech and the next see K. Muir, *Review
of English Studies* X, 1959: 286–89.)   28 **will** desire   28 **wit's regard**
what intelligence ought to regard   31–32 **inspired ... expiring** (pun)
33 **riot** profligacy   36 **betimes** (1) soon (2) early   38 **cormorant** glut-
ton (from the bird)

Against infection° and the hand of war,
This happy breed° of men, this little world,°   45
This precious stone set in the silver sea
Which serves it in the office of a wall,
Or as a moat defensive to a house,
Against the envy of less happier lands,
This blessed plot, this earth, this realm, this
      England,   50
This nurse, this teeming womb of royal kings,
Feared by their breed, and famous by their
      birth,
Renownèd for their deeds as far from home,
For Christian service° and true chivalry,
As is the sepulcher in stubborn° Jewry   55
Of the world's ransom, blessed Mary's son,
This land of such dear souls, this dear dear land—
Dear for her reputation through the world—
Is now leased out—I die pronouncing it—
Like to a tenement° or pelting° farm.°   60
England, bound in with the triumphant sea,
Whose rocky shore beats back the envious siege°
Of wat'ry Neptune, is now bound in with shame,
With inky blots, and rotten parchment bonds.
That England that was wont to conquer others   65
Hath made a shameful conquest of itself.
Ah! would the scandal vanish with my life,
How happy then were my ensuing death!

      Enter King and Queen, etc. [Aumerle, Bushy,
            Green, Bagot, Ross, and Willoughby.]

York. The King is come; deal mildly with his youth,
      For young hot colts being raged° do rage the more.   70

Queen. How fares our noble uncle, Lancaster?

Richard. What comfort, man? How is't with aged
      Gaunt?

----

44 **infection** moral infection   45 **happy breed** fortunate race   45 **little world** i.e., a world by itself   54 **Christian service** i.e., the Crusades   55 **stubborn** (because they rejected Christ)   60 **tenement** leased land or property   60 **pelting** paltry   40–60 **This ... farm** (the verb comes in line 59)   62 **siege** (perhaps a partial pun on "surge")   70 **raged** enraged

Gaunt. O, how that name befits my composition!
Old Gaunt indeed, and gaunt in being old!
75   Within me Grief hath kept a tedious fast;
And who abstains from meat that is not gaunt?
For sleeping England long time have I watched:
Watching breeds leanness, leanness is all gaunt.
The pleasure that some fathers feed upon
80   Is my strict fast°—I mean my children's looks—
And therein fasting hast thou made me gaunt;
Gaunt am I for the grave, gaunt as a grave°
Whose hollow womb inherits° naught but bones.

Richard. Can sick men play so nicely° with their
names?

85   *Gaunt.* No, misery makes sport to mock itself:
Since thou dost seek to kill my name in me,°
I mock my name, great King, to flatter thee.

Richard. Should dying men flatter with those that
live?

Gaunt. No, no, men living flatter those that die.

90   *Richard.* Thou, now a-dying, sayest thou flatterest me.

Gaunt. O no, thou diest, though I the sicker be.

Richard. I am in health, I breathe, and see thee ill.

Gaunt. Now he that made me knows I see thee ill;
Ill in myself to see, and in thee seeing ill.°
95   Thy deathbed is no lesser than thy land,
Wherein thou liest in reputation sick;
And thou, too careless patient° as thou art,
Commit'st thy anointed body to the cure
Of those physicians that first wounded thee.
100   A thousand flatterers sit within thy crown,
Whose compass is no bigger than thy head,

---

80 **Is my strict fast** I must go without   73–82 **name ... grave** (Coleridge defended the psychological truth of these puns)   83 **inherits** (the
grave will get only bones because Gaunt is wasted away)   84 **nicely** subtly and prettily   86 **kill my name in me** i.e., by banishing my son and
heir   94 **Ill ... ill** (1) bad eyesight (2) evil   97 **careless patient** one
who does not take proper steps to cure himself.

And yet incagèd in so small a verge°
The waste° is no whit lesser than thy land.
O, had thy grandsire° with a prophet's eye
Seen how his son's son should destroy his sons,°   *105*
From forth thy reach he would have laid thy
    shame,
Deposing thee before thou wert possessed,
Which art possessed° now to depose thyself.
Why, cousin,° wert thou regent of the world,
It were a shame to let this land by lease;   *110*
But for thy world° enjoying but this land
Is it not more than shame to shame it so?
Landlord of England art thou now, not king;
Thy state of law° is bondslave to the law,
And thou—

Richard. [*interrupting*] A lunatic, lean-witted fool,   *115*
Presuming on an ague's privilege,
Darest with thy frozen° admonition
Make pale our cheek, chasing the royal blood
With fury from his native residence.°
Now, by my seat's° right-royal majesty   *120*
Wert thou not brother to great Edward's son,
This tongue that runs so roundly° in thy head
Should run thy head from thy unreverent
    shoulders.

Gaunt. O, spare me not, my brother Edward's son,
For that I was his father Edward's son,   *125*
That blood already like the pelican°

102 **verge** limit (and possibly area within a radius of twelve miles around
the court)   103 **waste** (1) destruction of landlord's property by tenant
(2) useless expense (3) wide space   104 **grandsire** i.e., Edward III
105 **sons** i.e., Gloucester and Gaunt   107–108 **possessed ... possessed**
(1) possessed of the crown (2) possessed with devils   109 **cousin** kinsman   111 **world** cf. line 45   114 **state of law** legal status   117 **frozen**
(1) frigid in style (2) prompted by ague (3) cold, and so cooling me
119 **residence** i.e., his cheek   120 **seat's** throne's   122 **roundly** bluntly
126 **pelican** (thought to wound its breast to feed its young with its
blood—a symbol both of parental self-sacrifice and filial ingratitude)

Hast thou tapped out and drunkenly caroused:
My brother Gloucester, plain well-meaning soul—
Whom fair befall in heaven 'mongst happy souls!—
130   May be a precedent and witness good
That thou respect'st not spilling Edward's blood.
Join with the present sickness that I have,
And thy unkindness be like crooked° age
To crop at once a too-long-withered flower.
135   Live in thy shame, but die not shame with thee;
These words hereafter thy tormentors be.
Convey me to my bed, then to my grave;
Love they to live that love and honor have.

                    Exit [*Gaunt, borne by Attendants,*
                            and Northumberland].

Richard. And let them die that age and sullens° have,
140   For both hast thou, and both become the grave.

York. I do beseech your Majesty, impute his words
To wayward sickliness and age in him:
He loves you, on my life, and holds you dear
As Harry, Duke of Hereford, were he here.

Richard. Right, you say true, as Hereford's love, so
145   his,
As theirs, so mine; and all be as it is.°

                    [*Enter Northumberland.*]

Northumberland. My liege, old Gaunt commends him
      to your Majesty.

Richard. What says he?

Northumberland.   Nay, nothing, all is said;
His tongue is now a stringless instrument;
150   Words, life and all, old Lancaster hath spent.

York. Be York the next that must be bankrout° so!
Though death be poor, it ends a mortal woe.

Richard. The ripest fruit first falls, and so doth he;

133 **crooked** bent (and suggesting Time with a scythe; cf. line 134)   139
sullens sulks   146 **and all be as it is** let what will be, be   151 **bankrout**
bankrupt

His time is spent, our pilgrimage must be;
So much for that.° Now for our Irish wars.   *155*
We must supplant those rough rug-headed kernes°
Which live like venom,° where no venom else,
But only they, have privilege to live.
And for these great affairs do ask some charge,
Towards our assistance we do seize to us   *160*
The plate, coin, revenues, and movables
Whereof our uncle Gaunt did stand possessed.

York. How long shall I be patient? Ah, how long
Shall tender duty make me suffer wrong?
Not Gloucester's death, nor Hereford's banishment,   *165*
Nor Gaunt's rebukes,° nor England's private
    wrongs,°
Nor the prevention of poor Bolingbroke
About his marriage,° nor my own disgrace,°
Have ever made me sour° my patient cheek,
Or bend one wrinkle° on my Sovereign's face.   *170*
I am the last of noble Edward's sons,
Of whom thy father, Prince of Wales, was first:
In war was never lion raged more fierce,
In peace was never gentle lamb more mild,
Than was that young and princely gentleman.   *175*
His face thou hast, for even so looked he,
Accomplished with the number of thy hours;°
But when he frowned it was against the French,
And not against his friends; his noble hand
Did win what he did spend, and spent not that   *180*
Which his triumphant father's hand had won;

153–55 **The ... that** (cf. Bolingbroke's equally callous reception of Mowbray's death, 4.1. 103–04. He also changes the subject in the middle of the line)   156 **rug-headed kernes** shag-haired light-armed Irish foot soldiers   157 **venom** reptiles (alluding to the tradition that St. Patrick expelled snakes from Ireland)   166 **Gaunt's rebukes** rebukes suffered by Gaunt   166 **private wrongs** wrongs suffered by private citizens   167–68 **prevention ... marriage** (Richard prevented Bolingbroke's marriage in exile to the French King's cousin)   168 **my own disgrace** (unexplained; possibly we should accept the equally difficult original reading of Q1, "his own disgrace," corrected in all copies save one)   169 **sour** make sour   170 **wrinkle** frown   177 **Accomplished ... hours** when he was your age

His hands were guilty of no kindred blood,
But bloody with the enemies of his kin.
O, Richard, York is too far gone with grief,
185　Or else he never would compare between—

Richard. Why, uncle, what's the matter?

York.　　　　　　　　　　　　　O my liege,
Pardon me, if you please; if not, I pleased
Not to be pardoned, am content withal.
Seek you to seize and gripe° into your hands
190　The royalties° and rights of banished Hereford?
Is not Gaunt dead? and doth not Hereford live?
Was not Gaunt just? and is not Harry true?
Did not the one deserve to have an heir?
Is not his heir a well-deserving son?
195　Take° Hereford's rights away, and take from time
His charters and his customary rights,
Let not tomorrow then ensue° today;
Be not thyself. For how art thou a king
But by fair sequence and succession?°
200　Now afore God—God forbid I say true—
If you do wrongfully seize Hereford's rights,
Call in the letters patents that he hath
By his attorneys-general to sue
His livery,° and deny° his off'red homage,
205　You pluck a thousand dangers on your head,
You lose a thousand well-disposèd hearts,
And prick my tender patience to those thoughts
Which honor and allegiance cannot think.

Richard. Think what you will, we seize into our
　　　　hands
210　His plate, his goods, his money, and his lands.

York. I'll not be by° the while. My liege, farewell.
What will ensue hereof there's none can tell:

---

189 **gripe** clutch　190 **royalties** gifts from the King　195 **Take** if you take
197 **ensue** follow upon　199 **succession** (four syllables)　202–04 **Call . . .
livery** if you revoke the royal letters-patent that enable his attorneys to obtain for him his father's lands　204 **deny** refuse　211 **by** near

But by° bad courses may be understood
That their events° can never fall out good.   *Exit.*

Richard. Go, Bushy, to the Earl of Wiltshire°
    straight;   215
Bid him repair to us to Ely House,
To see this business. Tomorrow next
We will for Ireland—and 'tis time, I trow;
And we create in absence of ourself
Our uncle York Lord Governor of England,   220
For he is just, and always loved us well.°
Come on, our queen, tomorrow must we part;
Be merry, for our time of stay is short.

        [*Flourish.*] *Exeunt King and Queen. Manet°*
        Northumberland, [*with Willoughby, and Ross*].

Northumberland. Well, lords, the Duke of Lancaster is
    dead.

Ross. And living too, for now his son is duke.   225

Willoughby. Barely in title, not in revenues.

Northumberland. Richly in both, if justice had her
    right.

Ross. My heart is great, but it must break with
    silence
Ere't be disburdened with a liberal° tongue.

Northumberland. Nay, speak thy mind, and let him
    ne'er speak more   230
That speaks thy words again to do thee harm.

Willoughby. Tends that that thou would'st speak to
    the Duke of Hereford?
If it be so, out with it boldly, man;
Quick is mine ear to hear of good towards him.

Ross. No good at all that I can do for him,   235

---

213 **by** concerning   214 **events** outcomes   215 **Wiltshire** William le
Scrope, treasurer of England   221 **For . . . well** (in spite of York's criticisms of his conduct, Richard apparently appreciates his honesty)   223
s.d. **Manet** remains   229 **liberal** free

Unless you call it good to pity him,
Bereft, and gelded of his patrimony.

Northumberland. Now, afore God, 'tis shame such
    wrongs are borne
  In him a royal prince and many moe°
240 Of noble blood in this declining land!
  The King is not himself, but basely led
  By flatterers; and what they will inform
  Merely in hate 'gainst any of us all,
  That will the King severely prosecute
245 'Gainst us, our lives, our children, and our heirs.

Ross. The commons hath he pilled° with grievous
    taxes
  And quite lost their hearts. The nobles hath
    he fined
  For ancient quarrels and quite lost their hearts.

Willoughby. And daily new exactions are devised,
250 As blanks,° benevolences,° and I wot not what:
  But what, a° God's name, doth become of this?

Northumberland. Wars hath not wasted it, for warred
    he hath not,
  But basely yielded upon compromise
  That which his noble ancestors achieved with blows:
255 More hath he spent in peace than they in wars.

Ross. The Earl of Wiltshire hath the realm in farm.

Willoughby. The King's grown bankrout like a broken
  man.

Northumberland. Reproach and dissolution hangeth
  over him.

Ross. He hath not money for these Irish wars,
260 His burdenous taxations notwithstanding,
  But by the robbing of the banished Duke.

---

239 **moe** more   246 **pilled** plundered   250 **blanks** cf. 1.4.48.   250 **benevolences** forced loans (an anachronism, as they were introduced in
1473)   251 **a** in

Northumberland. His noble kinsman—most degen-
      erate king!
   But, lords, we hear this fearful tempest sing,
   Yet seek no shelter to avoid the storm:
   We see the wind sit sore upon our sails,   265
   And yet we strike° not, but securely perish.

Ross. We see the very wrack° that we must suffer,
   And unavoided is the danger now,
   For suffering so the causes of our wrack.

Northumberland. Not so; even through the hollow
      eyes of death   270
   I spy life peering, but I dare not say
   How near the tidings of our comfort is.

Willoughby. Nay, let us share thy thoughts, as thou
      dost ours.

Ross. Be confident to speak, Northumberland;
   We three are but thyself, and speaking so   275
   Thy words are but as thoughts: therefore be bold.

Northumberland. Then thus: I have from le Port
      Blanc, a bay
   In Brittaine,° received intelligence
   That Harry, Duke of Hereford, Rainold, Lord
      Cobham,
   [The son of Richard, Earl of Arundel,]°   280
   That late broke° from the Duke of Exeter,
   His brother, Archbishop, late of Canterbury,
   Sir Thomas Erpingham, Sir Thomas Ramston,
   Sir John Norbery, Sir Robert Waterton, and Francis
      Quoint—
   All these well furnished by the Duke of Brittaine   285
   With eight tall ships, three thousand men of war,°
   Are making hither with all due expedience,°

---

266 **strike** (a pun on striking sails and striking blows)   267 **wrack** wreck
278 **Brittaine** Brittany   280 **The . . . Arundel** (some such line, necessary
for the sense, is lacking, possibly because an Earl of Arundel was executed in October 1595)   281 **broke** escaped   286 **men of war** soldiers
287 **expedience** speed

And shortly mean to touch our northern shore.
Perhaps they had ere this, but that they stay
290 The first departing of the King for Ireland.
If then we shall shake off our slavish yoke,
Imp out° our drooping country's broken wing,
Redeem from broking pawn° the blemished
     crown,
Wipe off the dust that hides our scepter's gilt,°
295 And make high majesty look like itself,
Away with me in post° to Ravenspurgh;
But if you faint, as fearing to do so,
Stay, and be secret, and myself will go.

Ross. To horse, to horse, urge doubts to them that
     fear.

Willoughby. Hold out my horse,° and I will first be
300   there.   *Exeunt.*

[Scene 2. *Windsor Castle.*]

Enter the Queen, Bushy, Bagot.

Bushy. Madam, your Majesty is too much sad.
     You promised, when you parted with the King,
     To lay aside life-harming heaviness,
     And entertain a cheerful disposition.

5 *Queen.* To please the King I did: to please myself
     I cannot do it; yet I know no cause
     Why I should welcome such a guest as Grief,
     Save bidding farewell to so sweet a guest

292 **Imp out** engraft new feathers   293 **broking pawn** lending money
upon pawns, which was fraudulent (cf. 2.1.113)   294 **gilt** (pun on
"guilt")   296 **in post** with speed, with relays of horses   300 **Hold out
my horse** if my horse holds out

As my sweet Richard. Yet again methinks
Some unborn sorrow ripe in Fortune's womb   10
Is coming towards me; and my inward soul
With nothing trembles—at something it grieves
More than with parting from my lord the King.

Bushy. Each substance of a grief hath twenty
    shadows,°
Which shows like grief itself, but is not so;   15
For Sorrow's eye, glazèd with blinding tears,
Divides one thing entire to many objects,
Like perspectives° which, rightly gazed upon,
Show nothing but confusion; eyed awry,
Distinguish form. So your sweet Majesty,   20
Looking awry upon your lord's departure,
Find° shapes of grief more than himself to wail,°
Which looked on as it is, is nought but shadows
Of what it is not; then, thrice-gracious Queen,
More than your lord's departure weep not:
    more's not seen,   25
Or if it be, 'tis with false Sorrow's eye,
Which for things true weeps° things imaginary.

Queen. It may be so; but yet my inward soul
Persuades me it is otherwise. Howe'er it be,
I cannot but be sad—so heavy sad,   30
As, though on thinking on no thought I think,°
Makes me with heavy nothing faint and shrink.

Bushy. 'Tis nothing but conceit,° my gracious lady.

Queen. 'Tis nothing less:° conceit is still derived
From some forefather grief; mine is not so,   35
For nothing hath begot my something grief,
Or something hath the nothing that I grieve:°

2.2.   14 **shadows** i.e., illusory griefs   18 **perspectives** pictures constructed so that they look distorted when viewed directly ("rightly"), and
intelligible when viewed from the side ("awry")   22 **Find** (the subject
"you" is understood from "Majesty")   22 **wail** bewail   27 **weeps**
weeps for   31 **though . . . think** though I try to think about nothing
33 **conceit** fancy   34 **'Tis nothing less** it's anything except mere fancy
37 **something . . . grieve** the nothing that I grieve hath something in it

'Tis in reversion that I do possess,°
But what it is that is not yet known what,
40   I cannot name; 'tis nameless woe I wot.°

[Enter Green.]

Green. God save your Majesty! and well met, gentle-
    men.
I hope the King is not yet shipped for Ireland.

Queen. Why hopest thou so? 'Tis better hope he is,
For his designs crave° haste, his haste good
    hope:
45   Then wherefore dost thou hope he is not shipped?

Green. That he our hope might have retired his
    power
And driven into despair an enemy's hope,
Who strongly° hath set footing in this land:
The banished Bolingbroke repeals° himself,
50   And with uplifted arms is safe arrived
At Ravenspurgh.

Queen.   Now God in heaven forbid!

Green. Ah, madam! 'tis too true; and that° is worse,
The Lord Northumberland, his son, young Henry
    Percy,°
The lords of Ross, Beaumond, and Willoughby,
55   With all their powerful friends are fled to him.

Bushy. Why have you not proclaimed Northumberland
And all the rest° revolted faction, traitors?

Green. We have: whereupon the Earl of Worcester°
Hath broken his staff, resigned his stewardship,
60   And all the household servants fled with him
To Bolingbroke.

---

38 **'Tis ... possess** I am heir to it, and I shall know what it is when I
experience it   40 **wot** know   44 **crave** demand   48 **strongly** with a
strong force   49 **repeals** recalls   52 **that** what   53 **young Henry Percy**
(these words are repeated in the next scene, and either "Henry" or "his
son" may be spurious here)   57 **rest** remaining   58 **Worcester** Northumberland's brother, and the Lord Steward of the King's household

Queen. So, Green, thou art the midwife to my woe,
   And Bolingbroke, my sorrow's dismal heir;°
   Now hath my soul brought forth her prodigy,°
   And I, a gasping, new-delivered mother,   65
   Have woe to woe, sorrow to sorrow, joined.

Bushy. Despair not, madam.

Queen.   Who shall hinder me?
   I will despair and be at enmity
   With cozening Hope: he is a flatterer,
   A parasite, a keeper-back of Death,   70
   Who gently would dissolve the bands° of life
   Which false Hope lingers° in extremity.

              [Enter the Duke of York.]

Green. Here comes the Duke of York.

Queen. With signs of war° about his aged neck.
   O, full of careful business° are his looks!   75
   Uncle, for God's sake, speak comfortable words.°

York. Should I do so, I should belie my thoughts.
   Comfort's in heaven, and we are on the earth,
   Where nothing lives but crosses, cares, and grief.
   Your husband, he is gone to save far off,   80
   Whilst others come to make him lose at home.
   Here am I left to underprop his land,
   Who, weak with age, cannot support myself.
   Now comes the sick hour that his surfeit° made;
   Now shall he try his friends that flattered him.   85

              [Enter Servingman.]

Servingman. My lord, your son was gone before I
       came.

York. He was? Why so, go all which way it will.
   The nobles, they are fled, the commons cold,

---

63 **heir** offspring   64 **prodigy** monster   71 **dissolve the bands** unloose
the bonds   72 **lingers** causes to linger   74 **signs of war** (York is wear-
ing throat armor)   75 **careful business** anxious preoccupation   76 **comfortable** comforting (the phrase "comfortable words" is used in the
Anglican communion service)   84 **surfeit** overindulgence

And will, I fear, revolt on Hereford's side.
90   Sirrah, get thee to Plashy to my sister° Gloucester;
Bid her send me presently a thousand pound.
Hold, take my ring.

Servingman. My lord, I had forgot to tell your lord-
    ship:
Today as I came by I callèd there—
95   But I shall grieve you to report the rest.

York. What is't, knave?

Servingman. An hour before I came the Duchess
    died.°

York. God for his mercy, what a tide of woes
Comes rushing on this woeful land at once.
100   I know not what to do. I would to God—
So my untruth° had not provoked him to it—
The King had cut off my head with my brother's.
What! are there no posts dispatched for Ireland?
How shall we do for money for these wars?
Come, sister—cousin, I would say—pray pardon
105   me.
Go fellow, get thee home, provide some carts,
And bring away the armor that is there.

                              [*Exit Servingman.*]

Gentlemen, will you go muster men?
If I know how or which way to order these affairs,
110   Thus disorderly thrust into my hands,
Never believe me. Both are my kinsmen.
Th' one is my sovereign, whom both my oath
And duty bids defend; t'other again
Is my kinsman, whom the King hath wronged,
115   Whom conscience and my kindred bids to right.
Well, somewhat we must do. Come, cousin,
I'll dispose of° you. Gentlemen, go muster up
    your men,

90 **sister** sister-in-law   97 **died** (in fact she died later; but Shakespeare
wishes to give the effect of a succession of woes)   101 **untruth** disloy-
alty   117 **dispose of** make arrangements for

And meet me presently at Berkeley.
I should to Plashy too,
But time will not permit. All is uneven,   *120*
And everything is left at six and seven.°

    Exeunt Duke, Queen. Manent Bushy,
        [Bagot], Green.

Bushy. The wind sits° fair for news to go for Ire-
   land,
But none returns. For us to levy power
Proportionable° to the enemy
Is all unpossible.   *125*

Green. Besides, our nearness to the King in love
Is near the hate of those love not the King.

Bagot. And that is the wavering commons, for their
   love
Lies in their purses, and whoso empties them
By so much fills their hearts with deadly hate.   *130*

Bushy. Wherein the King stands generally
   condemned.

Bagot. If judgment lie in° them, then so do we,
Because we ever have been near the King.

Green. Well, I will for refuge straight to Bristow°
   Castle.
The Earl of Wiltshire is already there.   *135*

Bushy. Thither will I with you, for little office
The hateful commons will perform for us,
Except like curs to tear us all to pieces.
Will you go along with us?

Bagot. No, I will to Ireland to his Majesty.   *140*
Farewell; if heart's presages be not vain,
We three here part that ne'er shall meet again.

Bushy. That's as York thrives to beat back Bolingbroke.

121 **six and seven** i.e., in confusion   122 **sits** blows   124 **Proportionable**
proportional   132 **lie in** depends on   134 **Bristow** (old form of Bristol)

Green. Alas, poor Duke, the task he undertakes
145   Is numb'ring sands, and drinking oceans dry:
      Where one on his side fights, thousands will
          fly.
      Farewell at once, for once, for all, and ever.

Bushy. Well, we may meet again.

Bagot.   I fear me, never.
                                      [*Exeunt.*]

[Scene 3. *In Gloucestershire.*]

Enter [*Bolingbroke, Duke of*] *Hereford,* [*and*]
      Northumberland [*with soldiers*].

Bolingbroke. How far is it, my lord, to Berkeley now?

Northumberland. Believe me, noble lord,
      I am a stranger here in Gloucestershire.
      These high wild hills and rough uneven ways
5   Draws out our miles and makes them wearisome;
      And yet your fair discourse hath been as sugar,
      Making the hard way sweet and delectable.°
      But I bethink me what a weary way
      From Ravenspurgh to Cotshall° will be found
10   In Ross and Willoughby, wanting your company,
      Which I protest hath very much beguiled
      The tediousness and process° of my travel:
      But theirs is sweet'ned with the hope to have
      The present benefit which I possess;
15   And hope to joy is little less in joy
      Than hope enjoyed. By this the weary lords

2.3. 7 **delectable** (accents on first and third syllables)   9 **Cotshall**
Cotswold   12 **tediousness and process** tedious process

Shall make their way seem short as mine hath done,
By sight of what I have, your noble company.

Bolingbroke. Of much less value is my company
Than your good words. But who comes here?   20

Enter Harry Percy.

Northumberland. It is my son, young Harry Percy,
Sent from my brother Worcester whencesoever.°
Harry, how fares your uncle?

Percy. I had thought, my lord, to have learned his
health of you.

Northumberland. Why, is he not with the Queen?   25

Percy. No, my good lord, he hath forsook the court,
Broken his staff of office, and dispersed
The household of the King.

Northumberland.   What was his reason?
He was not so resolved when last we spake
together.

Percy. Because your lordship was proclaimèd
traitor;   30
But he, my lord, is gone to Ravenspurgh
To offer service to the Duke of Hereford,
And sent me over by Berkeley to discover
What power the Duke of York had levied there,
Then with directions to repair to Ravenspurgh.   35

Northumberland. Have you forgot the Duke of
Hereford, boy?

Percy. No, my good lord, for that is not forgot
Which ne'er I did remember. To my knowledge
I never in my life did look on him.

Northumberland. Then learn to know him now—this is
the Duke.   40

Percy. My gracious lord, I tender you my service,
Such as it is, being tender, raw, and young,

22 **whencesoever** from wherever he is

Which elder days shall ripen and confirm
To more approvèd service and desert.

45 *Bolingbroke.* I thank thee, gentle Percy, and be sure
I count myself in nothing else so happy
As in a soul rememb'ring my good friends;
And as my fortune ripens with thy love,
It shall be still thy true love's recompense:
My heart this covenant makes, my hand thus
50   seals it.

Northumberland. How far is it to Berkeley, and what
    stir
Keeps good old York there with his men of war?

Percy. There stands the castle by yon tuft of trees,
Manned with three hundred men, as I have heard,
And in it are the Lords of York, Berkeley, and
55   Seymour,
None else of name and noble estimate.

[*Enter Ross and Willoughby.*]

Northumberland. Here come the Lords of Ross and
    Willoughby,
Bloody with spurring, fiery red with haste.

Bolingbroke. Welcome, my lords, I wot your love
    pursues
60 A banished traitor. All my treasury
Is yet but unfelt° thanks, which more enriched
Shall be your love° and labor's recompense.

Ross. Your presence makes us rich, most noble lord.

Willoughby. And far surmounts our labor to attain it.

Bolingbroke. Evermore thank's the exchequer of the
65   poor,
Which till my infant° fortune comes to years
Stands for my bounty. But who comes here?

[*Enter Berkeley.*]

61 **unfelt** intangible   62 **love** love's   66 **infant** (and so unable to possess property)

Northumberland. It is my Lord of Berkeley, as I
   guess.

Berkeley. My Lord of Hereford, my message is to
   you.

Bolingbroke. My lord, my answer is—to Lancaster;°   70
   And I am come to seek that name in England;
   And I must find that title in your tongue
   Before I make reply to aught you say.

Berkeley. Mistake me not, my lord; 'tis not my
      meaning
   To race one title° of your honor out.   75
   To you, my lord, I come—what lord you will—
   From the most gracious regent of this land,
   The Duke of York, to know what pricks you on
   To take advantage of the absent time,°
   And fright our native peace with self-borne° arms?   80

   [*Enter York, attended.*]

Bolingbroke. I shall not need transport my words by
      you:
   Here comes his Grace in person. My noble uncle!

   [*Kneels.*]

York. Show me thy humble heart, and not thy knee,
   Whose duty is deceivable° and false.

Bolingbroke. My gracious uncle—   85

York. Tut, tut! Grace me no grace, nor uncle me no
      uncle;
   I am no traitor's uncle, and that word "grace"
   In an ungracious mouth is but profane.
   Why have those banished and forbidden legs
   Dared once to touch a dust of England's ground?   90

---

70 **to Lancaster** (Bolingbroke is about to reply, but in the middle of the
sentence he changes his mind, to say that he will answer only in the
name of Lancaster)   75 **race one title** erase title (with pun on "tittle")
79 **absent time** time of the King's absence   80 **self-borne** borne for
one's own cause   84 **deceivable** deceptive

But then, more "why?" Why have they dared to
    march
So many miles upon her peaceful bosom,
Frighting her pale-faced villages with war,
And ostentation of despisèd° arms?
95 Com'st thou because the anointed King is hence?
Why, foolish boy, the King is left behind,
And in my loyal bosom lies his power.
Were I but now the lord of such hot youth
As when brave Gaunt, thy father, and myself
100 Rescued the Black Prince, that young Mars of men,
From forth the ranks of many thousand French,
O, then, how quickly should this arm of mine,
Now prisoner to the palsy, chastise thee,
And minister correction to thy fault!

Bolingbroke. My gracious uncle, let me know my
105   fault:
On what condition stands it, and wherein?

York. Even in condition of the worst degree
In gross rebellion and detested treason.
Thou art a banished man, and here art come
110 Before the expiration of thy time,
In braving arms against thy sovereign.

Bolingbroke. As I was banished, I was banished
    Hereford,
But as I come, I come for Lancaster.
And, noble uncle, I beseech your Grace,
115 Look on my wrongs with an indifferent° eye.
You are my father, for methinks in you
I see old Gaunt alive. O, then, my father,
Will you permit that I shall stand condemned,
A wandering vagabond, my rights and royalties
120 Plucked from my arms perforce, and given away
To upstart unthrifts?° Wherefore was I born?
If that my cousin king be King in England,

94 **despisèd** despicable   115 **indifferent** impartial   121 **unthrifts** prodigals

It must be granted I am Duke of Lancaster.
You have a son, Aumerle, my noble cousin:
Had you first died, and he been thus trod down,   125
He should have found his uncle Gaunt a father,
To rouse his wrongs and chase them to the bay.°
I am denied to sue my livery here,
And yet my letters patents give me leave.
My father's goods are all distrained and sold,   130
And these, and all, are all amiss employed.
What would you have me do? I am a subject;
And° I challenge law, attorneys are denied me;
And therefore personally I lay my claim
To my inheritance of free descent.   135

Northumberland. The noble Duke hath been too much
   abused.

Ross. It stands your Grace upon° to do him right.

Willoughby. Base men by his endowments are made
   great.

York. My lords of England, let me tell you this:
I have had feeling of my cousin's wrongs,   140
And labored all I could to do him right;
But in this kind to come in braving arms,
Be his own carver,° and cut out his way,
To find out right with wrong—it may not be:
And you that do abet him in this kind   145
Cherish rebellion, and are rebels all.

Northumberland. The noble Duke hath sworn his
   coming is
But for his own; and for the right of that
We all have strongly sworn to give him aid:
And let him never see joy that breaks that oath.   150

York. Well, well, I see the issue of these arms.
I cannot mend it, I must needs confess,
Because my power is weak and all ill left:°

127 **bay** quarry's last stand   133 **And** if   137 **It stands your Grace upon** it behooves your Grace   143 **Be his own carver** i.e., be a law to himself   153 **ill left** left inadequate (?) left in disorder (?)

           But if I could, by Him that gave me life,
155   I would attach° you all, and make you stoop
           Unto the sovereign mercy of the King.
           But since I cannot, be it known unto you
           I do remain as neuter.° So fare you well—
           Unless you please to enter in the castle,
160   And there repose you for this night.

    Bolingbroke. An offer, uncle, that we will accept.
           But we must win your grace to go with us
           To Bristow Castle, which they say is held
           By Bushy, Bagot, and their complices,°
165   The caterpillars of the commonwealth,°
           Which I have sworn to weed and pluck away.

    York. It may be I will go with you, but yet I'll pause,
           For I am loath to break our country's laws.
           Nor friends, nor foes, to me welcome you are.
170   Things past redress are now with me past care.

                                            Exeunt.

                    [Scene 4. *In Wales.*]

    Enter Earl of Salisbury, and a Welsh Captain.°

    Captain. My Lord of Salisbury, we have stayed ten
                 more days.
           And hardly keep our countrymen together,
           And yet° we hear no tidings from the King;
           Therefore we will disperse ourselves. Farewell.

5   *Salisbury.* Stay yet another day, thou trusty Welshman;
           The King reposeth all his confidence in thee.

    155 **attach** arrest 158 **neuter** neutral 164 **complices** accomplices
    165 **The ... commonwealth** (common Elizabethan expression, ulti-
    mately Biblical, for those who preyed on society) 2.4 s.d *Captain* (possi-
    bly Owen Glendower, mentioned in 3.1.43) 3 **yet** so far

Captain. 'Tis thought the King is dead: we will not
    stay.
  The bay trees in our country are all withered,
  And meteors fright the fixèd stars of heaven,
  The pale-faced moon looks bloody on the earth,   *10*
  And lean-looked° prophets whisper fearful change;
  Rich men look sad, and ruffians dance and leap,
  The one in fear to lose what they enjoy,°
  The other to enjoy by rage° and war.
  These signs forerun the death or fall of kings.   *15*
  Farewell; our countrymen are gone and fled,
  As well assured Richard their king is dead.   [*Exit.*]

Salisbury. Ah, Richard! With the eyes of heavy mind
  I see thy glory like a shooting star
  Fall to the base earth from the firmament;   *20*
  Thy sun sets weeping in the lowly west,
  Witnessing storms to come, woe and unrest;°
  Thy friends are fled to wait upon thy foes,
  And crossly° to thy good all fortune goes.   [*Exit.*]

---

11 **lean-looked** lean-looking   13 **enjoy** possess   14 **to enjoy by rage** in hope of enjoying by violent action   21–22 **sun . . . unrest** (Richard's badge was a sun obscured by or breaking from clouds)   24 **crossly** adversely

[ACT 3

Scene 1. *Bristol. Before the Castle.*]

*Enter [Bolingbroke] Duke of Hereford, York, North-
umberland, [other Lords, Soldiers,] Bushy and Green
prisoners.*

Bolingbroke. Bring forth these men.
　　Bushy and Green, I will not vex your souls,
　　Since presently° your souls must part° your bodies,
　　With too much urging your pernicious lives,
5　　For 'twere no charity; yet, to wash your blood
　　From off my hands, here in the view of men,
　　I will unfold some causes of your deaths.
　　You have misled a prince, a royal king,
　　A happy° gentleman in blood and lineaments,
10　　By you unhappied and disfigured clean;
　　You have in manner with your sinful hours
　　Made a divorce° betwixt his queen and him,
　　Broke the possession of a royal bed,
　　And stained the beauty of a fair queen's cheeks
　　With tears, drawn from her eyes by your foul
15　　　　wrongs.°
　　Myself a prince, by fortune of my birth,

3.1. 3 **presently** immediately　3 **part** part from　9 **happy** fortunate　11–12
in manner ... divorce you have made a kind of divorce　11–15 **You ...
wrongs** (there is no suggestion elsewhere in the play that Richard was es-
tranged from his queen, though Holinshed does refer to his adultery. If the
accusation is one of homosexuality, it may echo Marlowe's *Edward II*; and
in *Woodstock* Queen Ann complains of Richard's favorites. But Bolingbroke is making a propaganda speech)

52

Near to the King in blood, and near in love
Till you did make him misinterpret me,
Have stooped my neck under your injuries,
And sighed my English breath in foreign clouds,   20
Eating the bitter bread of banishment,
Whilst you have fed upon my signories,°
Disparked° my parks, and felled my forest woods,
From my own windows torn my household coat,°
Raced out my impresse,° leaving me no sign,   25
Save men's opinions and my living blood,
To show the world I am a gentleman.°
This and much more, much more than twice all this,
Condemns you to the death. See them delivered over
To execution and the hand of death.   30

Bushy. More welcome is the stroke of death to me
Than Bolingbroke to England. Lords, farewell.

Green. My comfort is that heaven will take our souls
And plague injustice with the pains of hell.

Bolingbroke. My Lord Northumberland, see them
  dispatched.°   35

[*Exeunt Northumberland with Bushy and Green.*]

Uncle, you say the Queen is at your house;
For God's sake, fairly let her be intreated.°
Tell her I send to her my kind commends;°
Take special care my greetings be delivered.

York. A gentleman of mine I have dispatched   40
With letters of your love to her at large.°

Bolingbroke. Thanks, gentle uncle. Come, Lords, away
To fight with Glendower° and his complices;
A while to work, and after holiday.   *Exeunt.*

22 **signories** estates   23 **Disparked** thrown open   24 **From ... coat**
broke the coat of arms in stained glass   25 **Raced out my impresse** erased
my impresa (emblem)   16–27 **Myself ... gentleman** (Bolingbroke's real
complaint. He does not mention the forced loans and the farming of
the land)   35 **dispatched** executed   37 **intreated** treated   38 **commends**
commendations, greetings   41 **at large** in full   43 **Glendower** (cf. note
in 2.4.s.d. Perhaps Bolingbroke does not know that the Welsh army has dis-
banded)

[Scene 2. *The coast of Wales, near
Barkloughly Castle.*]

*Enter the King, Aumerle, [the Bishop of]
Carlisle, etc. [Drums, flourish, and colors.]*

Richard. Barkloughly Castle call they this at hand?

Aumerle. Yea, my lord. How brooks° your Grace the
    air
    After your late tossing on the breaking seas?

Richard. Needs must I like it well. I weep for joy
5   To stand upon my kingdom once again.
    Dear earth, I do salute° thee with my hand,
    Though rebels wound thee with their horses' hoofs.
    As a long-parted mother with her child
    Plays fondly with her tears and smiles in meeting,
10   So weeping, smiling, greet I thee, my earth,
    And do thee favors with my royal hands.
    Feed not thy sovereign's foe, my gentle earth,
    Nor with thy sweets comfort his ravenous sense;
    But let thy spiders, that suck up thy venom,
15   And heavy-gaited toads lie in their way,
    Doing annoyance to the treacherous feet
    Which with usurping steps do trample thee;
    Yield stinging nettles to mine enemies;
    And when they from thy bosom pluck a flower,
20   Guard it, I pray thee, with a lurking adder
    Whose double tongue may with a mortal° touch
    Throw death upon thy sovereign's enemies.
    Mock not my senseless° conjuration, lords:

3.2. 2 **brooks** enjoys   6 **salute** greet with a gesture   21 **mortal** deadly
23 **senseless** addressed to senseless things

This earth shall have a feeling, and these stones
Prove armèd soldiers, ere her native king   25
Shall falter under foul rebellion's arms.

Carlisle. Fear not, my lord; that power that made
          you king
Hath power to keep you king in spite of all.
The means that heavens yield must be embraced
And not neglected. Else heaven would,   30
And we will not:° heaven's offer we refuse,
The proffered means of succor and redress.

Aumerle. He means, my lord, that we are too remiss,
Whilst Bolingbroke through our security
Grows strong and great in substance and in power.   35

Richard. Discomfortable° cousin, know'st thou not
That when the searching eye of heaven is hid
Behind the globe° and lights the lower world,°
Then thieves and robbers range abroad unseen
In murders and in outrage boldly here: 40
But when from under this terrestrial ball
He fires the proud tops of the eastern pines
And darts his light through every guilty hole,
Then murders, treasons, and detested sins,
The cloak of night being plucked from off their
          backs,   45
Stand bare and naked, trembling at themselves?
So when this thief, this traitor, Bolingbroke,
Who all this while hath reveled in the night
Whilst we were wand'ring with the Antipodes,
Shall see us rising in our throne, the east,   50
His treasons will sit blushing in his face,
Not able to endure the sight of day,
But self-affrighted tremble at his sin.
Not all the water in the rough rude sea
Can wash the balm° off from an anointed king;   55
The breath of worldly° men cannot depose

30–31 **Else ... not** otherwise we go against the will of heaven   36 **Discomfortable** discomforting   38 **globe** earth   38 **lower world** antipodes
55 **balm** (cf. 4.1.206)   56 **worldly** earthly

The deputy elected by the Lord.
For every man that Bolingbroke hath pressed°
To lift shrewd° steel against our golden crown,
God for his Richard hath in heavenly pay
A glorious angel;° then, if angels fight,
Weak men must fall, for heaven still guards the
    right.

Enter Salisbury.

Welcome, my lord. How far off lies your power?°

Salisbury. Nor near, nor farther off, my gracious
    lord,
Than this weak arm. Discomfort guides my tongue,
And bids me speak of nothing but despair.
One day too late, I fear me, noble lord,
Hath clouded all thy happy days on earth.
O, call back yesterday, bid time return,
And thou shalt have twelve thousand fighting men.
Today, today, unhappy day too late,
O'erthrows thy joys, friends, fortune, and thy state;
For all the Welshmen, hearing thou wert dead,
Are gone to Bolingbroke, dispersed and fled.

Aumerle. Comfort, my liege, why looks your Grace
    so pale?

Richard. But now the blood of twenty thousand men
Did triumph in my face, and they are fled;
And till so much blood thither come again,
Have I not reason to look pale and dead?
All souls that will be safe fly from my side,
For Time hath set a blot upon my pride.

Aumerle. Comfort, my liege, remember who you are.

Richard. I had forgot myself: am I not King?
Awake, thou coward majesty! Thou sleepest.
Is not the King's name twenty thousand names?
Arm, arm, my name! a puny subject strikes
At thy great glory. Look not to the ground,

58 **pressed** conscripted   59 **shrewd** sharp   59–61 **crown ... angel** (possibly a pun on these two coins)   63 **power** army

Ye favorites of a king, are we not high?
High° be our thoughts. I know my uncle York
Hath power enough to serve our turn. But who
    comes here?   *90*

            Enter Scroop.

Scroop. More health and happiness betide my liege
Than can my care-tuned° tongue deliver him.

Richard. Mine ear is open, and my heart prepared;
The worst is worldly loss thou canst unfold.
Say, is my kingdom lost? Why, 'twas my care,   *95*
And what loss is it to be rid of care?
Strives Bolingbroke to be as great as we?
Greater he shall not be; if he serve God,
We'll serve Him too, and be his fellow so.
Revolt our subjects? That we cannot mend: *100*
They break their faith to God as well as us.
Cry woe, destruction, ruin, and decay:
The worst is death, and death will have his day.

Scroop. Glad am I that your Highness is so armed
To bear the tidings of calamity.   *105*
Like an unseasonable stormy day
Which makes the silver rivers drown their shores
As if the world were all dissolved to tears,
So high above his limits swells the rage
Of Bolingbroke, covering your fearful land   *110*
With hard bright steel and hearts harder than steel.
White beards have armed their thin and hairless
    scalps
Against thy majesty; boys with women's voices
Strive to speak big,° and clap their female° joints
In stiff unwieldy arms against thy crown;   *115*
Thy very beadsmen° learn to bend their bows
Of double-fatal° yew against thy state;
Yea, distaff-women manage° rusty bills°

---

89 **High** i.e., high in name and place   92 **care-tuned** tuned to the key of
sorrow   114 **speak big** assume men's voices   114 **female** weak, effeminate   116 **beadsmen** pensioners who pray for their benefactors   117
double-fatal (the berry is poisonous and the wood used for bows)
118 **manage** wield   118 **bills** wooden shafts with spiked blades

Against thy seat: both young and old rebel,
120   And all goes worse than I have power to tell.

Richard. Too well, too well thou tell'st a tale so ill.
Where is the Earl of Wiltshire? Where is Bagot?
What is become of Bushy? Where is Green?
That they have let the dangerous enemy
125   Measure our confines with such peaceful° steps?
If we prevail, their heads shall pay for it.
I warrant they have° made peace with Bolingbroke.

Scroop. Peace have they made with him indeed, my
lord.

Richard. O, villains, vipers, damned without
redemption!
130   Dogs easily won to fawn on any man!
Snakes in my heart-blood warmed that sting my
heart!
Three Judases, each one thrice worse than Judas!
Would they make peace? Terrible hell
Make war upon their spotted° souls for this!

135   *Scroop.* Sweet love, I see, changing his property,°
Turns to the sourest and most deadly hate.
Again uncurse their souls: their peace is made
With heads and not with hands; those whom you
curse
Have felt the worst of death's destroying wound,
140   And lie full low, graved in the hollow ground.

Aumerle. Is Bushy, Green, and the Earl of Wiltshire
dead?

Scroop. Ay, all of them at Bristow lost their heads.

Aumerle. Where is the Duke, my father, with his
power?°

Richard. No matter where—of comfort no man
speak.

---

125 **peaceful** i.e., unopposed   127 **they have** (pronounced "they've")
134 **spotted** sinful   135 **property** distinctive quality   143 **power** army

Let's talk of graves, of worms, and epitaphs,   *145*
Make dust our paper, and with rainy eyes
Write sorrow on the bosom of the earth.
Let's choose executors and talk of wills:
And yet not so, for what can we bequeath
Save our deposèd bodies to the ground?   *150*
Our lands, our lives, and all are Bolingbroke's,
And nothing can we call our own, but death
And that small model° of the barren earth
Which serves as paste and cover° to our bones.
For God's sake let us sit upon the ground   *155*
And tell sad stories of the death of kings:
How some have been deposed, some slain in war,
Some haunted by the ghosts they have deposed,
Some poisoned by their wives, some sleeping killed,
All murdered—for within the hollow° crown   *160*
That rounds the mortal temples of a king
Keeps Death his court, and there the antic° sits,
Scoffing his state and grinning at his pomp,
Allowing him a breath, a little scene,
To monarchize,° be feared, and kill with looks,   *165*
Infusing him with self and vain conceit,°
As if this flesh which walls about our life
Were brass impregnable; and, humored° thus,
Comes at the last, and with a little pin
Bores thorough° his castle wall, and farewell king!   *170*
Cover your heads, and mock not flesh and blood
With solemn reverence; throw away respect,
Tradition, form, and ceremonious duty;
For you have but mistook me all this while:
I live with bread like you, feel want,   *175*
Taste grief, need friends—subjected° thus,
How can you say to me, I am a king?

---

153 **model** (variously explained as mold, grave mound, and microcosm)
154 **paste and cover** (an image taken from pie crust, since this was sometimes called a coffin)   160 **hollow** empty circle, vain, transitory   162 **antic** clown   165 **monarchize** play the monarch   166 **self and vain conceit**
empty estimate of self   168 **humored** (perhaps "Death thus amused" or
"the King thus indulged")   170 **thorough** through   176 **subjected** made
a subject and subject to the ordinary needs of man

Carlisle. My lord, wise men ne'er sit and wail their
    woes,
    But presently° prevent the ways to wail.
180   To fear the foe, since fear oppresseth strength,
    Gives in your weakness strength unto your foe;
    And so your follies fight against yourself.
    Fear and be slain, no worse can come to fight,°
    And fight and die is death destroying death,
185   Where fearing dying pays death servile breath.°

Aumerle. My father hath a power; inquire of him,
    And learn to make a body of a limb.°

Richard. Thou chid'st me well. Proud Bolingbroke, I
    come
    To change° blows with thee for our day of doom.
190   This ague fit of fear is overblown;°
    An easy task it is to win our own.
    Say, Scroop, where lies our uncle with his power?°
    Speak sweetly, man, although thy looks be sour.

Scroop. Men judge by the complexion of the sky
195   The state and inclination of the day;
    So may you by my dull and heavy eye.
    My tongue hath but a heavier tale to say.
    I play the torturer by small and small°
    To lengthen out the worst that must be spoken:
200   Your uncle York is joined with Bolingbroke,
    And all your northern castles yielded up,
    And all your southern gentlemen in arms
    Upon his party.°

Richard.   Thou hast said enough.
    Beshrew thee,° cousin, which° didst lead me
    forth
205   Of that sweet way° I was in to despair.

---

179 **presently** immediately   183 **to fight** by fighting   185 **pays . . . breath**
makes us slaves to death   187 **body of a limb** make a whole out of a part
189 **change** exchange   190 **overblown** blown over   192 **power** army
198 **small and small** little by little   203 **Upon his party** on his side   204
Beshrew thee ill befall you   204 **which** who   205 **way** path, habit

What say you now? What comfort have we now?
By heaven, I'll hate him everlastingly
That bids me be of comfort any more.
Go to Flint Castle: there I'll pine away;
A king, woe's slave, shall kingly woe obey.   *210*
That power I have, discharge, and let them go
To ear the land that hath some hope to grow,°
For I have none. Let no man speak again
To alter this, for counsel is but vain.

Aumerle. My liege, one word.

Richard.   He does me double wrong   *215*
That wounds me with the flatteries of his tongue.
Discharge my followers, let them hence away,
From Richard's night to Bolingbroke's fair day.

                                        [*Exeunt.*]

[Scene 3. *Wales, before Flint Castle.*]

*Enter [with drum and colors] Bolingbroke, York,
Northumberland, [Attendants and Soldiers].*

Bolingbroke. So that by this intelligence we learn
The Welshmen are dispersed, and Salisbury
Is gone to meet the King, who lately landed
With some few private friends upon this coast.

Northumberland. The news is very fair and good, my
       lord;   *5*
Richard not far from hence hath hid his head.

York. It would beseem the Lord Northumberland

212 **To . . . grow** to cultivate the fertile ground, i.e., desert to Bolingbroke

To say "King Richard." Alack, the heavy day
When such a sacred king should hide his head.

Northumberland. Your Grace mistakes; only to be
10   brief
Left I his title out.

York.   The time hath been
Would you have been so brief° with him, he would
Have been so brief with you to shorten you,
For taking so the head,° your whole head's length.

Bolingbroke. Mistake° not, uncle, further than you
15   should.

York. Take not, good cousin, further than you
should,
Lest you mis-take:° the heavens are over our
heads.

Bolingbroke. I know it, uncle, and oppose not myself
Against their will. But who comes here?

Enter Percy.

20   Welcome, Harry. What, will not this castle yield?

Percy. The castle royally is manned, my lord,
Against thy entrance.

Bolingbroke.   Royally!
Why, it contains no king?

Percy.   Yes, my good lord,
It doth contain a king: King Richard lies
25   Within the limits of yon lime and stone;
And with him are the Lord Aumerle, Lord
Salisbury,
Sir Stephen Scroop, besides a clergyman
Of holy reverence—who, I cannot learn.

Northumberland. O, belike it is the Bishop of Carlisle.

3.3. **11–12 The . . . brief** there was a time when if you had been so curt
14 **taking so the head** (1) chopping off the title (2) acting without re-
straint   15 **Mistake** take amiss   17 **mis-take** transgress, take what is
not yours, i.e., the crown

Bolingbroke. Noble lord,   30
   Go to the rude ribs° of that ancient castle,
   Through brazen trumpet send the breath of parley
   Into his ruined ears, and thus deliver:
   Henry Bolingbroke
   On both his knees doth kiss King Richard's hand,   35
   And sends allegiance and true faith of heart
   To his most royal person; hither come
   Even at his feet to lay my arms and power,
   Provided that my banishment repealed,
   And lands restored again be freely granted;   40
   If not, I'll use the advantage of my power,
   And lay the summer's dust with showers of blood
   Rained from the wounds of slaughtered
     Englishmen—
   The which,° how far off from the mind of
     Bolingbroke
   It is such crimson tempest should bedrench   45
   The fresh green lap of fair King Richard's land,
   My stooping duty tenderly° shall show.
   Go, signify as much, while here we march
   Upon the grassy carpet of this plain.
   Let's march without the noise of threat'ning drum,   50
   That from this castle's tattered° battlements
   Our fair appointments° may be well perused.
   Methinks King Richard and myself should meet
   With no less terror than the elements
   Of fire and water,° when their thund'ring shock   55
   At meeting tears the cloudy cheeks of heaven.
   Be he the fire, I'll be the yielding water;
   The rage be his, whilst on the earth I rain°
   My waters—on the earth, and not on him.
   March on, and mark King Richard how he looks.   60

*The trumpets sound [parle without, and answer
within; then a flourish]. Richard appeareth on*

---

31 **ribs** protecting walls   44 **The which** as to which   47 **tenderly** so-
licitously   51 **tattered** crenelated, dilapidated   52 **appointments** arms
and equipment   55 **fire and water** lightning and rain clouds   58 **rain**
(pun on "reign")

*the walls [with the Bishop of Carlisle, Aumerle, Scroop,
Salisbury].*

See, see King Richard doth himself appear,
As doth the blushing discontented sun
From out the fiery portal of the East,
When he perceives the envious clouds are bent
65   To dim his glory, and to stain the track
Of his bright passage to the Occident.

York. Yet looks he like a king: behold his eye,
As bright as is the eagle's, lightens forth°
Controlling majesty. Alack, alack for woe,
70   That any harm should stain so fair a show.

Richard. [*To Northumberland*] We are amazed,
        and thus long have we stood
To watch the fearful bending of thy knee,
Because we thought ourself thy lawful king:
And if we be, how dare thy joints forget
75   To pay their awful° duty to our presence?
If we be not, show us the hand of God
That hath dismissed us from our stewardship;
For well we know no hand of blood and bone
Can gripe the sacred handle of our scepter,
80   Unless he do profane, steal, or usurp;
And though you think that all, as you have done,
Have torn their souls by turning° them from us,
And we are barren and bereft of friends,
Yet know, my master, God omnipotent,
85   Is mustering in his clouds on our behalf
Armies of pestilence, and they shall strike
Your children yet unborn and unbegot
That lift your vassal hands against my head,
And threat the glory of my precious crown.
90   Tell Bolingbroke—for yon methinks he stands—
That every stride he makes upon my land
Is dangerous treason. He is come to open
The purple testament of bleeding war;

_____

68 lightens forth flashes   **75 awful** reverential   **82 torn ... turning** (pun)

But ere the crown he looks for live in peace
Ten thousand bloody crowns° of mothers' sons   *95*
Shall ill become the flower of England's face,
Change the complexion of her maid-pale peace
To scarlet indignation, and bedew
Her pastor's° grass with faithful English blood.

Northumberland. The King of heaven forbid our lord
    the King   *100*
Should so with civil and uncivil arms
Be rushed upon. Thy thrice-noble cousin,
Harry Bolingbroke, doth humbly kiss thy hand,
And by the honorable tomb he swears
That stands upon your royal grandsire's bones,   *105*
And by the royalties of both your bloods—
Currents that spring from one most gracious
    head—
And by the buried hand of warlike Gaunt,
And by the worth and honor of himself,
Comprising all that may be sworn or said,   *110*
His coming hither hath no further scope°
Than for his lineal royalties,° and to beg
Infranchisement° immediate on his knees;
Which on thy royal party° granted once,
His glittering arms he will commend to rust,   *115*
His barbèd° steeds to stables, and his heart
To faithful service of your Majesty.
This swears he, as he is a prince and just;
And, as I am a gentleman, I credit him.

Richard. Northumberland, say thus the King returns,°   *120*
His noble cousin is right welcome hither,
And all the number of his fair demands
Shall be accomplished without contradiction.
With all the gracious utterance thou hast
Speak to his gentle hearing kind commends.°   *125*

---

95 **crowns** (punning on the *crown* of line 94)   99 **pastor's** (the King
was the shepherd of his kingdom)   111 **scope** aim   112 **lineal royalties**
hereditary rights   113 **Infranchisement** recall from banishment and
restitution of his lands   114 **party** side   116 **barbèd** armored   120 **returns** answers   125 **commends** greetings

[*To Aumerle*] We° do debase ourselves, cousin,
    do we not,
To look so poorly° and to speak so fair?
Shall we call back Northumberland, and send
Defiance to the traitor and so die?

Aumerle. No, good my lord; let's fight with gentle
130   words,
    Till time lend friends, and friends their helpful
    swords.

Richard. O God! O God! that e'er this tongue of mine,
    That laid the sentence of dread banishment
    On yon proud man, should take it off again
135   With words of sooth!° O, that I were as great
    As is my grief, or lesser than my name!°
    Or that I could forget what I have been!
    Or not remember what I must be now!
    Swell'st thou, proud heart? I'll give thee scope to
    beat,
140   Since foes have scope to beat both thee and me.

Aumerle. Northumberland comes back from
    Bolingbroke.

Richard. What must the King do now? Must he
    submit?
    The King shall do it. Must he be deposed?
    The King shall be contented. Must he lose
145   The name of king? a° God's name, let it go.
    I'll give my jewels for a set of beads;°
    My gorgeous palace for a hermitage;
    My gay apparel for an almsman's gown;
    My figured° goblets for a dish of wood;
150   My scepter for a palmer's° walking-staff;
    My subjects for a pair of carvèd saints;
    And my large kingdom for a little grave,
    A little, little grave, an obscure grave;

---

126 **We** (the speech prefix is repeated in the quarto perhaps because a line
of Northumberland's has dropped out) 127 **poorly** abjectly 135 **sooth**
flattery 136 **name** i.e., king 145 **a** in 146 **set of beads** rosary 149 **figured** ornamented 150 **palmer's** pilgrim's

Or I'll be buried in the King's highway,
Some way of common trade,° where subjects' feet   *155*
May hourly trample on their sovereign's head;
For on my heart they tread now whilst I live,
And buried once, why not upon my head?
Aumerle, thou weep'st, my tender-hearted cousin:
We'll make foul weather with despisèd tears;   *160*
Our sighs and they shall lodge° the summer corn,
And make a dearth in this revolting land:
Or shall we play the wantons° with our woes
And make some pretty match with shedding tears,
As thus, to drop them still° upon one place,   *165*
Till they have fretted° us a pair of graves
Within the earth; and, therein laid, "there lies
Two kinsmen digged their graves with weeping
    eyes":
Would not this ill do well? Well, well, I see
I talk but idly, and you laugh at me.   *170*
Most mighty prince, my Lord Northumberland,
What says King Bolingbroke? Will his Majesty
Give Richard leave to live till Richard die?
You make a leg,° and Bolingbroke says "Ay."

Northumberland. My lord, in the base court° he
    doth attend   *175*
To speak with you; may it please you to come
    down?

Richard.   Down, down I come, like glist'ring
    Phaethon,°
Wanting the manage° of unruly jades.
In the base court! Base court where kings grow
    base,
To come at traitors' calls, and do them grace: *180*
In the base court, come down: down court,
    down king,

155 **trade** coming and going   161 **lodge** beat down   163 **play the wan-**
tons be unrestrained   165 **still** always   166 **fretted** worn   174 **make a**
leg curtsy   175 **base court** basse cour, the lower and outer courtyard
177 **Phaethon** (he drove the sun chariot of his father, Apollo, and was
struck by Zeus's thunderbolt)   178 **manage** art of managing horses

For night owls shriek where mounting larks should
    sing.

Bolingbroke. What says his Majesty?

Northumberland.   Sorrow and grief of heart
    Makes him speak fondly° like a frantic man;
    Yet he is come.

   [*Enter King Richard and Attendants, below.*]

185 *Bolingbroke.*   Stand all apart,
    And show fair duty to his Majesty.

                    He kneels down.

    My gracious lord.

Richard. Fair cousin, you debase your princely knee
    To make the base earth proud with kissing it.
190 Me rather° had my heart might feel your love,
    Than my unpleased eye see your courtesy.
    Up, cousin, up, your heart is up, I know,
    Thus high° at least, although your knee be low.

Bolingbroke. My gracious lord, I come but for mine
    own.

Richard. Your own is yours, and I am yours, and
195   all.

Bolingbroke. So far be mine, my most redoubted°
    lord,
    As my true service shall deserve your love.

Richard. Well you deserve: they well deserve to have
    That know the strong'st and surest way to get.
200 Uncle, give me your hands; nay, dry your eyes;
    Tears show their love, but want their remedies.°
    Cousin, I am too young to be your father,
    Though you are old enough to be my heir.
    What you will have, I'll give, and willing too,

---

184 **fondly** foolishly   190 **Me rather** I would sooner   193 **Thus high**
(pointing to his crown)   196 **redoubted** dreaded   201 **want their**
remedies i.e., cannot provide a cure for themselves or for the grief
which causes them

For do we must what force will have us do.   205
Set on towards London, cousin, is it so?

Bolingbroke. Yea, my good lord.

Richard.   Then I must not say no.
                              [*Flourish. Exeunt.*]

[Scene 4. *The Duke of York's garden.*]

*Enter the Queen with [two Ladies,] her
Attendants.*

Queen. What sport shall we devise here in this garden,
  To drive away the heavy thought of care?

Lady. Madame,° we'll play at bowls.

Queen. 'Twill make me think the world is full of rubs,°
  And that my fortune runs against the bias.°   5

Lady. Madame, we'll dance.

Queen. My legs can keep no measure in delight,
  When my poor heart no measure° keeps in grief:
  Therefore no dancing, girl; some other sport.

Lady. Madame, we'll tell tales.   10

Queen. Of sorrow, or of joy?

Lady.   Of either, madame.

Queen. Of neither, girl.
  For if of joy, being altogether wanting,

3.4. 3 **Madame** (spelled thus in the quarto, possibly to suggest that the
ladies came with the Queen from France) 4 **rubs** obstacles by which
bowls were diverted from their proper course 5 **bias** the form of the
bowl which imparts an oblique motion 7–8 **measure . . . measure** (1)
time to music (2) a stately dance (3) moderation

It doth remember° me the more of sorrow;
15   Or if of grief, being altogether had,
It adds more sorrow to my want of joy:
For what I have I need not to repeat,
And what I want it boots° not to complain.

Lady. Madame, I'll sing.

Queen.   'Tis well that thou hast cause;
But thou should'st please me better, would'st thou
20   weep.

Lady. I could weep, madame, would it do you good.

Queen. And I could sing, would weeping do me good,
And never borrow any tear of thee.

            *Enter Gardeners, [one the master, the other
                      two his men].*

But stay, here come the gardeners.
25   Let's step into the shadow of these trees.
My wretchedness unto a row of pins,
They will talk of state,° for every one doth so
Against a change;° woe is forerun with woe.

Gardener. [*To one Servant*] Go, bind thou up
            young dangling apricocks,°
30   Which like unruly children make their sire
Stoop with oppression° of their prodigal° weight;
Give some supportance° to the bending twigs.
[*To the other*] Go thou, and like an executioner
Cut off the heads of too fast growing sprays
35   That look too lofty in our commonwealth:
All must be even in our government.
You thus employed, I will go root away
The noisome weeds which without profit suck
The soil's fertility from wholesome flowers.

40   *Man.* Why should we, in the compass of a pale,°
Keep law and form and due proportion,

14 **remember** remind   18 **boots** avails   27 **state** the realm   28 **Against
a change** when a change is expected   29 **apricocks** apricots   31 **oppression** weighing down   31 **prodigal** wasteful   32 **supportance** support
40 **pale** fenced-in land

Showing, as in a model,° our firm estate,
When our sea-wallèd garden, the whole land,
Is full of weeds, her fairest flowers choked up,
Her fruit trees all unpruned, her hedges ruined,   45
Her knots° disordered, and her wholesome herbs
Swarming with caterpillars?°

Gardener.   Hold thy peace.
He that hath suffered this disordered spring
Hath now himself met with the fall of leaf:
The weeds which his broad spreading leaves did
    shelter,   50
That seemed in eating him to hold him up,
Are plucked up root and all by Bolingbroke—
I mean the Earl of Wiltshire, Bushy, Green.

Man. What, are they dead?

Gardener.   They are; and Bolingbroke
Hath seized the wasteful King. O, what pity is it   55
That he had not so trimmed and dressed° his land
As we this garden! We at time of year
Do wound the bark, the skin of our fruit trees,
Lest being overproud in sap and blood
With too much riches it confound itself;   60
Had he done so to great and growing men,
They might have lived to bear, and he to taste
Their fruits of duty. Superfluous branches
We lop away, that bearing boughs may live:
Had he done so, himself had borne the crown,   65
Which waste of idle hours hath quite thrown down.

Man. What, think you the King shall be deposed?

Gardener. Depressed° he is already, and deposed
'Tis doubt he will be. Letters came last night
To a dear friend of the good Duke of York's,   70
That tell black tidings.

Queen.   O, I am pressed to death

---

42 **as in a model** in miniature 46 **knots** laid-out flower beds 47 **cater-pillars** (cf. 2.3.165) 56 **dressed** tended 68 **depressed** lowered in fortune

Through want of speaking!°

[*Comes forward.*]

Thou, old Adam's likeness, set to dress this
    garden,
How dares thy harsh rude tongue sound this
    unpleasing news?
What Eve, what serpent hath suggested° thee
To make a second fall of cursèd man?
Why dost thou say King Richard is deposed?
Dar'st thou, thou little better thing than earth,
Divine his downfall? Say, where, when and how
Cam'st thou by this ill tidings? Speak, thou wretch.

Gardener. Pardon me, madam; little joy have I
To breathe this news, yet what I say is true:
King Richard he is in the mighty hold°
Of Bolingbroke. Their fortunes both are weighed:
In your lord's scale is nothing but himself
And some few vanities that make him light;
But in the balance of great Bolingbroke
Besides himself are all the English peers,
And with that odds he weighs King Richard down.
Post you to London, and you will find it so;
I speak no more than everyone doth know.

Queen. Nimble mischance, that art so light of foot,
Doth not thy embassage belong to me,
And am I last that knows it? O, thou thinkest
To serve me last that I may longest keep
Thy sorrow in my breast! Come, ladies, go
To meet at London London's king in woe.
What, was I born to this, that my sad look
Should grace the triumph of great Bolingbroke?
Gard'ner, for telling me these news of woe,
Pray God, the plants thou graft'st may never grow.

Exit [with Ladies].

71-72 **O ... speaking** (referring to the torture of pressing to death ad-
ministered to prisoners who refused to speak)   75 **suggested** tempted
83 **hold** custody

Gardener. Poor queen, so that thy state might be no
    worse,
  I would my skill were subject to thy curse.
  Here did she fall a tear; here in this place
  I'll set a bank of rue, sour herb of grace;   *105*
  Rue even for ruth° here shortly shall be seen,
  In the remembrance of a weeping queen.

                                                    Exeunt.

106 **ruth** pity

[ACT 4

Scene 1. *Westminster Hall.*]

Enter Bolingbroke, with the Lords [Aumerle,
Northumberland, Percy, Fitzwater, Surrey, the
Bishop of Carlisle, the Abbot of Westminster,
another Lord, Herald, and Officers] to Parlia-
ment.

Bolingbroke. Call forth Bagot.

              Enter Bagot [with Officers].

Now, Bagot, freely speak thy mind,
What thou dost know of noble Gloucester's death,
Who wrought it with° the King, and who performed
5 The bloody office of his timeless° end.

Bagot. Then set before my face the Lord Aumerle.

Bolingbroke. Cousin, stand forth, and look upon that
    man.

Bagot. My Lord Aumerle, I know your daring tongue
Scorns to unsay what once it hath delivered.
In that dead time° when Gloucester's death was
10   plotted,
I heard you say, "Is not my arm of length,
That reacheth from the restful English court

4.1. 4 **wrought it with** persuaded   5 **timeless** untimely (or everlasting)
10 **dead time** (variously interpreted: past time, deadly time, midnight
hour)

74

As far as Callice° to mine uncle's head?"
Amongst much other talk that very time
I heard you say that you had rather refuse   15
The offer of an hundred thousand crowns
Than Bolingbroke's return to England;
Adding withal, how blest this land would be
In this your cousin's death.

Aumerle.   Princes and noble Lords,
What answer shall I make to this base man?   20
Shall I so much dishonor my fair stars
On equal terms° to give him chastisement?
Either I must, or have mine honor soiled
With the attainder° of his slanderous lips.
There is my gage, the manual° seal of death,   25
That marks thee out for hell: I say thou liest,
And will maintain what thou hast said is false
In thy heart-blood, though being all too base
To stain the temper° of my knightly sword.

Bolingbroke. Bagot, forbear, thou shalt not take it up.   30

Aumerle. Excepting one, I would he were the best
In all this presence that hath moved me so.°

Fitzwater. If that thy valor stand on sympathy,°
There is my gage, Aumerle, in gage° to thine;
By that fair sun which shows me where thou
    stand'st,   35
I heard thee say, and vauntingly thou spak'st it,
That thou wert cause of noble Gloucester's death.
If thou deniest it twenty times, thou liest,
And I will turn thy falsehood to thy heart,
Where it was forgèd, with my rapier's point.   40

Aumerle. Thou dar'st not, coward, live to see that day.

---

13 **Callice** Calais   22 **On equal terms** (Aumerle was Bagot's superior
and could therefore refuse to fight with him)   24 **attainder** accusation
25 **manual** by my own hand (punning on a seal fixed to a document and
his glove)   29 **temper** i.e., excellence   31–32 **Excepting ... so** I wish
I had been angered by the highest in rank present, except Bolingbroke
33 **stand on sympathy** depends on correspondence of rank   34 **in gage**
in pledge

Fitzwater. Now, by my soul, I would it were this hour!

Aumerle. Fitzwater, thou art damned to hell for this.

Percy. Aumerle, thou liest, his honor is as true
45　　In this appeal as thou art all unjust;
　　　And that thou art so, there I throw my gage,
　　　To prove it on thee to the extremest point
　　　Of mortal breathing;° seize it if thou dar'st.

Aumerle. And if° I do not, may my hands rot off,
50　　And never brandish more revengeful steel
　　　Over the glittering helmet of my foe.

Another Lord. I task the earth to the like,° forsworn
　　　　　Aumerle,
　　　And spur thee on with full as many lies
　　　As may be hollowed° in thy treacherous ear
55　　From sun to sun:° there is my honor's pawn;
　　　Engage° it to the trial if thou darest.

Aumerle. Who sets me else?° By heaven, I'll throw°
　　　　　at all!
　　　I have a thousand spirits in one breast
　　　To answer twenty thousand such as you.

60　*Surrey.* My lord Fitzwater, I do remember well
　　　The very time Aumerle and you did talk.

Fitzwater. 'Tis very true; you were in presence° then,
　　　And you can witness with me this is true.

Surrey. As false, by heaven, as heaven itself is true!

Fitzwater. Surrey, thou liest.

65　*Surrey.*　　　　　　　　　　Dishonorable boy,
　　　That lie shall lie so heavy on my sword,
　　　That it shall render vengeance and revenge,
　　　Till thou, the lie-giver, and that lie do lie
　　　In earth as quiet as thy father's skull.

47–48 **extremest … breathing** to the death　49 **And if** if indeed　52
task … like lay on the earth the task of bearing another gage　54 **hollowed**
shouted　55 **sun to sun** sunrise to sunset　56 **Engage** (pun on "gage" and
"engage")　57 **Who sets me else** who else puts up a stake against me
57 **throw** (metaphor from dicing)　62 **in presence** present (or in attendance
at court)

In proof whereof, there is my honor's pawn;   70
Engage it to the trial if thou dar'st.

Fitzwater. How fondly° dost thou spur a forward°
    horse!
If I dare eat, or drink, or breathe, or live,
I dare meet Surrey in a wilderness,
And spit upon him, whilst I say he lies,   75
And lies, and lies. There is my bond of faith,
To tie thee to my strong correction.°
As I intend to thrive in this new world,°
Aumerle is guilty of my true appeal.
Besides, I heard the banished Norfolk say   80
That thou, Aumerle, did'st send two of thy men
To execute the noble Duke at Callice.

Aumerle. Some honest Christian trust me with a
    gage.°
That Norfolk lies, here do I throw down this,
If he may be repealed to try his honor.   85

Bolingbroke. These differences shall all rest under
    gage°
Till Norfolk be repealed; repealed he shall be,
And, though mine enemy, restored again
To all his lands and signories.° When he is
    returned,
Against Aumerle we will inforce his trial.   90

Carlisle. That honorable day shall never be seen.
Many a time hath banished Norfolk fought
For Jesu Christ in glorious Christian field,
Streaming° the ensign of the Christian cross
Against black pagans, Turks, and Saracens;   95
And, toiled° with works of war, retired himself
To Italy, and there at Venice gave
His body to that pleasant country's earth,
And his pure soul unto his captain, Christ,

72 **fondly** foolishly   72 **forward** willing   77 **correction** punishment
78 **new world** i.e., of the new reign   83 **Some . . . gage** (he has used both
his own gloves)   86 **under gage** i.e., prorogued   89 **signories** estates
94 **streaming** flying   96 **toiled** exhausted with toil

100   Under whose colors he had fought so long.

Bolingbroke. Why, Bishop, is Norfolk dead?

Carlisle. As surely as I live, my lord.

Bolingbroke. Sweet peace conduct his sweet soul to
     the bosom
     Of good old Abraham!° Lords appellants,°
105   Your differences shall all rest under gage,
     Till we assign you to your days of trial.

               Enter York.

York. Great Duke of Lancaster, I come to thee
     From plume-plucked° Richard, who with willing
     soul
     Adopts thee heir, and his high scepter yields
110   To the possession of thy royal hand.
     Ascend his throne, descending now from him,
     And long live Henry, fourth of that name!

Bolingbroke. In God's name, I'll ascend the regal
     throne.

Carlisle. Marry,° God forbid!
115   Worst° in this royal presence may I speak,
     Yet best beseeming me to speak the truth.
     Would God that any in this noble presence
     Were enough noble to be upright judge
     Of noble Richard. Then true noblesse would
120   Learn° him forbearance from so foul a wrong.
     What subject can give sentence on his king?
     And who sits here that is not Richard's subject?
     Thieves are not judged, but they are by to hear,
     Although apparent° guilt be seen in them;
125   And shall the figure° of God's majesty,
     His captain, steward, deputy elect,°
     Anointed, crownèd, planted many years,

---

104 **Abraham** cf. Luke 16:22   104 **appellants** those who are appealing
or accusing each other   108 **plume-plucked** i.e., humbled   114 **Marry**
(a light oath, from "By the Virgin Mary")   115 **Worst** i.e., least in rank
or competence   120 **Learn** teach   124 **apparent** manifest   125 **figure**
image   126 **elect** chosen

Be judged by subject° and inferior breath,
And he himself not present? O, forfend° it, God,
That in a Christian climate souls refined°   130
Should show so heinous, black, obscene° a deed!
I speak to subjects and a subject speaks,
Stirred up by God thus boldly for his king.
My Lord of Hereford here, whom you call king,
Is a foul traitor to proud Hereford's king;   135
And if you crown him, let me prophesy
The blood of English shall manure the ground,
And future ages groan for this foul act;
Peace shall go sleep with Turks and infidels,
And, in this seat of peace, tumultuous wars   140
Shall kin with° kin, and kind° with kind, confound;
Disorder, horror, fear, and mutiny
Shall here inhabit, and this land be called
The field of Golgotha° and dead men's skulls.
O, if you raise this house against this house,°   145
It will the woefullest division prove
That ever fell upon this cursèd earth!°
Prevent it, resist it, let it not be so,
Lest child, child's children, cry against you woe.

Northumberland. Well have you argued, sir; and for
    your pains   150
Of capital treason we arrest you here.
My Lord of Westminster, be it your charge
To keep him safely till his day of trial.
May it please you, lords, to grant the Commons'
    suit?°

Bolingbroke. Fetch hither Richard, that in common
    view   155
He may surrender; so we shall proceed
Without suspicion.

---

128 **subject** of a subject   129 **forfend** avert   130 **refined** purified by
the Christian environment   131 **obscene** offensive   141 **with** by means
of   141 **kind** race   144 **Golgotha** cf. Mark 15:22 "a place of dead mens
skulles" (Bishops' Bible)   145 **O . . . house** cf. Mark 3:25   147 **cursèd**
earth earth cursed by civil war   154 **suit** (that the charges against the
King should be published)

York.   I will be his conduct.°

                                                    Exit.

Bolingbroke. Lords, you that here are under our
     arrest,
     Procure your sureties for your days of answer.
160 Little are we beholding to your love,
     And little looked for at your helping hands.

              Enter Richard and York.

Richard. Alack, why am I sent for to a king,
     Before I have shook off the regal thoughts
     Wherewith I reigned? I hardly yet have learned
165 To insinuate,° flatter, bow, and bend my knee.
     Give Sorrow leave a while to tutor me
     To this submission. Yet I well remember
     The favors° of these men: were they not mine?
     Did they not sometime cry "All hail!" to me?
170 So Judas° did to Christ: but he in twelve°
     Found truth in all but one; I, in twelve thousand,
          none.
     God save the King! Will no man say "Amen"?
     Am I both priest and clerk?° Well, then, amen.
     God save the King, although I be not he;
175 And yet amen, if heaven do think him me.
     To do what service am I sent for hither?

York. To do that office° of thine own good will,
     Which tired majesty did make thee offer:
     The resignation of thy state and crown
     To Henry Bolingbroke.

180 *Richard.*   Give me the crown.
     Here, cousin, seize the crown. Here, cousin,
     On this side my hand, and on that side yours.
     Now is this golden crown like a deep well
     That owes° two buckets, filling one another,

---

157 **conduct** conductor   165 **insinuate** progress by devious ways   168 **favors** (1) faces (2) benefits   170 **Judas** cf. Matthew 26:49   170 **twelve** i.e., the apostles   173 **clerk** (employed to utter responses to the priest's prayers) 177 **office** (York corrects Richard's "service")   184 **owes** owns

The emptier ever dancing in the air,   *185*
The other down, unseen, and full of water.
That bucket down and full of tears am I,
Drinking my griefs, whilst you mount up on high.

Bolingbroke. I thought you had been willing to resign.

Richard. My crown I am, but still my griefs are mine: *190*
You may my glories and my state depose,
But not my griefs; still am I King of those.

Bolingbroke. Part of your cares you give me with
       your crown.

Richard. Your cares° set up, do not pluck my cares
       down.
My care is loss of care, by old care done;   *195*
Your care is gain of care, by new care won.°
The cares I give, I have, though given away;
They 'tend° the crown, yet still with me they stay.

Bolingbroke. Are you contented to resign the crown?

Richard. Ay, no; no, ay: for I must nothing be.   *200*
Therefore no, no, for I resign to thee.
Now, mark me how I will undo° myself.
I give this heavy weight from off my head,
And this unwieldy scepter from my hand,
The pride of kingly sway from out my heart;   *205*
With mine own tears I wash away my balm,°
With mine own hands I give away my crown,
With mine own tongue deny my sacred state,
With mine own breath release all duteous oaths;
All pomp and majesty I do forswear;   *210*
My manors, rents, revenues,° I forgo;
My acts, decrees, and statutes I deny:
God pardon all oaths that are broke to me,

---

194 **cares** (the word is used in several different senses in lines 194–97—
sorrows, responsibilities, diligence or carefulness, anxiety)   195–96
My . . . won my sorrow is loss of responsibility by failing to take pains;
your anxiety is gain of responsibility won by your new carefulness
198 **'tend** attend on   202 **undo** (1) strip (2) ruin   206 **balm** anointing
ointment used at coronation   211 **revenues** (accent on second syllable)

God keep all vows unbroke are° made to thee.
215 Make me, that nothing have, with nothing grieved,
And thou with all pleased, that hast all achieved.
Long may'st thou live in Richard's seat to sit,
And soon lie Richard in an earthy pit.
God save King Henry, unkinged Richard says,
220 And send him many years of sunshine days.
What more remains?

Northumberland.   No more, but that you read
These accusations, and these grievous crimes,
Committed by your person and your followers,
Against the state and profit of this land:
225 That by confessing them, the souls of men
May deem that you are worthily° deposed.

Richard. Must I do so? and must I ravel out°
My weaved-up follies? Gentle Northumberland,
If thy offenses were upon record,°
230 Would it not shame thee, in so fair a troop,°
To read a lecture of them?° If thou would'st,
There should'st thou find one heinous article,
Containing the deposing of a king,
And cracking the strong warrant of an oath,
235 Marked with a blot, damned in the book of heaven.
Nay, all of you that stand and look upon me,
Whilst that my wretchedness doth bait myself,
Though some of you, with Pilate,° wash your
     hands,
Showing an outward pity: yet you Pilates
240 Have here delivered me to my sour° cross,
And water cannot wash away your sin.

Northumberland. My lord, dispatch,° read o'er these
     articles.

Richard. Mine eyes are full of tears, I cannot see:
And yet salt water blinds them not so much,

214 **are** that are   226 **worthily** deservedly   227 **ravel out** unweave
229 **record** (accent on second syllable)   230 **troop** assembly   231
read a lecture of them read them aloud   238 **Pilate** cf. Matthew 27:24.
240 **sour** bitter   242 **dispatch** hurry up

But they can see a sort° of traitors here.   245
Nay, if I turn mine eyes upon myself,
I find myself a traitor with the rest;
For I have given here my soul's consent
T' undeck the pompous° body of a king;
Made glory base, and sovereignty a slave,   250
Proud majesty a subject, state a peasant.

Northumberland. My lord——

Richard. No lord of thine, thou haught,° insulting
   man,
Nor no man's lord: I have no name, no title,
No, not that name was given me at the font   255
But 'tis usurped.° Alack, the heavy day!
That I have worn so many winters out,
And know not now what name to call myself.
O, that I were a mockery king of snow,
Standing before the sun of Bolingbroke,   260
To melt myself away in water drops!
Good king, great king—and yet not greatly good—
And if my word be sterling° yet in England,
Let it command a mirror hither straight,
That it may show me what a face I have,   265
Since it is bankrout° of his majesty.

Bolingbroke. Go some of you, and fetch a looking
   glass.   [*Exit Attendant.*]

Northumberland. Read o'er this paper while the glass
   doth come.

Richard. Fiend, thou torments me, ere I come to hell.

Bolingbroke. Urge it no more, my Lord Northumberland.   270

Northumberland. The Commons will not then be
   satisfied.

Richard. They shall be satisfied: I'll read enough,

---

245 **sort** group, pack   249 **pompous** splendid   253 **haught** haughty
255–56 **No . . . usurped** (Richard was rumored to be a bastard)   263 **ster-
ling** current   266 **bankrout** bankrupt

When I do see the very book indeed,
Where all my sins are writ,° and that's myself.

Enter one with a glass.

275 Give me the glass, and therein will I read.
No deeper wrinkles yet? Hath Sorrow struck
So many blows upon this face of mine,
And made no deeper wounds? O, flatt'ring glass!
Like to my followers in prosperity,
280 Thou dost beguile me. Was this face the face
That every day under his household roof
Did keep ten thousand men? Was this the face
That, like the sun,° did make beholders wink?
Was this the face that faced° so many follies,
285 And was at last outfaced by Bolingbroke?
A brittle glory shineth in this face,
As brittle as the glory is the face,

[*Throws glass down.*]

For there it is, cracked in a hundred shivers.
Mark, silent king, the moral of this sport:
290 How soon my sorrow hath destroyed my face.

Bolingbroke. The shadow° of your sorrow hath
   destroyed
The shadow° of your face.

Richard.   Say that again.
"The shadow of my sorrow"? Ha, let's see.
'Tis very true, my grief lies all within,
295 And these external manners of laments
Are merely shadows to the unseen grief
That swells with silence in the tortured soul.°
There lies the substance: and I thank thee, King,
For thy great bounty, that not only giv'st
300 Me cause to wail, but teachest me the way

273–74 **book . . . writ** (cf. Psalms 139:16)   283 **sun** (cf. 3.2.50)   284
faced brazened out, countenanced   291 **shadow** outward show   292
shadow reflection   294–97 **my . . . soul** (Bolingbroke had implied that
Richard was putting on an act; Richard replies that his visible grief is a
reflection of a deeper grief he is feeling)

How to lament the cause. I'll beg one boon,
And then be gone, and trouble you no more.
Shall I obtain it?

Bolingbroke.   Name it, fair cousin.

Richard. Fair cousin? I am greater than a king:
    For when I was a king, my flatterers   305
    Were then but subjects; being now a subject,
    I have a king here to° my flatterer.
    Being so great, I have no need to beg.

Bolingbroke. Yet ask.

Richard. And shall I have?   310

Bolingbroke. You shall.

Richard. Then give me leave to go.

Bolingbroke. Whither?

Richard. Whither you will, so I were from your
    sights.

Bolingbroke. Go some of you, convey him to the
    Tower.   315

Richard. O, good! "Convey"! Conveyers° are you
    all,
    That rise thus nimbly by a true king's fall.

        [*Exeunt Richard, some Lords, and Guards.*]

Bolingbroke. On Wednesday next we solemnly set
    down°
    Our coronation: Lords, prepare yourselves.

        Exeunt. Manent [*the Abbot of*] *Westminster,*
        [*the Bishop of*] *Carlisle, Aumerle.*

Abbot. A woeful pageant have we here beheld.   320

Carlisle. The woe's to come; the children yet unborn
    Shall feel this day as sharp to them as thorn.

---

307 **to** for   316 **Conveyers** thieves ("convey" was a euphemism for
"steal")   318 **set down** appoint

Aumerle. You holy clergymen, is there no plot
    To rid the realm of this pernicious blot?

325 *Abbot.* My lord,
    Before I freely speak my mind herein,
    You shall not only take the sacrament
    To bury mine intents,° but also to effect
    Whatever I shall happen to devise.
330   I see your brows are full of discontent,
    Your hearts of sorrow, and your eyes of tears.
    Come home with me to supper: I will lay
    A plot shall show us all a merry day.   *Exeunt.*

328 **bury mine intents** conceal my plans

[ACT 5

Scene 1. *London. A Street.*]

Enter the Queen with her Attendants.

Queen. This way the King will come, this is the way
　To Julius Caesar's ill-erected Tower,°
　To whose flint bosom my condemnèd lord
　Is doomed a prisoner by proud Bolingbroke.
　Here let us rest, if this rebellious earth　　　　　　　　　5
　Have any resting for her true king's queen.

　　　Enter Richard [and Guard].

　But soft, but see, or rather do not see
　My fair rose wither; yet look up, behold,
　That you in pity may dissolve to dew,
　And wash him fresh again with true-love tears.　　　10
　Ah, thou the model where old Troy did stand!°
　Thou map of honor, thou King Richard's tomb,
　And not King Richard, thou most beauteous inn,
　Why should hard-favored grief be lodged in thee,
　When triumph is become an alehouse° guest?　　　15

Richard. Join not with grief, fair woman, do not so,
　To make my end too sudden; learn, good soul,

5.1. 2 **Tower** (the Tower of London was built, according to legend, by
Julius Caesar, *ill-erected* because it was used as a prison)　11 **model
where old Troy did stand** outline of the walls where Troy once stood,
i.e., ruined majesty—suggested by London's old name of Trinovantum,
New Troy　15 **alehouse** (Bolingbroke, contrasted with Richard, the
beauteous inn)

To think our former state a happy dream,
From which awaked, the truth of what we are
20   Shows us but this: I am sworn brother, sweet,
To grim Necessity, and he and I
Will keep a league till death. Hie thee to France,
And cloister thee in some religious house:°
Our holy lives must win a new world's crown,
Which our profane hours here have stricken
25   down.°

Queen. What! is my Richard both in shape and mind
Transformed and weakened? Hath Bolingbroke
Deposed thine intellect? Hath he been in thy heart?
The lion dying thrusteth forth his paw
30   And wounds the earth, if nothing else, with rage
To be o'erpow'red, and wilt thou, pupil-like,
Take the correction mildly, kiss the rod,
And fawn on Rage with base humility,
Which art a lion and the king of beasts?

35   *Richard.* A king of beasts indeed: if aught but beasts,
I had been still a happy king of men.
Good sometimes° queen, prepare thee hence for
   France.
Think I am dead, and that even here thou takest
As from my deathbed thy last living leave.
40   In winter's tedious nights sit by the fire
With good old folks, and let them tell thee tales
Of woeful ages long ago betid;°
And ere thou bid good night, to quite their griefs°
Tell thou the lamentable tale of me,
45   And send the hearers weeping to their beds.
For why,° the senseless brands will sympathize°
The heavy accent of thy moving tongue,
And in compassion weep the fire out:
And some° will mourn in ashes, some coal-black,

---

23 **religious house** convent   25 **our profane ... down** our careless
lives have endangered our hopes of heaven   37 **sometimes** sometime,
former   42 **betid** happened   43 **quite their griefs** requite, or cap, their
tragic stories   46 **For why** because of this   46 **sympathize** correspond
to   49 **some** (of the brands)

For the deposing of a rightful king.   50

Enter Northumberland.

Northumberland. My lord, the mind of Bolingbroke is
　　changed:
　You must to Pomfret,° not unto the Tower.
　And, madam, there is order ta'en° for you:
　With all swift speed you must away to France.

Richard. Northumberland, thou ladder wherewithal   55
　The mounting Bolingbroke ascends my throne,
　The time shall not be many hours of age
　More than it is, ere foul sin, gathering head,°
　Shall break into corruption. Thou shalt think,
　Though he divide the realm and give thee half,   60
　It is too little, helping him° to all;
　He shall think that thou which knowest the way
　To plant unrightful kings, wilt know° again,
　Being ne'er so little urged another way,
　To pluck him headlong from the usurped throne.   65
　The love of wicked men converts° to fear,
　That fear to hate, and hate turns one or both
　To worthy° danger and deservèd death.

Northumberland. My guilt be on my head, and there
　　an end.°
　Take leave and part, for you must part°
　　forthwith.   70

Richard. Doubly divorced! Bad men, you violate
　A twofold marriage: 'twixt my crown and me,
　And then betwixt me and my married wife.
　Let me unkiss the oath 'twixt thee and me—
　And yet not so, for with a kiss 'twas made.   75
　Part us, Northumberland; I towards the north,
　Where shivering cold and sickness pines° the clime;

---

52 **Pomfret** Pontefract Castle, in Yorkshire   53 **there is order ta'en**
arrangements have been made   58 **gathering head** (metaphor from a
boil)   61 **helping him** seeing that you helped him   63 **know** know
how   66 **converts** changes   68 **worthy** deserved   69 **there an end**
i.e., that's all I have to say   70 **part, for you must part** part from your
queen, for you must depart   77 **pines** causes to pine

My wife to France, from whence, set forth in
    pomp,
She came adornèd hither like sweet May,
80   Sent back like Hallowmas,° or short'st of day.°

Queen. And must we be divided? Must we part?

Richard. Ay, hand from hand, my love, and heart
    from heart.

Queen. Banish us both, and send the King with me.

Richard. That were some love, but little policy.

85   *Queen.* Then whither he goes, thither let me go.

Richard. So two together weeping make one woe.
    Weep thou for me in France, I for thee here;
    Better far off than, near, be ne'er the near.°
    Go count thy way with sighs, I mine with groans.

90   *Queen.* So longest way shall have the longest moans.

Richard. Twice for one step I'll groan, the way being
    short,
    And piece the way out° with a heavy heart.
    Come, come, in wooing sorrow, let's be brief,
    Since, wedding it, there is such length in grief.°
95   One kiss shall stop our mouths, and dumbly part:
    Thus give I mine, and thus take I thy heart.

Queen. Give me mine own again, 'twere no good part
    To take on me to keep and kill thy heart.
    So now I have mine own again, be gone,
100   That I may strive to kill it with a groan.

Richard. We make woe wanton° with this fond delay:
    Once more adieu, the rest let sorrow say.

                  Exeunt, [different ways].

80 **Hallowmas** Nov. 1   80 **short'st of day** Dec. 22   88 **ne'er the near**
never the nearer (proverbial)   92 **piece the way out** lengthen (with possible pun on "pace")   94 **Since ... grief** we are wedded to sorrow till
death and shall have plenty of time to grieve   101 **wanton** unrestrained
(with secondary sense of promiscuous)

[Scene 2. *The Duke of York's palace.*]

Enter Duke of York and the Duchess.

Duchess. My lord, you told me you would tell the
　　rest,
　　When weeping made you break the story off,
　　Of our two cousins' coming into London.

York. Where did I leave?

Duchess.　　　　　　　At that sad stop, my lord,
　　Where rude misgoverned° hands from widows'
　　　　tops　　　　　　　　　　　　　　　　　　　　　5
　　Threw dust and rubbish on King Richard's head.

York. Then, as I said, the Duke, great Bolingbroke,
　　Mounted upon a hot and fiery steed,
　　Which his aspiring rider seemed to know,°
　　With slow but stately pace kept on his course,　　　10
　　Whilst all tongues cried "God save thee, Boling-
　　　　broke!"
　　You would have thought the very windows spake:
　　So many greedy looks of young and old
　　Through casements darted their desiring eyes
　　Upon his visage; and that all the walls　　　　　　15
　　With painted imagery° had said at once,
　　"Jesu preserve thee! Welcome, Bolingbroke!"
　　Whilst he, from the one side to the other turning,
　　Bareheaded, lower than his proud steed's neck,
　　Bespake them thus: "I thank you, countrymen."　　20
　　And thus still doing, thus he passed along.

5.2. 5 **rude misgoverned** uncivilized and wrongly directed　9 **rider
seemed to know** seemed to know his rider　16 **painted imagery**
painted cloths, resembling tapestry

Duchess. Alack, poor Richard! Where rode he the
    whilst?

York. As in a theater the eyes of men,
    After a well-graced° actor leaves the stage,
25   Are idly° bent on him that enters next,
    Thinking his prattle to be tedious;
    Even so, or with much more contempt, men's eyes
    Did scowl on gentle Richard; no man cried "God
      save him!"
    No joyful tongue gave him his welcome home,
30   But dust was thrown upon his sacred head;
    Which with such gentle° sorrow he shook off,
    His face still combating with tears and smiles,
    The badges° of his grief and patience,
    That had not God for some strong purpose steeled
    The hearts of men, they must perforce° have
35   melted,
    And barbarism itself have pitied him.
    But heaven hath a hand in these events,
    To whose high will we bound our calm contents.°
    To Bolingbroke are we sworn subjects now,
40   Whose state and honor I for aye° allow.

             [*Enter Aumerle.*]

Duchess. Here comes my son, Aumerle.

York.   Aumerle that was,
    But that is lost for being Richard's friend;
    And, madam, you must call him Rutland now.
    I am in Parliament pledge for his truth°
45   And lasting fealty to the new-made king.

Duchess. Welcome, my son; who are the violets° now
    That strew the green lap of the new-come spring?

Aumerle. Madam, I know not, nor I greatly care not.

---

24 **well-graced** accomplished   25 **idly** without interest   31 **gentle** noble   33 **badges** signs   35 **perforce** inevitably   38 **bound our calm
contents** limit our wishes to calm content   40 **aye** ever   44 **truth** loyalty   46 **violets** favorites in the new court

God knows I had as lief° be none as one.

York. Well, bear you well in this new spring of time,　　50
　　Lest you be cropped before you come to prime.
　　What news from Oxford?° Do these jousts and
　　　triumphs hold?°

Aumerle. For aught I know, my lord, they do.

York. You will be there, I know.

Aumerle. If God prevent me not, I purpose so.　　55

York. What seal° is that that hangs without thy
　　bosom?
　　Yea, look'st thou pale? Let me see the writing.

Aumerle. My lord, 'tis nothing.

York.　　　　　　　　No matter, then, who see it.
　　I will be satisfied: let me see the writing.

Aumerle. I do beseech your Grace to pardon me:　　60
　　It is a matter of small consequence,
　　Which for some reasons I would not have seen.

York. Which for some reasons, sir, I mean to see.
　　I fear, I fear——

Duchess.　　　　　What should you fear?
　　'Tis nothing but some band° that he is ent'red
　　　into　　65
　　For gay apparel 'gainst° the triumph day.

York. Bound to himself? What doth he with a bond
　　That he is bound to? Wife, thou art a fool.
　　Boy, let me see the writing.

Aumerle. I do beseech you, pardon me. I may not
　　show it.　　70

York. I will be satisfied. Let me see it, I say!

49 **had as lief** would find it as pleasant　52 **Oxford** (cf. line 99)
Aumerle would give a start　52 **Do . . . hold** will these tournaments
and triumphal celebrations be held　56 **seal** (which would be hanging
from the document on an attached strip of parchment)　65 **band** bond
66 **'gainst** in preparation for

He plucks it out of his bosom and reads it.

Treason, foul treason, villain, traitor, slave!

Duchess. What is the matter, my lord?

York. Ho, who is within there? Saddle my horse.
75   God for his mercy!° What treachery is here!

Duchess. Why, what is it, my lord?

York. Give me my boots, I say! Saddle my horse!
Now, by mine honor, by my life, my troth,
I will appeach° the villain.

Duchess.   What is the matter?

80   *York.* Peace, foolish woman.

Duchess. I will not peace. What is the matter,
Aumerle?

Aumerle. Good mother, be content; it is no more
Than my poor life must answer.

Duchess.   Thy life answer?

York. Bring me my boots: I will unto the King.

His man enters with his boots.

Duchess. Strike him, Aumerle. Poor boy, thou art
85   amazed.°
Hence, villain, never more come in my sight.

York. Give me my boots, I say.

Duchess. Why, York, what wilt thou do?
Wilt thou not hide the trespass of thine own?
90   Have we more sons? Or are we like to have?
Is not my teeming date° drunk up with time?
And wilt thou pluck my fair son from mine age?
And rob me of a happy mother's name?
Is he not like thee? Is he not thine own?

95   *York.* Thou fond,° mad woman,
Wilt thou conceal this dark conspiracy?

75 **God for his mercy** Lord have mercy upon us   79 **appeach** peach,
inform against   85 **amazed** dazed   91 **teeming date** time of childbearing   95 **fond** foolish

A dozen of them here have ta'en the sacrament
And interchangeably° set down their hands
To kill the King at Oxford.

Duchess.   He shall be none;
We'll keep him here. Then what is that to him?   *100*

York. Away, fond woman, were he twenty times my
    son,
I would appeach him.

Duchess.   Had'st thou groaned for him
As I have done, thou would'st be more pitiful.
But now I know thy mind; thou dost suspect
That I have been disloyal to thy bed,   *105*
And that he is a bastard, not thy son:
Sweet York, sweet husband, be not of that mind;
He is as like thee as a man may be,
Not like to me, or any of my kin,
And yet I love him.

York.   Make way, unruly woman.   *110*

                                   Exit.

Duchess. After, Aumerle! Mount thee upon his horse;
Spur, post,° and get before him to the King,
And beg thy pardon ere he do accuse thee.
I'll not be long behind; though I be old,
I doubt not but to ride as fast as York;   *115*
And never will I rise up from the ground
Till Bolingbroke have pardoned thee. Away!
    Be gone!   *[Exeunt.]*

98 interchangeably reciprocally   **112 post** hasten

[Scene 3. *Windsor Castle.*]

Enter [Bolingbroke, now] the King, with his
Nobles [Percy and others].

Bolingbroke. Can no man tell me of my unthrifty°
    son?°
  'Tis full three months since I did see him last.
  If any plague° hang over us, 'tis he.
  I would to God, my lords, he might be found:
5 Inquire at London, 'mongst the taverns there,
  For there, they say, he daily doth frequent
  With unrestrainèd loose companions,
  Even such, they say, as stand in narrow lanes,
  And beat our watch° and rob our passengers;°
10 While he, young wanton and effeminate° boy,
  Takes on the point of honor° to support
  So dissolute a crew.

Percy. My lord, some two days since I saw the Prince,
  And told him of those triumphs held at Oxford.

15 *Bolingbroke.* And what said the gallant?

Percy. His answer was, he would unto the stews,°
  And from the commonest creature pluck a glove,
  And wear it as a favor, and with that
  He would unhorse the lustiest challenger.

20 *Bolingbroke.* As dissolute as desperate; but yet
  Through both° I see some sparks of better hope,
  Which elder years may happily bring forth.

5.3. 1 **unthrifty** prodigal   1 **son** (Prince Hal of *Henry IV*)   3 **plague** (he
is thinking of the prophecies of Richard and Carlisle)   9 **watch** watchmen
9 **passengers** wayfarers   10 **effeminate** voluptuous   11 **Takes on the
point of honor** undertakes as a point of honor   16 **stews** brothels
21 **both** i.e., dissoluteness and desperateness

But who comes here?

Enter Aumerle, amazed.

Aumerle.   Where is the King?

Bolingbroke.   What means
Our cousin, that he stares and looks so wildly?

Aumerle. God save your Grace! I do beseech your
    Majesty   25
To have some conference° with your Grace
    alone.

Bolingbroke. Withdraw yourselves, and leave us here
    alone.
                  [Exeunt Percy and Lords.]
What is the matter with our cousin now?

Aumerle. For ever may my knees grow to the earth,

               [Kneels.]

My tongue cleave to my roof within my mouth,   30
Unless a pardon° ere I rise or speak.

Bolingbroke. Intended, or committed, was this fault?
If on the first,° how heinous e'er it be,
To win thy after-love I pardon thee.

Aumerle. Then give me leave that I may turn the key,   35
  That no man enter till my tale be done.

Bolingbroke. Have thy desire.

      *[Aumerle locks the door.] The Duke of
      York knocks at the door and crieth.*

York. *[Within]* My liege, beware, look to thy-
    self:
Thou hast a traitor in thy presence there.

Bolingbroke. Villain, I'll make thee safe.°   40
          [Draws his sword.]

Aumerle. Stay thy revengeful hand; thou hast no cause
    to fear.

---

26 **conference** conversation   31 **Unless a pardon** unless I have a pardon
33 **on the first** of the former kind   40 **safe** harmless (by killing him)

York. Open the door, secure,° foolhardy King!
  Shall I for love speak treason° to thy face?
  Open the door, or I will break it open.

                    [*Bolingbroke opens.*]

                    [*Enter York.*]

45 *Bolingbroke.* What is the matter, uncle? Speak.

                    [*He relocks door.*]

  Recover breath. Tell us, how near is danger,
  That we may arm us to encounter it.

York. Peruse this writing here, and thou shalt know
  The treason that my haste forbids° me show.

Aumerle. Remember, as thou read'st, thy promise
50   passed.°
  I do repent me, read not my name there;
  My heart is not confederate with my hand.

York. It was, villain, ere thy hand did set it down.
  I tore it from the traitor's bosom, King:
55 Fear, and not love, begets his penitence.
  Forget° to pity him, lest thy pity prove
  A serpent that will sting thee to the heart.

Bolingbroke. O heinous, strong° and bold con-
      spiracy!
  O loyal father of a treacherous son!
60 Thou sheer immaculate and silver fountain,
  From whence this stream, through muddy passages,
  Hath held his° current, and defiled himself,°
  Thy overflow of good converts° to bad;
  And thy abundant goodness shall excuse
65 This deadly blot in thy digressing° son.

York. So shall my virtue be his vice's bawd,
  And he shall spend mine honor with his shame,

---

42 **secure** overconfident   43 **treason** (by calling him a fool)   49 **haste forbids** (because he is out of breath)   50 **passed** given   56 **Forget** forget your promise   58 **strong** dangerous   62 **his** its   62 **himself** itself   63 **converts** changes   65 **digressing** transgressing

As thriftless sons their scraping° fathers' gold.
Mine honor lives when his dishonor dies,
Or my shamed life in his dishonor lies.　　　70
Thou kill'st me in his life, giving him breath;
The traitor lives, the true man's put to death.

Duchess. [*Within*] What ho! My liege, for God's
　　sake, let me in!

Bolingbroke. What shrill-voiced suppliant makes this
　　eager cry?

Duchess. A woman, and thy aunt, great King—'tis I.　　75
Speak with me, pity me, open the door;
A beggar begs that never begged before.

Bolingbroke. Our scene is alt'red from a serious thing,
And now changed to "The Beggar and the King."°
My dangerous cousin, let your mother in:　　80
I know she is come to pray for your foul sin.

[*Aumerle unlocks door during York's speech.*]

York. If thou do pardon, whosoever pray,°
More sins for this forgiveness prosper may.

[*Enter Duchess.*]

This fest'red joint cut off, the rest rest° sound;
This let alone will all the rest confound.　　85

Duchess. O King, believe not this hardhearted man:
Love loving not itself, none other can.°

York. Thou frantic woman, what dost thou make
　　here?
Shall thy old dugs once more a traitor rear?°

Duchess. Sweet York, be patient. Hear me, gentle
　　liege.　　　90

[*Kneels.*]

68 **scraping** parsimonious　79 **The Beggar and the King** (referring to
the title, but not to the contents, of the ballad about King Cophetua and
the Beggar Maid)　82 **whosoever pray** whoever prays　84 **rest rest**
those that remain stay　87 **Love . . . can** i.e., if he does not love his son
he cannot love anyone, even you　89 **rear** raise him to life (with a pun
on the usual sense)

Bolingbroke. Rise up, good aunt.

Duchess.   Not yet, I thee beseech.
  For ever will I walk upon my knees,
  And never see day that the happy sees,
  Till thou give joy—until thou bid me joy—
95 By pardoning Rutland, my transgressing boy.

Aumerle. Unto my mother's prayers I bend my knee.

                    [*Kneels.*]

York. Against them both my true joints bended be;

                    [*Kneels.*]

  Ill may'st thou thrive, if thou grant any grace.

Duchess. Pleads he in earnest? Look upon his face.
100 His eyes do drop no tears, his prayers are in jest;
  His words come from his mouth, ours from our
      breast;
  He prays but faintly, and would be denied;
  We pray with heart and soul, and all beside;
  His weary joints would gladly rise, I know;
105 Our knees still kneel till to the ground they grow;
  His prayers are full of false hypocrisy,
  Ours of true zeal and deep integrity;
  Our prayers do outpray his—then let them have
  That mercy which true prayer ought to have.

Bolingbroke. Good aunt, stand up.

110 *Duchess.*   Nay, do not say "Stand up";
  Say "Pardon" first, and afterwards "Stand up";
  And if I were thy nurse thy tongue to teach,
  "Pardon" should be the first word of thy speech.
  I never longed to hear a word till now.
115 Say "Pardon," King; let pity teach thee how.
  The word is short, but not so short as sweet:
  No word like "pardon" for kings' mouths so meet.

York. Speak it in French, King; say "Pardonne
  moy."°

118 **Pardonne moy** pray excuse me, i.e., "No" (*moy* rhymes with *destroy*)

Duchess. Dost thou teach pardon pardon to destroy?
Ah, my sour husband, my hardhearted lord!   *120*
That sets the word itself against the word.
Speak "Pardon" as 'tis current in our land:
The chopping° French we do not understand.
Thine eye begins to speak; set thy tongue there,
Or in thy piteous heart plant thou thine ear,   *125*
That hearing how our plaints and prayers do
    pierce,
Pity may move thee "Pardon" to rehearse.°

Bolingbroke. Good aunt, stand up.

Duchess.   I do not sue to stand.
Pardon is all the suit° I have in hand.

Bolingbroke. I pardon him as God shall pardon me.   *130*

Duchess. O, happy vantage of a kneeling knee!
Yet° am I sick for fear; speak it again.
Twice saying "Pardon" doth not pardon twain,°
But makes one pardon strong.

Bolingbroke.   With all my heart
I pardon him.

Duchess. [*Standing*]   A god on earth° thou art.   *135*

[*York and Aumerle rise.*]

Bolingbroke. But for our trusty° brother-in-law,° and
    the abbot,
With all the rest of that consorted crew,
Destruction straight shall dog them at the heels.
Good uncle, help to order several powers
To Oxford, or where'er these traitors are;   *140*
They shall not live within this world, I swear,
But I will have them if I once know where.
Uncle, farewell, and cousin, too, adieu.

123 **chopping** changing the meaning of words   127 **rehearse** repeat (a perfect rhyme with "pierce" in the 16th century)   129 **suit** (1) suit of cards (2) petition   132 **Yet** still   133 **twain** (1) two people (2) divide   135 **god on earth** (the Homilies taught this; and, as Portia says, "earthly power doth then show likest God's/When mercy seasons justice")   136 **trusty** (ironical)   136 **brother-in-law** (Duke of Exeter, Richard's half-brother, who had married Bolingbroke's sister)

Your mother well hath prayed, and prove you
    true.°

Duchess. Come, my old° son, I pray God make thee
145   new.   *Exeunt.*

[Scene 4. *Windsor Castle.*]

Enter Sir Pierce Exton & [a Man].

Exton. Didst thou not mark the King, what words he
    spake?
  "Have I no friend will rid me of this living fear?"
  Was it not so?

Man.   These were his very words.

Exton. "Have I no friend?" quoth he: he spake it
    twice,
5   And urged it twice together, did he not?

Man. He did.

Exton. And speaking it, he wishtly° looked on me,
  As who should say, "I would thou wert the man
  That would divorce this terror from my heart"—
10   Meaning the King at Pomfret. Come, let's go:
  I am the King's friend, and will rid his foe.

                                    [*Exeunt.*]

144 **true** loyal   145 **old** unregenerate   5.4.   7 **wishtly** (probably "wish-
fully," with an undertone of "wistly," i.e., intently)

[Scene 5. *Pomfret Castle.*]

Enter Richard alone.

Richard. I have been studying how I may compare
   This prison where I live unto the world:
   And for because the world is populous,
   And here is not a creature but myself,
   I cannot do it. Yet I'll hammer it out: 5
   My brain I'll prove the female to my soul,
   My soul the father, and these two beget
   A generation° of still°-breeding thoughts;
   And these same thoughts people this little world,
   In humors° like the people of this world,   10
   For no thought is contented. The better sort,
   As thoughts of things divine are intermixed
   With scruples,° and do set the word itself
   Against the word;° as thus: "Come, little ones";°
   And then again,   15
   "It is as hard to come as for a camel
   To thread the postern of a small needle's° eye."°
   Thoughts tending to ambition, they do plot
   Unlikely wonders: how these vain weak nails
   May tear a passage thorough the flinty ribs   20
   Of this hard world, my ragged° prison walls;
   And, for° they cannot, die in their own pride.°
   Thoughts tending to content flatter themselves
   That they are not the first of fortune's slaves,
   Nor shall not be the last, like seely° beggars   25
   Who sitting in the stocks refuge° their shame,

5.5. 8 **generation** offspring   8 **still** constantly   10 **humors** psychological characteristics   13 **scruples** doubts   14 **word** passage of Scripture
14 **Come, little ones** Matthew 19:14ff.   17 **needle's** (monosyllabic)
16–17 **It . . . eye** Matthew 19:24ff.   21 **ragged** rugged   22 **for** because
22 **pride** prime   25 **seely** (silly) simple-minded   26 **refuge** protect
themselves from

That many have, and others must, sit there;
And in this thought they find a kind of ease,
Bearing their own misfortunes on the back
30   Of such as have before endured the like.
Thus play I in one person many people,
And none contented; sometimes am I king,
Then treasons make me wish myself a beggar,
And so I am. Then crushing penury
35   Persuades me I was better when a king.
Then am I kinged again and, by and by,
Think that I am unkinged by Bolingbroke,
And straight am nothing. But whate'er I be,
Nor I, nor any man that but man is,
40   With nothing shall be pleased, till he be eased
With being nothing.°

The music plays.

Music do I hear.
Ha—ha! Keep time! How sour sweet music is
When time is broke, and no proportion° kept;
So is it in the music of men's lives:
45   And here have I the daintiness of ear
To check° time broke in a disordered°
      string,
But for the concord of my state and time,°
Had not an ear to hear my true time broke.
I wasted time,° and now doth Time° waste me:
For now hath Time made me his numb'ring°
50   clock;
My thoughts are minutes, and with sighs they jar°
Their watches° on unto mine eyes, the outward
      watch°
Whereto my finger, like a dial's point,°
Is pointing still,° in cleansing them from tears.

39–41 **nor any man . . . nothing** i.e., man is never content until he is no
more   43 **proportion** musical time   46 **check** rebuke   46 **disordered**
out of its place, a bar wrong   47 **time** the times   49 **time** measured duration   49 **Time** Father Time   50 **numb'ring** counting hours and minutes   51 **jar** tick (of a clock), making a discord   52 **watches** intervals
of time   52 **outward watch** dial (with pun on a man keeping watch)
53 **dial's point** hand of clock   54 **still** continually

Now, sir, the sound that tells what hour it is   *55*
Are clamorous groans which strike upon my
   heart,
Which is the bell. So sighs, and tears, and groans,
Show minutes, times, and hours; but my time
Runs posting on in Bolingbroke's proud joy,
While I stand fooling here, his Jack-of-the-
   clock.°   *60*
This music mads me: let it sound no more.
For though it have holp° madmen to their wits,
In me it seems it will make wise men mad.
Yet blessing on his heart that gives it me,
For 'tis a sign of love; and love to Richard   *65*
Is a strange brooch° in this all-hating world.

Enter a Groom of the stable.

Groom. Hail, royal Prince!

Richard.   Thanks, noble° peer!
The cheapest of us is ten groats too dear.
What art thou? And how comest thou hither,
Where no man never comes, but that sad dog   *70*
That brings me food to make misfortune live?°

Groom. I was a poor groom of thy stable, King,
When thou wert King, who, traveling towards
   York,
With much ado at length have gotten leave
To look upon my sometimes° royal master's face.   *75*
O, how it erned° my heart, when I beheld
In London streets, that coronation day,
When Bolingbroke rode on roan Barbary,°
That horse that thou so often hast bestrid,
That horse that I so carefully have dressed.°   *80*

---

60 **Jack-of-the-clock** mannikin to strike the hours   62 **holp** helped   66
strange brooch rare jewel   67 **royal . . . noble** (a royal was worth ten
shillings, a noble six shillings and eight pence; a groat, fourpence.
Richard is saying that to call him "royal" now is to price him too high,
since he is now the peer, the equal, of the groom)   71 **make misfortune
live** perpetuate my unfortunate life   75 **sometimes** former   76 **erned**
grieved   78 **Barbary** (here the name of the horse, as well as the breed)
80 **dressed** groomed

Richard. Rode he on Barbary? Tell me, gentle° friend,
How went he under him?

Groom. So proudly as if he disdained the ground.

Richard. So proud that Bolingbroke was on his back!
85   That jade hath eat bread from my royal hand;
This hand hath made him proud with clapping°
him.
Would he not stumble? Would he not fall down,
Since pride must have a fall, and break the neck
Of that proud man that did usurp his back?
90   Forgiveness, horse! Why do I rail on thee,
Since thou created to be awed by man
Wast born to bear? I was not made a horse,
And yet I bear a burden like an ass,
Spurred, galled,° and tired by jauncing° Boling-
broke.

Enter one, [a Keeper,] to Richard with meat.

95 *Keeper.* Fellow, give place; here is no longer stay.

Richard. If thou love me, 'tis time thou wert away.

Groom. What my tongue dares not, that my heart
shall say.   *Exit Groom.*

Keeper. My lord, wilt please you to fall to?°

Richard. Taste° of it first, as thou art wont to do.

100 *Keeper.* My lord, I dare not; Sir Pierce of Exton
Who lately came from the King, commands the
contrary.

Richard. The devil take Henry of Lancaster, and thee!
Patience is stale, and I am weary of it.

Keeper. Help, help, help!

*The murderers [Exton and Servants]
rush in.*

81 **gentle** (implying groom is of gentle birth) 86 **clapping** patting 94
galled made sore 94 **jauncing** making the horse prance (and perhaps
himself prancing and triumphant) 98 **fall to** start eating 99 **Taste** (he
suspects poison)

Richard. How now! What means Death in this rude
    assault?°   *105*
Villain, thy own hand yields thy death's instrument.

    [*Snatches a weapon and kills one.*]

Go thou, and fill another room° in hell!

    [*He kills another.*] *Here Exton strikes*
        him down.

That hand shall burn in never-quenching fire
That staggers° thus my person. Exton, thy fierce
    hand
Hath with the King's blood stained the King's own
    land.   *110*
Mount, mount, my soul; thy seat is up on high,
Whilst my gross flesh sinks downward here to die.

    [*Dies.*]

Exton. As full of valor as of royal blood!
Both have I spilled. O, would the deed were good!
For now the devil that told me I did well   *115*
Says that this deed is chronicled in hell.
This dead king to the living king I'll bear.
Take hence the rest, and give them burial here.

    [*Exeunt with the bodies.*]

[Scene 6. *Windsor Castle.*]

    [*Flourish.*] *Enter Bolingbroke with the*
    Duke of York, [*other Lords and Attendants*].

Bolingbroke. Kind uncle York, the latest news we
    hear
Is that the rebels have consumed with fire

105 **What . . . assault?** what does death mean by assaulting me so vio-
lently?   107 **room** place   109 **staggers** makes to stagger

Our town of Ciceter° in Gloucestershire,
But whether they be ta'en or slain we hear not.

Enter Northumberland.

5   Welcome, my lord; what is the news?

Northumberland. First, to thy sacred state wish I all
         happiness;
      The next° news is, I have to London sent
      The heads of Salisbury, Spencer, Blunt, and Kent,°
      The manner of their taking may appear
10   At large discoursèd in this paper here.

Bolingbroke. We thank thee, gentle Percy, for thy
         pains,
      And to thy worth will add right worthy gains.°

Enter Lord Fitzwater.

Fitzwater. My lord, I have from Oxford sent to
         London
      The heads of Brocas° and Sir Bennet Seely,
15   Two of the dangerous consorted° traitors
      That sought at Oxford thy dire overthrow.

Bolingbroke. Thy pains, Fitzwater, shall not be
         forgot:
      Right noble is thy merit well I wot.

Enter Henry Percy [and the Bishop of Carlisle].

Percy. The grand conspirator, Abbot of Westminster,
20   With clog of conscience and sour melancholy,
      Hath yielded up his body to the grave;
      But here is Carlisle living, to abide
      Thy kingly doom, and sentence of his pride.

Bolingbroke. Carlisle, this is your doom:
      Choose out some secret place, some reverend
25   room°

5.6. 8 **Ciceter** Cirencester   7 **next** most important   8 **Spencer, Blunt,
and Kent** Lord Spencer, formerly Earl of Gloucester; Sir Thomas Blunt;
Earl of Kent   12 **right worthy gains** well-deserved reward   14 **Brocas**
Sir Leonard (or Bernard) Brocas   15 **consorted** associated   25 **reverend room** place of religious retirement

More than thou hast,° and with it joy° thy life.
So° as thou liv'st in peace, die free from strife;
For though mine enemy thou hast ever been,
High sparks of honor in thee have I seen.

Enter Exton with [Attendants bearing]
the coffin.

Exton. Great King, within this coffin I present   *30*
Thy buried fear:° herein all breathless lies
The mightiest of thy greatest enemies,
Richard of Bordeaux,° by me hither brought.

Bolingbroke. Exton, I thank thee not, for thou hast
    wrought
A deed of slander with thy fatal hand   *35*
Upon my head and all this famous land.

Exton. From your own mouth, my lord, did I this deed.

Bolingbroke. They love not poison that do poison
    need,
Nor do I thee; though I did wish him dead,
I hate the murderer, love him murderèd.   *40*
The guilt of conscience take thou for thy labor,
But neither my good word, nor princely favor.
With Cain go wander thorough shades of night,
And never show thy head by day nor light.
                                            [*Exit Exton.*]
Lords, I protest, my soul is full of woe,   *45*
That blood should sprinkle me to make me grow.
Come, mourn with me for what I do lament,
And put on sullen black incontinent.°
I'll make a voyage to the Holy Land,
To wash this blood off from my guilty hand.   *50*
March sadly after; grace my mournings here,
In weeping after this untimely bier.
                                            [*Exeunt.*]

FINIS

26 **More than thou hast** i.e., more religious and less political   26 **joy** enjoy   27 **So** provided that   31 **buried fear** (cf. *living fear,* 5.4.2)   33 **Bordeaux** (Richard's birthplace)   48 **incontinent** forthwith

Textual Note

Richard II was first published in 1597, after 29 August, when it was registered. The First Quarto (Q1) appeared with the following title page: "THE/ Tragedie of King Ri-/ chard the se-/ cond./ *As it hath beene publikely acted/ by the right Honourable the/ Lorde Chamberlaine his Ser-/ uants./* LONDON/ Printed by Valentine Simmes for Androw Wise, and/ are to be sold at his shop in Paules church yard at/ the signe of the Angel./ 1597."

The play is thought to have been printed from a transcript of Shakespeare's manuscript, but it may preserve some of his spelling and punctuation. Some critics (Cairncross, Brooks, Ure) think that the text is memorially contaminated in a few places (i.e., the transcriber introduced mistakes through his memory of other lines of the play and also of *Richard III*). The First Quarto forms the basis of the present edition, except for the abdication scene, which was omitted from the first three quartos and included in the Fourth (1608). The play was included in the First Folio (1623), probably from a corrected text of Q5 (1615). The Folio text (F) enables us to correct Q1 in a number of places, and it provides the best text of the abdication scene; but many of its readings are "sophistications"—unnecessary alterations—for which Shakespeare was not responsible.

The present edition modernizes spelling and punctuation, amplifies abbreviations and regularizes speech prefixes, corrects obvious typographical errors, adjusts the position of stage directions, and in a few cases alters the lineation. Q1 is not divided into acts or scenes; the present edition uses the divisions established by the Globe editors, who used those of F but who added one at 5.4. F indicates the divisions in Latin; they are translated here. Other deviations from Q1 (and for the abdication scene from F) are listed below. The adopted reading is given in italics; if it is not taken from F a note in a bracket explains that it is taken (for example) from Q5 or (again, for example) from an editor's emendation—indicated by [ed]. Next is given the original reading in roman.

1.1.118 *my scepter's* scepters   139 *But* Ah but   152 *gentlemen* Gentleman   162 *When . . . when?* When Harry? when obedience bids   192 *parle* parlee

1.2.47 *sit* set   58 *it* is

1.3.26 *demand of* [ed] ask   33 *comest* [Q5] comes   84 *innocency* [ed] innocence   172 *then but* but   180 *you owe* y'owe   221 *night* nightes   238 *had it* [ed] had't

1.4.1 s.d. *Bagot* [ed] Bushie   20 *cousin, cousin* Coosens Coosin   23 *Bagot . . . Green* [Q6] [Q1] omits; F has "heere Bagot and Greene"]   53 *Bushy, what news?* [Q1 omits, but prints the s.d. "Enter Bushie with newes"]   65 *All* [ed; Q and F omit]

2.1.18 *fond* [ed] found [the emendation to "fond" is plausible; but it is possible that "found" was an error caused by the similar endings of adjacent lines— "soundes" and "sound"—or that a line was omitted by mistake]   48 *as a* as   102 *incagèd* inraged   113 *not* [ed] not, not   124 *brother* [Q2] brothers   156 *kernes* kerne   177 *the a* 232 *that that* [ed] that   257 *King's* King   280 *The . . . Arundel* [ed; Q and F omit]   283 *Thomas Ramston* [Holinshed] Iohn Ramston   284 *Quoint* Coines

2.2.16 *eye* eyes   25 *more's* more is   31 *though* thought   53 *Henry* H   88 *cold* [ed] they are cold   112 *Th'one* Tone   137 *The . . . will* [ed] Will the hateful commons

2.3.36 *Hereford* Herefords   98 *the lord* lord

3.2.32 *succor* [ed] succors   38 *and* [ed] that   40 *boldly* [ed] bouldy   72 *O'erthrows* Ouerthrowes

3.3.13 *with you to* to   17 *mis-take* [ed] mistake   30 *lord* Lords   59 *waters—on* [ed] water's on   118 *prince and* [ed] princesse

3.4.11 *joy* [ed] griefe   21 *good.* good?   26 *pins* pines   57 *We at* [ed] at   80 *Cam'st* Canst

4.1.22 *him* them   54 *As* [ed] As it   55 *sun to sun* [ed] sinne to sinne   76 *my bond* bond   154–319 [for this passage, here printed from F, Q1 has only "Let it be so, and loe on wednesday next, / We solemnly proclaime our Coronation, / Lords be ready all"]   182 *and on* [Q4] on   182 *yours* [Q4] thine   250 *and* [Q4] a   254 *Nor* [Q4] No, nor   275 *the* [Q4] that   284 *was* [Q4] Is   284 *that* [Q4] which   285 *And* [Q4] That   288 *a* [Q4] an   295 *manners* [Q4] manner   332 *I will* [ed] Ile

5.1.25 *stricken* throwne

5.2.55 *prevent me* [ed] preuent   78 *life, my* [ed] life, by my   116 *And* An

5.3.10 *While* [ed] Which   20 *but yet* [ed] yet   35 *that I* that   67 *and* an   110 *Bolingbroke* Yorke   134–35 *With . . . him* [ed] I pardon him with al my heart   143 *cousin, too* [Q6] cousin

5.4.1 s.d. *Enter* Manet

5.5.27 *sit* set   79 *bestrid* bestride

5.6.8 *Salisbury . . . Blunt* Oxford, Salisbury, Blunt   12 s.d. *Fitzwater* [Q6] Fitzwaters   43 *thorough* [ed] through [Q] through the [F]

The Sources of *Richard II*

The following have been suggested as possible sources of the play:

1. *The Chronicles* of Raphael Holinshed (1587), pp. 493–540.
2. *The Union of the Two Noble and Illustrate Famelies of Lancastre and Yorke* by Edward Hall (1548).
3. *The Cronycles of Englande* by Sir John Froissart (translated by Lord Berners, 1525).
4. J. Créton's *Histoire du Roy d'Angleterre*
5. *Chronique de la Traïson et Mort de Richart Deux*
6. Le Beau's *Chronique de Richard II depuis l'an 1377 jusques à l'an 1399.*
   (4, 5, and 6 were in manuscript until the nineteenth century)
7. *Thomas of Woodstock* (anonymous play).
8. *The First Fowre Bookes of the Civile Wars* by Samuel Daniel (1595).
9. *A Myrroure for Magistrates* (1559)
10. A lost play.

As we have seen, Professor J. Dover Wilson believes that the main source was this lost play, the author of which used Nos. 1–6 of the works listed above. The theory presupposes that this unknown dramatist displayed a historical erudition beyond Shakespeare's customary range, although there are few signs of erudition in his companion piece, *The Troublesome Reign of King John*. As it is known that Shakespeare did in other plays combine several different sources, it is easier to believe that he followed the same practice in *Richard II* than that some unknown hack writer went to the same trouble.

If, then, we are skeptical of the existence of the lost play we can examine briefly the evidence for Shakespeare's use of the remaining nine hypothetical sources. There is no doubt that he had read parts of Holinshed, Hall, and *The Mirror for Magistrates*; almost certainly he knew Berners' Froissart and Daniel's poem; and there are enough apparent echoes of *Woodstock* to make it highly probable that he knew it, probably in the theater. Whether he had read the three French manuscripts or not is much more dubious.

It is significant that Shakespeare begins his play with the quarrel between Mowbray and Bolingbroke, for this is the point at which Hall begins his story; but, apart from this, the influence of Hall is apparently very slight.

It has been argued by Professor J. Dover Wilson (following Paul Reyher) that Shakespeare's characterization of John of Gaunt was suggested by Froissart who, in his chapter on "How the Duke of Lancaster Died," speaks of his grief at his son's banishment, and at the King's misgovernment:

> For he saw well that if he long persevered and were suffered to continue, the realm was likely to be utterly lost. With these imaginations and other, the Duke fell sick, whereon he died.

Froissart also mentions Richard's joy at Gaunt's death, and in an earlier passage he makes Gaunt say:

> Our nephew, the King of England, will shame all ere he cease. He believeth too lightly evil counsel who shall destroy him; and simply, if he live long, he will lose his realm, and that hath been gotten with much cost and travail by our predecessors and by us.

Froissart, too, but not Holinshed, mentions the rumor that Richard was not the son of the Black Prince. This is found also in *Traïson*.

Mr. A. P. Rossiter, however, thought that the character of Gaunt could have been derived from *Woodstock*, Stow, and Hall. There is no doubt that Shakespeare was acquainted with *Woodstock*, for he echoes it in a number of places, as in the accusation that Richard had become England's landlord:

> Rent out our kingdom like a pelting farm . . .
> And thou no king, but landlord now become.

It is not possible to prove that Shakespeare read the three French manuscript chronicles, but they were not entirely inaccessible. Holinshed, Hall, and Daniel all used Créton's poem, and Holinshed refers to *Traïson* as "an old French pamphlet belonging to John Stow." If Shakespeare had wished to follow up Holinshed's references, the chances are that he could have done so, although the evidence that he actually did so has not convinced many scholars.

A messenger in Créton's poem describes the way people of all ages flocked to Bolingbroke's standard:

> Then might you have beheld young and old, the feeble and the strong, make a clamor, and regarding neither right nor wrong stir themselves up with one accord . . . they began to flee towards the Duke . . . he brings young and old under subjection.

So Scroop (3.2.112ff.), after describing the white beards and boys who have joined Bolingbroke, adds "both young and old rebel." In the same scene, Richard's appeals to heaven, the use of Salisbury as a messenger of evil tidings, and the account of successive disasters—

> you may be sure he was not fain to smile, for, on all sides, one after another, came pouring in upon him mischief and trouble—

are all to be found in the corresponding scene of the play. The most striking parallel, however, is the comparison of Richard's betrayal and suffering to that of Christ. In the prose section of Créton's account, he compares the rejection of Richard by the people to the rejection of Christ by the Jews:

> Then spake Duke Henry quite aloud to the commons of the said city. "Fair sirs, behold your king! consider what you will do with him!" And they made answer with a loud voice, "We will

have him taken to Westminster." And so he delivered him unto them. At this hour did he remind me of Pilate, who caused our Lord Jesus Christ to be scourged at the stake, and afterwards had him brought before the multitude of the Jews, saying, "Fair Sirs, behold your king!" who replied, "let him be crucified!" Then Pilate washed his hands of it, saying, "I am innocent of the just blood." And so he delivered our Lord unto them. Much in the like manner did Duke Henry, when he gave up his rightful lord to the rabble of London, in order that, if they should put him to death, he might say, "I am innocent of this deed."

In *Traïson* there are several similar passages. The author compares Northumberland to Judas; and a few pages later Richard compares himself to Christ, who was likewise "undeservedly sold and given into the hands of his enemies." Although Holinshed refers to a prelate as a Pilate, and although Shakespeare elsewhere associates treachery with Judas, the emphasis on the Christ parallel is to be found only in Créton, *Traïson*, and Shakespeare. There are a few minor parallels with *Traïson*. "Daring-hardy" (1.3.43) may translate *hardie* in precisely the same context, and "base court" (3.3.175) may likewise translate *basse cour*. There seems, therefore, to be a slight balance of probability that Shakespeare had read both Créton's poem and *Traïson*, but there is less probability that he had read Le Beau's chronicle.

About seventy parallels have been listed with Daniel's *Civil Wars*. Some of these, however, are not peculiar to Daniel's poem, and others may be explained by the fact that both poets amplified their sources independently. But enough parallels remain to convince all recent editors (Dover Wilson, Black, Ure) that Shakespeare was influenced by Daniel, especially in 2.1, 4.1, 5.1, and 5.2. Shakespeare and Daniel both altered the age of the Queen, making her a woman instead of a child; Shakespeare was clearly indebted to Daniel for the account of the entry of Richard and Bolingbroke into London; and there are clear echoes of Daniel in Gaunt's speech on England:

Why Neptune hast thou made us stand alone
Divided from the world, for this say they?

* * *

A place there is where proudly raised there stands
A huge aspiring rock neighboring the skies
Whose surly brow imperiously commands
The sea his bounds that at his proud feet lies:
And spurns the waves that in rebellious bands
Assault his empire and against him rise: . . .
With what contagion France didst thou infect
The land by thee made proud to disagree?

Although we have argued that Shakespeare consulted a number of different sources, there is little doubt that the great bulk of his material came from Holinshed. The only scenes that did not largely derive from the *Chronicles* are the following:

1.2. No direct source has been discovered
2.1.1–152. Partly based on Froissart and Daniel
2.2. Largely invention
3.4. No source
5.1. Possibly suggested by Daniel
5.2.1–40. Probably suggested by Daniel

It will be observed from the relevant passages from Holinshed given below that Shakespeare sometimes combines widely separated facts for a single scene, that he telescopes events, and that on occasion he rearranges the order of historical happenings.

Of telescoping perhaps the best example is 2.1. Bolingbroke had been banished in September 1398; his father died in the following February; Richard left for Ireland in May; and Bolingbroke landed at Ravenspurgh in July. But in Shakespeare's scene Gaunt is dying immediately after his son's banishment—in 1.4 we have a description of Bolingbroke's leave-taking and of Gaunt's illness—but before the end of the scene we are told that Bolingbroke has already sailed from Brittany. A period of nine months elapses in the course of the scene. By this telescoping Shakespeare is able to link the death of Gaunt with the banishment of Bolingbroke, to link the confiscation of his estates with the necessities of the Irish campaign, and to link the support Bolingbroke receives with Richard's conduct and with the patriotic admonitions of Gaunt. The scene is dramatically effective on the stage, in spite of the impossibilities revealed in the study; and the fact that Bolingbroke is returning to England before he can have heard of the confiscation of his estates, and yet pretends later that this was his motive for returning from exile, is an example of the deliberate ambiguity with which the character is presented.

The fourth act provides a good example of Shakespeare's rearrangement of historical facts, although there is no essential distortion of historical truth. Bagot's accusation of Aumerle took place on October 16, Fitzwater's accusation two days later; Carlisle's speech (which was not, as in the play, associated with Bolingbroke's claim of the crown) was a week later, on October 23; the abdication took place in the Tower (not in Westminster Hall) on September 29; and the Abbot of Westminster's entertainment of the conspirators was not until December 17. Although Swinburne complained that the quarrel at the beginning of the scene was "a morally chaotic introduction of incongruous causes, inexplicable plaintiffs, and incomprehensible defendants," it reminds us, just before the abdication, of Gloucester's death, its ultimate cause; and it provides Aumerle with a motive for rebellion. Carlisle's speech, one of the most significant moments in the whole tetralogy, is much more dramatic in its place as a warning to the characters in the play and to us of the results of Bolingbroke's usurpation at the moment of its happening. It is obviously more dramatic for Richard to go through the ritual of his abdication in public than before the commissioners in the Tower; and the Abbot's plot is properly introduced at a moment when our sympathies have been fully aroused for Richard, especially when we realize that the plot to restore him to the throne is the direct cause of his murder. Some details of the scene may have been suggested by other sources—Froissart, Hall, Daniel, *The Mirror for Magistrates*, the *Homilies*, and even *Traïson*.

Finally, an example may be given of Shakespeare's omissions. In Holinshed's account, Northumberland persuades Richard to leave Conway Castle, ambushing him on the way to Flint, and conveying him to Flint Castle as a prisoner. Shakespeare omits this incident, following Froissart, who merely says that Richard rode to Flint, and prepared to defend the castle there.

RAPHAEL HOLINSHED

From Chronicles of England, Scotland, and Ireland

[Numerals in brackets refer to acts and scenes that deal with Holinshed's material.]

It fell out that in this parliament holden at Shrewsbury, Henry, Duke of Hereford, accused Thomas Mowbray, Duke of Norfolk, of certain words which he should utter in talk had betwixt them, as they rode together lately before betwixt London and Brainford, sounding highly to the King's dishonor. And for further proof thereof, he presented a supplication to the King, wherein he appealed the Duke of Norfolk in field of battle for a traitor, false and disloyal to the King and enemy unto the realm. This supplication was read before both the dukes in presence of the King: which done, the Duke of Norfolk took upon him to answer it, declaring that whatsoever the Duke of Hereford had said against him other than well, he lied falsely like an untrue knight as he was. And when the King asked of the Duke of Hereford what he said to it, he, taking his hood off his head, said: "My sovereign lord, even as the supplication which I took you importeth, right so I say for truth, that Thomas Mowbray, Duke of Norfolk, is a traitor, false and disloyal to your royal majesty, your crown, and to all the states of your realm."

Then the Duke of Norfolk being asked what he said to this, he answered: "Right dear lord, with your favor that I make answer unto your cousin here, I say (your reverence saved) that Henry of Lancaster, Duke of Hereford, like a false and disloyal traitor as he is, doth lie, in that he hath or shall say of me otherwise than well." "No more," said the king, "we have heard enough"; and herewith commanded the Duke of Surrey, for that turn Marshal of England, to arrest in his name the two dukes. The Duke of Lancaster, father to the Duke of Hereford, the Duke of York, the Duke of Aumerle, Constable of England, and the Duke of Surrey, Marshal of the realm, undertook as pledges body for body for the Duke of Hereford; but the Duke of Norfolk was not suffered to put in pledges, and so under arrest was led unto Windsor Castle and there guarded with keepers that were appointed to see him safely kept.

Now after the dissolving of the parliament at Shrewsbury there was a day appointed six weeks after, for the King to come unto Windsor to hear and to take some order betwixt the two dukes, which had thus appealed each other. There was a great scaffold erected within the castle of Windsor for the King to sit with the lords and prelates of his realm: and so at the day appointed, he with the said lords and prelates being come thither and set in their places, the Duke of Hereford, appellant, and the Duke of Norfolk, defendant, were sent for to come and appear before the King, sitting there in his seat of justice. And then began Sir John Bushy to speak for the King, declaring to the lords how they should understand, that where the Duke of Hereford had presented a supplication to the King, who was there set to minister justice to all men that would demand the same, as appertained to his royal majesty, he therefore would now hear what the parties could say one against other, and withal the King commanded the dukes of Aumerle and Surrey, the one being Constable, and the other Marshal, to go unto the two dukes, appellant and defendant, requiring them on his behalf to grow to some agreement: and, for his part, he would be ready to pardon all that had been said or done amiss betwixt them, touching any harm or dishonor to him or his realm: but they answered both assuredly that it was not possible to have any peace or agreement made betwixt them.

[1.1] When he heard what they had answered, he commanded that they should be brought forthwith before his presence, to hear what they would say. Herewith an herald in the King's name with loud voice commanded the dukes to come before the King, either of them to show his reason, or else to make peace together without more delay. When they were come before the King and lords, the King spake himself to them, willing them to agree, and make peace together: for it is (said he) the best way ye can take. The Duke of Norfolk with due reverence hereunto answered it could not be so brought to pass, his honor saved. Then the King asked of the Duke of Hereford what it was that he demanded of the Duke of Norfolk, and "what is the matter that ye cannot make peace together and become friends?"

Then stood forth a knight; who asking and obtaining license to speak for the Duke of Hereford, said: "Right dear and sovereign lord, here is Henry of Lancaster, Duke of Hereford and Earl of Derby, who saith, and I for him likewise say, that Thomas Mowbray, Duke of Norfolk, is a false and disloyal traitor to you and your royal majesty and to your whole realm: and likewise the Duke of Hereford saith and I for him, that Thomas Mowbray, Duke of Norfolk, hath received eight thousand nobles to pay the soldiers that keep your town of Calais, which he hath not done as he ought; and furthermore the said Duke of Norfolk hath been the occasion of all the treason that hath been contrived in your realm for the space of these eighteen years, and by his false suggestions and malicious counsel, he hath caused to die and to be murdered your right dear uncle, the Duke of Gloucester, son to King Edward. Moreover the Duke of Hereford saith, and I for him, that he will prove this with his body against the body of the said Duke of Norfolk within lists." The King herewith waxed angry, and asked the Duke of Hereford if these were his words; who answered: "Right dear lord, they are my words; and hereof I require right, and the battle against him."

There was a knight also that asked license to speak for the Duke of Norfolk, and obtaining it, began to answer thus: "Right dear sovereign lord, here is Thomas Mowbray, Duke of Norfolk, who answereth and saith, and I for him, that all which Henry of Lancaster hath said and declared (saving thé reverence due to the King and his council) is a lie; and the said Henry of Lancaster hath falsely and wickedly lied as a false and disloyal knight, and both hath been and is a traitor against you, your crown, royal majesty and realm. This will I prove and defend as becometh a loyal knight to do with my body against his. Right dear lord, I beseech you, therefore, and your council, that it may please you in your royal discretion to consider and mark what Henry of Lancaster, Duke of Hereford, such a one as he is, hath said."

The King then demanded of the Duke of Norfolk if these were his words, and whether he had any more to say. The Duke of Norfolk then answered for himself: "Right dear sir, true it is that I have received so much gold to pay your people of the town of Calais; which I have done, and I do avouch that your town of Calais is as well kept at your commandment as ever it was at any time before, and that there never hath been by any of Calais any complaint made unto you of me. Right dear and my sovereign lord, for the voyage that I made into France about your marriage, I never received either gold or silver of you, nor yet for the voyage that the Duke of Aumerle and I made into Almaine, where we spent great treasure. Marry, true it is that once I laid an ambush to have slain the Duke of Lancaster, that there sitteth: but nevertheless he hath pardoned me thereof, and there was good peace betwixt us, for the which I yield him hearty thanks. This is that which I have to answer, and I am ready to defend myself against mine adversary; I beseech you, therefore, of right, and to have the battle against him in upright judgment."

After this, when the King had communed with his council a little, he commanded the two dukes to stand forth, that their answers might be heard. The King then caused them once again to be asked if they would agree and make peace together, but they both flatly answered that they would not: and withal the Duke of Hereford cast down his gage, and the Duke of Norfolk took it up. The King perceiving this demeanor betwixt them, sware by Saint John Baptist that he would never seek to make peace betwixt them again. And therefore Sir John Bushy in name of the King and his council declared that the King and his council had commanded and ordained that they should have a day of battle appointed them at Coventry. Here writers disagree about the day that was appointed: for some say it was upon a Monday in August; other upon Saint Lambert's day, being the seventeenth of September, other on the eleventh of September; but true it is that the King assigned them not only the day but also appointed them lists and place for the combat, and thereupon great preparation was made, as to such a matter appertained.

[1.3] At the time appointed, the King came to Coventry, where the two dukes were ready, according to the order prescribed therein, coming thither in great array, accompanied with the lords and gentlemen of their lineages. The King caused a sumptuous scaffold or theater and royal lists there to be erected and prepared. The Sunday before they should fight, after dinner, the Duke of Hereford came to the King (being lodged about a quarter of a mile without the town in a tower that belonged to Sir William Bagot) to take his leave of him. The morrow after, being the day appointed for the combat, about the spring of the day, came the Duke of Norfolk to the court to take leave likewise of the King. The Duke of Hereford armed him in his tent, that was set up near to the lists, and the Duke of Norfolk put on his armor betwixt the gate and the barrier of the town in a beautiful house, having a fair perclois of wood towards the gate, that none might see what was done within the house.

The Duke of Aumerle that day, being High Constable of England, and the Duke of Surrey, Marshal, placed themselves betwixt them, well armed and appointed; and when they saw their time, they first entered into the lists with a great company of men appareled in silk sendall, embroidered with silver, both richly and curiously, every man having a tipped staff to keep the field in order. About the hour of prime came to the barriers of the lists the Duke of Hereford, mounted on a white courser, barded with green and blue velvet embroidered sumptuously with swans and antelopes of goldsmiths' work, armed at all points. The Constable and Marshal came to the barriers, demanding of him what he was; he answered: "I am Henry of Lancaster, Duke of Hereford, which am come hither to do mine endeavor against Thomas Mowbray, Duke of Norfolk, as a traitor untrue to God, the King, his realm, and me." Then incontinently he sware upon the holy evangelists that his quarrel was true and just, and upon that point he required to enter the lists. Then he put up his sword, which before he held naked in his hand, and putting down his visor, made a cross on his horse, and with spear in hand, entered into the lists, and descended from his horse, and set him down in a chair of green velvet at the one end of the lists, and there reposed himself, abiding the coming of his adversary.

Soon after him, entered into the field with great triumph King Richard, accompanied with all the peers of the realm. . . . When the King was set in his seat, which was richly hanged and adorned, a knight-at-arms made open proclamation, prohibiting all men in the name of the King and of the High Constable and Marshal to enterprise or attempt to approach or touch any part of the lists upon pain of death, except such as were appointed to order or marshal the field. The proclamation ended, another herald cried: "Behold here Henry of Lancaster, Duke of Hereford, appellant, which is entered into the lists royal to do his devoir against Thomas Mowbray, Duke of Norfolk, defendant, upon pain to be found false and recreant."

The Duke of Norfolk hovered on horseback at the entry of the lists, his horse being barded with crimson velvet, embroidered richly with lions of silver and mulberry trees; and when he had made his oath before the Constable and Marshal that his quarrel was just and true, he entered the field manfully, saying aloud: "God aid him that hath the right." And then he departed from his horse, and sat him down in his chair, which was of crimson velvet, curtained about with white and red damask. The lord delivered the one spear himself to the Duke of Hereford, and sent the other to the Duke of Norfolk by a knight. Then the herald proclaimed that the traverses and chairs should be removed, commanding them on the king's behalf to mount on horseback and address themselves to the battle and combat.

The Duke of Hereford was quickly horsed, and closed his bavier, and cast his spear into the rest, and when the trumpet sounded set forward courageously towards his enemy six or seven paces. The Duke of Norfolk was not fully set forward, when the King cast down his warder, and the heralds cried "Ho, ho!" Then the King caused their spears to be taken from them, and commanded them to repair again to their chairs, where they remained two long hours, while the King and his council deliberately consulted what order was best to be had in so weighty a cause. Finally, after they had devised and fully determined what should be done therein, the heralds cried silence; and Sir John Bushy, the King's secretary, read the sentence and determination of the King and his council in a long roll, the effect whereof was that Henry, Duke of Hereford, should within fifteen days depart out of the realm, and not to return before the term of ten years were expired, except by the King he should be repealed again, and this upon pain of death; and that Thomas Mowbray, Duke of Norfolk, because he had sown sedition in the realm by his words, should likewise avoid the realm, and never to return again into England, nor approach the borders or confines thereof upon pain of death; and that the King would stay the profits of his lands, till he had levied thereof such sums of money as the Duke had taken up of the King's treasurer for the wages of the garrison of Calais, which were still unpaid.

When these judgments were once read, the King called before him both the parties, and made them to swear that the one should never come in place where the other was, willingly; nor keep any company together in any foreign region; which oath they both received humbly, and so went their ways. The Duke of Norfolk departed sorrowfully out of the realm into Almaine, and at the last came to Venice, where he for thought and melancholy deceased: for he was in hope (as writers record) that he should have been borne out in the matter by the King, which when it fell out otherwise, it grieved him not a little. The Duke of Hereford took his leave of the King at Eltham, who there released four years of his banishment: so he took journey over into Calais, and from thence went into France, where he remained. A wonder it was to see what number of people ran after him in every town and street where he came, before he took the sea, lamenting and bewailing his departure, as who would say, that when he departed, the only shield, defense and comfort of the commonwealth was vaded and gone.

At his coming into France, King Charles, hearing the cause of his banishment (which he esteemed to be very slight), received him gently, and him honorably entertained, insomuch that he had by favor obtained in marriage the only daughter of the Duke of Berrie, uncle to the French King, if King Richard had not been a let in that matter, who being thereof certified [2.1.167–68], sent the Earl of Salisbury with all speed into France, both to surmise by untrue suggestion heinous offenses against him, and also to require the French King that in no wise he would suffer his cousin to be matched in marriage with him that was so manifest an offender. This was a pestilent kind of proceeding against that nobleman then being in a foreign country, having been so honorably received as he was at his entrance into France, and upon view and good liking of his behavior there, so forward in marriage with a lady of noble lineage. . . .

[1.4.48] But yet to content the King's mind, many blank charters were devised and brought into the city, which many of the substantial and wealthy citizens were fain to seal, to their great charge, as in the end appeared. And the like charters were sent abroad into all shires within the realm, whereby great grudge and murmuring arose among the people: for when they were so sealed, the King's officers wrote in the same what liked them, as well for charging the parties with payment of money, as otherwise.

[2.1] In this mean time, the Duke of Lancaster departed out of this life at the Bishop of Ely's place in Holborn. . . . The death of this duke gave occasion of increasing more hatred in the people of this realm toward the King, for he seized into his hands all the goods that belonged to him, and also received all the rents and revenues of his lands which ought to have descended unto the Duke of Hereford by lawful inheritance, in revoking his letters patents, which he had granted to him before, by virtue whereof he might make his attorneys-general to sue livery for him, of any manner of inheritances or possessions that might from thenceforth fall unto him, and that his homage might be respited, with making reasonable fine: whereby it was evident that the King meant his utter undoing.

This hard dealing was much misliked of all the nobility, and cried out against of the meaner sort: but namely the Duke of York was therewith sore moved, who before this time had borne things with so patient a mind as he could, though the same touched him very near, as the death of his brother, the Duke of Gloucester, the banishment of his nephew, the said Duke of Hereford, and other moe injuries in great number, which for the slippery youth of the King he passed over for the time, and did forget as well as he might. But now perceiving that neither law, justice, nor equity could take place where the King's willful will was bent upon any wrongful purpose, he considered that the glory of the public wealth of his country must needs decay, by reason of the King his lack of wit, and want of such as would (without flattery) admonish him of his duty: and therefore he thought it the part of a wise man to get him in time to a resting place, and to leave the following of such an unadvised captain as with a leaden sword would cut his own throat. Hereupon he with the Duke of Aumerle his son went to his house at Langley, rejoicing that nothing had mishappened in the commonwealth through his device or consent. The common bruit ran that the King had set to farm the realm of England unto Sir William Scroop, Earl of Wiltshire, and then Treasurer of England, to Sir John Bushy, Sir John Bagot, and Sir Henry Green, knights.

About the same time, the Earl of Arundel's son, named Thomas, which was kept in the Duke of Exeter's house, escaped out of the realm by means of one William Scot, mercer, and went to his uncle Thomas Arundel, late Archbishop of Canterbury, as then sojourning at Cullen.

[1.4] King Richard being destitute of treasure to furnish such a princely port as he maintained, borrowed great sums of money of many of the great lords and peers of his realm, both spiritual and temporal, and likewise of other mean persons, promising them in good earnest, by delivering to them his letters patents for assurance, that he would repay the money so borrowed at a day appointed: which notwithstanding, he never paid.

[2.4] In this year in a manner throughout all the realm of England, old bay trees withered, and afterwards, contrary to all men's thinking, grew green again, a strange sight, and supposed to import some unknown event.

[1.4] In this mean time the King being advertised that the wild Irish daily wasted and destroyed the towns and villages within the English pale, and had slain many of the soldiers which lay there in garrison for defense of that country, determined to make eftsoons a voyage thither, and prepared all things necessary for his passage now against the spring. . . .

[2.1] The King departed toward Bristow, from thence to pass into [2.2] Ireland, leaving the Queen with her train still at Windsor: he appointed for his lieutenant general in his absence his uncle the Duke of York: and so in the month of April, as diverse authors write, he set forward from Windsor, and finally took shipping at Milford, and from thence with two hundred ships and a puissant power of men of arms and archers he sailed into Ireland. . . .

Now whilst he was thus occupied in devising how to reduce them into subjection, and taking orders for the good stay and quiet government of the country, divers of the nobility, as well prelates as other, and likewise many of the magistrates and rulers of the cities, towns, and commonalty here in England, perceiving daily how the realm drew to utter ruin, not like to be recovered to the former state of wealth whilst King Richard lived and reigned (as they took it), devised with great deliberation and considerate advice, to send and signify by letters unto Duke Henry, whom they now called (as he was indeed) Duke of Lancaster and Hereford, requiring him with all convenient speed to convey himself into England, promising him all their aid, power, and assistance, if he, expelling King Richard, as a man not meet for the office he bare, would take upon him the scepter, rule, and diadem of his native land and region.

[2.1] He therefore being thus called upon by messengers and letters from his friends, and chiefly through the earnest persuasion of Thomas Arundel, late Archbishop of Canterbury, who (as before ye have heard) had been removed from his see and banished the realm by King Richard's means, got him down to Britaine [Brittany], together with the said

Archbishop, where he was joyfully received of the Duke and
Duchess, and found such friendship at the Duke's hands that
there were certain ships rigged and made ready for him, at a
place in base Britaine, called Le port blanc, as we find in the
chronicles of Britaine: and when all his provision was made
ready, he took the sea, together with the said Archbishop of
Canterbury, and his nephew Thomas Arundel, son and heir
to the late Earl of Arundel, beheaded at the Tower Hill, as
you have heard. There were also with him Reginald, Lord
Cobham, Sir Thomas Erpingham, and Sir Thomas Ramston,
knights, John Norbury, Robert Waterton and Francis Coint,
esquires: few else were there, for (as some write) he had not
past fifteen lances, as they termed them in those days, that
is to say, men of arms, furnished and appointed as the use
then was. Yet other write, that the Duke of Britaine delivered unto him three thousand men of war to attend him, and
that he had eight ships well furnished for the war, where
Froissart yet speaketh but of three. Moreover, where Froissart and also the chronicles of Britaine avouch that he should
land at Plymouth, by our English writers it seemeth otherwise: for it appeareth by their assured report, that he approaching to the shore, did not straight take land, but lay
hovering aloof, and showed himself now in this place, and
now in that, to see what countenance was made by the
people, whether they meant enviously to resist him, or
friendly to receive him.

[2.2] When the Lord Governor, Edmund Duke of York,
was advertised that the Duke of Lancaster kept still the sea
and was ready to arrive (but where he meant first to set foot
on land, there was not any that understood the certainty) he
sent for the Lord Chancellor, Edmund Stafford, Bishop of
Exeter, and for the Lord Treasurer, William Scroop, Earl of
Wiltshire, and other of the King's Privy Council, as John
Bushy, William Bagot, Henry Green, and John Russell,
knights; of these he required to know what they thought good
to be done in this matter, concerning the Duke of Lancaster
being on the seas. Their advice was to depart from London
unto St. Albans, and there to gather an army to resist the
Duke in his landing; but to how small purpose their counsel
served, the conclusion thereof plainly declared, for the most

part that were called, when they came thither, boldly
protested that they would not fight against the Duke of Lancaster, whom they knew to be evil dealt withal.

[2.2] The Lord Treasurer, Bushy, Bagot and Green, perceiving that the commons would cleave unto and take part
with the Duke, slipped away, leaving the Lord Governor of
the realm and the Lord Chancellor to make what shift they
could for themselves. Bagot got him to Chester, and so escaped into Ireland; the other fled to the castle of Bristow, in
hope there to be in safety. The Duke of Lancaster, after he
had coasted alongst the shore a certain time and had got some
intelligence how the people's minds were affected towards
him, landed about the beginning of July in Yorkshire, at a
place sometime called Ravenspur betwixt Hull and Bridling-
ton, and with him not past threescore persons, as some write:
but he was so joyfully received of the lords, knights, and gentlemen of those parts that he found means, by their help,
forthwith to assemble a great number of people that were
willing to take his part. The first that came to him were the
lords of Lincolnshire and other countries adjoining, as the
Lords Willoughby, Ross, Darcy, and Beaumont.

[2.3] At his coming unto Doncaster, the Earl of Northumberland and his son Sir Henry Percy, wardens of the
marches against Scotland, with the Earl of Westmoreland,
came unto him, where he sware unto those lords that he
would demand no more but the lands that were to him descended by inheritance from his father, and in right of his
wife. Moreover, he undertook to cause the payment of taxes
and tallages to be laid down, and to bring the King to good
government, and to remove from him the Cheshire men,
which were envied of many, for that the King esteemed of
them more than of any other, happily because they were
more faithful to him than other, ready in all respects to obey
his commandments and pleasure. From Doncaster having
now got a mighty army about him, he marched forth with all
speed through the countries, coming by Evesham unto
Berkeley. Within the space of three days all the King's castles in those parts were surrendered unto him.

The Duke of York, whom King Richard had left as governor of the realm in his absence, hearing that his nephew, the

Duke of Lancaster, was thus arrived and had gathered an army, he also assembled a puissant power of men of arms and archers (as before ye have heard) but all was in vain, for there was not a man that willingly would thrust out one arrow against the Duke of Lancaster or his partakers, or in any wise offend him or his friends. The Duke of York therefore passing forth towards Wales to meet the King, at his coming forth of Ireland, was received into the castle of Berkeley, and there remained till the coming thither of the Duke of Lancaster, whom when he perceived that he was not able to resist, on the Sunday after the feast of Saint James, which as that year came about fell upon the Friday, he came forth into the church that stood without the castle, and there communed with the Duke of Lancaster. With the Duke of York were the Bishop of Norwich, the Lord Berkeley, the Lord Seymour, and other; with the Duke of Lancaster were these: Thomas Arundel, Archbishop of Canterbury that had been banished, the Abbot of Leicester, the Earls of Northumberland and Westmoreland, Thomas Arundel, son to Richard late Earl of Arundel, the Baron of Greystoke, the Lords Willoughby and Ross, with divers other lords, knights, and other people, which daily came to him from every part of the realm. Those that came not were spoiled of all they had, so as they were never able to recover themselves again, for their goods being then taken away were never restored. And thus what for love, and what for fear of loss, they came flocking unto him from every part.

At the same present there was arrested, and committed to safe custody, the Bishop of Norwich, Sir William Elmam, and Sir Walter Burley, knights, Laurence Drew and John Golofer, esquires. On the morrow after, the foresaid Dukes with their power went towards Bristow, where, at their coming, they showed themselves before the town and castle, being an huge multitude of people. There were enclosed within the castle the Lord William Scroop, Earl of Wiltshire and Treasurer of England, Sir Henry Green and Sir John Bushy, knights, who prepared to make resistance; but when it would not prevail, they were taken and brought forth bound as prisoners into the camp before the Duke of Lancaster. On the morrow next ensuing, they were arraigned

before the Constable and Marshal, and found guilty of treason, for misgoverning the King and realm, and forthwith
had their heads smit off. Sir John Russell was also taken
there, who, feigning himself to be out of his wits, escaped
their hands for a time.

It fortuned at the same time in which the Duke of Hereford or Lancaster (whe're ye list to call him) arrived thus in
England, the seas were so troubled by tempests, and the
winds blew so contrary for any passage to come over forth
of England to the King remaining still in Ireland, that for the
space of six weeks he received no advertisements from
thence; yet, at length, when the seas became calm, and the
wind once turned anything favorable, there came over a
ship, whereby the King understood the manner of the
Duke's arrival, and all his proceedings till that day in which
the ship departed from the coast of England, whereupon he
meant forthwith to have returned over into England, to
make resistance against the Duke: but through persuasion of
the Duke of Aumerle (as was thought) he stayed till he
might have all his ships and other provision fully ready for
his passage.

In the meantime, he sent the Earl of Salisbury over into
England to gather a power together by help of the King's
friends in Wales and Cheshire with all speed possible, that
they might be ready to assist him against the Duke upon his
arrival—for he meant himself to follow the Earl within six
days after. The Earl, passing over into Wales, landed at
Conway and sent forth letters to the King's friends, both in
Wales and Cheshire, to levy their people and to come with
all speed to assist the King, whose request with great desire
and very willing minds they fulfilled, hoping to have found
the King himself at Conway, insomuch that within four
days' space there were to the number of forty thousand men
assembled, ready to march with the King against his enemies, if he had been there himself in person.

[2.4] But when they missed the King, there was a bruit
spread amongst them that the King was surely dead, which
wrought such an impression and evil disposition in the
minds of the Welshmen and others that for any persuasion
which the Earl of Salisbury might use, they would not go

forth with him till they saw the King: only they were contented to stay fourteen days to see if he should come or not.
But when he came not within that term, they would no
longer abide, but scaled and departed away; whereas if the
King had come before their breaking up, no doubt but they
would have put the Duke of Hereford in adventure of a field.
So that the King's lingering of time before his coming over
gave opportunity to the Duke to bring things to pass as he
could have wished, and took from the King all occasion to
recover afterwards any forces sufficient to resist him.

[3.2] At length, about eighteen days after that the King
had sent from him the Earl of Salisbury, he took the sea, together with the Dukes of Aumerle, Exeter, Surrey, and
divers of the nobility, with the Bishops of London, Lincoln,
and Carlisle. They landed near the castle of Barclowlie in
Wales, about the feast of Saint James the Apostle, and
stayed awhile in the same castle, being advertised of the
great forces which the Duke of Lancaster had got together
against him, wherewith he was marvelously amazed, knowing certainly that those which were thus in arms with the
Duke of Lancaster against him would rather die than give
place, as well for the hatred as fear which they had conceived at him. Nevertheless he, departing from Barclowlie,
hasted with all speed towards Conway, where he understood
the Earl of Salisbury to be still remaining.

He therefore, taking with him such Cheshire men as he
had with him at that present, in whom all his trust was reposed, he doubted not to revenge himself of his adversaries,
and so at the first he passed with a good courage: but when
he understood as he went thus forward, that all the castles,
even from the borders of Scotland unto Bristow, were delivered unto the Duke of Lancaster, and that likewise the nobles
and commons, as well of the south parts as the north, were
fully bent to take part with the same Duke against him; and
further, hearing how his trusty councilors had lost their
heads at Bristow, he became so greatly discomforted that,
sorrowfully lamenting his miserable state, he utterly de-
spaired of his own safety, and calling his army together,
which was not small, licensed every man to depart to his
own home.

The soldiers being well bent to fight in his defense, besought him to be of good cheer, promising with an oath to stand with him against the Duke, and all his partakers, unto death: but this could not encourage him at all, so that in the night next ensuing, he stole from his army, and with the Dukes of Exeter and Surrey, the Bishop of Carlisle and Sir Stephan Scroop, and about half a score others, he got him to the castle of Conway, where he found the Earl of Salisbury, determining there to hold himself till he might see the world at some better stay, for what counsel to take to remedy the mischief thus pressing upon him he wist not. On the one part he knew his title just, true, and infallible; and his conscience clear, pure, and without spot of envy or malice; he had also no small affiance in the Welshmen and Cheshire men. On the other side, he saw the puissance of his adversaries, the sudden departing of them whom he most trusted, and all things turned upside down. He evidently saw, and manifestly perceived, that he was forsaken of them by whom in time he might have been aided and relieved, where now it was too late, and too far overpassed.

This surely is a very notable example, and not unworthy of all princes to be well weighed and diligently marked, that this Henry of Lancaster should be thus called to the Kingdom, and have the help and assistance almost of all the whole realm, which perchance never thereof thought or yet dreamed; and that King Richard should thus be left desolate, void, and in despair of all hope and comfort, in whom if there were any offense, it ought rather to be imputed to the frailty of wanton youth than to the malice of his heart: but such is the deceivable judgment of man, which not regarding things present with due consideration, thinketh ever that things to come shall have good success, with a pleasant and delightful end. But in this dejecting of the one, and advancing of the other, the providence of God is to be respected, and his secret will to be wondered at. . . .

Sir Thomas Percy, Earl of Worcester, Lord Steward of the King's house, either being so commanded by the King, or else upon displeasure (as some write) for that the King had proclaimed his brother, the Earl of Northumberland, traitor, broke his white staff, which is the representing sign and token of his office, and without delay went to Duke Henry. . . .

The King herewith sent to Beaumaris and after to Caernarvon: but finding no provision either of victuals or other things in those castles, he came back to Conway. . . . [3.3] After this, the Duke, with advice of his council, sent the Earl of Northumberland unto the King, accompanied with four hundred lances and a thousand archers, who coming to the castle of Flint, had it delivered unto him, and from thence he hasted forth towards Conway. But before he approached near the place, he left his power behind him, hid closely in two ambushes behind a craggy mountain, beside the highway that leadeth from Flint to Conway.

This done, taking not past four or five with him, he passed forth, till he came before the town, and then sending an herald to the King, requested a safe conduct from the King, that he might come and talk with him: which the King granted, and so the Earl of Northumberland, passing the water, entered the castle, and coming to the King, declared to him, that if it might please his grace to undertake that there should be a parliament assembled, in the which justice might be had against such as were enemies to the commonwealth, and had procured the destruction of the Duke of Gloucester and other noblemen, and herewith pardon the Duke of Hereford of all things wherein he had offended him, the Duke would be ready to come to him on his knees, to crave him forgiveness, and as an humble subject to obey him in all dutiful services. The King . . . upon the Earl's oath for assurance that the same should be performed in each condition, agreed to go with the Earl to meet the Duke, and hereupon taking their horses, they rode forth, but the Earl rode before, as it were, to prepare dinner for the King at Rutland, but coming to the place where he had left his people, he stayed there with them. . . .

[*The King is trapped in the ambush, given dinner at Rutland, and taken to Flint.*]

The King had very few about him of his friends, except only the Earl of Salisbury, the Bishop of Carlisle, the Lord Stephan Scroop, Sir Nicholas Fereby, a son also of the Countess of Salisbury, and Jenico Dartois, a Gascoigne that still ware the cognizance or device of his master, King Richard, that is to say, a white hart, and would not put it from him, neither for persuasions nor threats. . . .

King Richard being thus come unto the castle of Flint, on the Monday the eighteenth of August, and the Duke of Hereford being still advertised from hour to hour by posts how the Earl of Northumberland sped, the morrow following, being Tuesday, and the nineteenth of August, he came thither and mustered his army before the King's presence, which undoubtedly made a passing fair show, being very well ordered by the Lord Henry Percy, that was appointed general or rather (as we may call him) master of the camp, under the Duke, of the whole army. There were come already to the castle, before the approaching of the main army, the Archbishop of Canterbury, the Duke of Aumerle, the Earl of Worcester, and divers other. The Archbishop entered first, and then followed the other, coming into the first ward.

The King, that was walking aloft on the braies of the walls to behold the coming of the Duke afar off, might see that the Archbishop and the other were come, and (as he took it) to talk with him. Whereupon he forthwith came down unto them, and beholding that they did their due reverence to him on their knees, he took them up, and drawing the Archbishop aside from the residue, talked with him a good while and, as it was reported, the Archbishop willed him to be of good comfort, for he should be assured not to have any hurt as touching his person; but he prophesied not as a prelate, but as a Pilate. For, was it no hurt, think you, to his person to be spoiled of his royalty, to be deposed from his crown, to be translated from principality to prison, and to fall from honor into horror? All which befell him to his extreme heart-grief, no doubt: which to increase, means, alas, there were many; but to diminish, helps, God wot, but a few. . . .

Then the Earl of Northumberland, passing forth of the castle to the Duke, talked with him awhile in sight of the King, being again got up to the walls to take better view of the army, being now advanced within two bowshots of the castle, to the small rejoicing, ye may be sure, of the sorrowful

King. The Earl of Northumberland, returning to the castle, appointed the King to be set to dinner, for he was fasting till then, and after he had dined, the Duke came down to the castle himself, and entered the same all armed, his bassenet only excepted, and being within the first gate he stayed there, till the King came forth of the inner part of the castle unto him.

The King, accompanied with the Bishop of Carlisle, the Earl of Salisbury, and Sir Stephan Scroop, knight, who bare the sword before him, and a few other, came forth into the utter ward, and sat down in a place prepared for him. Forthwith, as the Duke got sight of the King, he showed a reverend duty as became him, in bowing his knee, and coming forward did so likewise the second and third time, till the King took him by the hand, and lift him up, saying: "Dear cousin, you are welcome." The Duke, humbly thanking him, said: "My sovereign Lord and King, the cause of my coming at this present is (your honor saved) to have again restitution of my person, my lands and heritage, through your favorable license." The King hereunto answered: "Dear cousin, I am ready to accomplish your will, so that ye may enjoy all that is yours, without exception."

Meeting thus together, they came forth of the castle, and the King there called for wine, and after they had drunk, they mounted on horseback, and rode that night to Flint, and the next day unto Chester, the third unto Nantwich ... and so came to London.

[5.2.] Neither was the King permitted all this while to change his apparel, but rode still through all these towns simply clothed in one suit of raiment, and yet he was in his time exceeding sumptuous in apparel. . . . And so he was brought the next way to Westminster.

As for the Duke, he was received with all the joy and pomp that might be of the Londoners, and was lodged in the Bishop's palace by Paul's church. It was a wonder to see what great concourse of people and what number of horses came to him on the way as he thus passed the countries, till his coming to London, where, upon his approach to the city, the mayor rode forth to receive him, and a great number of other citizens. Also the clergy met him with procession, and such joy appeared in the countenances of the people, uttering the same also with words, as the like not lightly been seen. For in every town and village where he passed, children rejoiced, women clapped their hands, and men cried out for joy. But to speak of the great numbers of people that flocked together in the fields and streets of London at his coming, I here omit; neither will I speak of the presents, welcomings, lauds, and gratifications made to him by the citizens and commonalty. . . .

The next day after his coming to London, the King from Westminster was had to the Tower, and there committed in safe custody. Many evil-disposed persons, assembling themselves together in great numbers, intended to have met with him, and to have taken him from such as had the conveying of him, that they might have slain him. But the mayor and aldermen gathered to them the worshipful commoners and grave citizens, by whose policy, and not without much ado, the other were revoked from their evil purpose. . . .

[4.1.] After this was a parliament called by the Duke of Lancaster, using the name of King Richard in the writs directed forth to the lords and other states for their summons. This parliament began the thirteenth day of September, in the which many heinous points of misgovernance and injurious dealings in the administration of his kingly office were laid to the charge of this noble prince, King Richard, the which (to the end the Commons might be persuaded that he was an unprofitable prince to the commonwealth and worthy to be deposed) were in grossed up in 33 solemn articles, heinous to the ears of all men. . . .

Then for so much as these articles and other heinous and detestable accusations were laid against him in open parliament, it was thought by the most part that he was worthy to be deposed from all kingly honor and princely government: and to bring the matter without slander the better to pass, divers of the King's servants, which by license had access to his person, comforted him (being with sorrow almost consumed and in manner half dead) in the best wise they could, exhorting him to regard his health and save his life.

And first, they advised him willingly to suffer himself to

be deposed, and to resign his right of his own accord, so that the Duke of Lancaster might without murder or battle obtain the scepter and diadem, after which (they well perceived) he gaped: by mean whereof they thought he might be in perfect assurance of his life long to continue. . . . The King being now in the hands of his enemies, and utterly despairing of all comfort, was easily persuaded to renounce his crown and princely pre-eminence, so that in hope of life only he agreed to all things that were of him demanded. And so . . . he renounced and voluntarily was deposed from the royal crown and kingly dignity, the Monday being the nine and twentieth day of September and feast of St. Michael the Archangel, in the year of our Lord 1399, and in the three and twentieth year of his reign. . . .

[*Declaration of the Commissioners.*] Within the said place of the Tower . . . was rehearsed unto the King by the mouth of the foresaid Earl of Northumberland that beforetime at Conway . . . the King . . . promised . . . that he for insufficiency which he knew himself to be of to occupy so great a charge as to govern the realm of England, he would gladly leave off and renounce his right and title. . . . Upon the same afternoon the King looking for the coming of the Duke of Lancaster, at last the said Duke, with the Archbishop of Canterbury and the persons afore recited, entered the foresaid chamber, bringing with them . . . divers other. Where, after due obeisance done by them unto the King, he familiarly and with a glad countenance (as to them and us appeared) talked with the said Archbishop and Duke a good season; and that communication finished, the King, with glad countenance in presence of us and the other above rehearsed, said openly that he was ready to renounce and resign all his kingly majesty in manner and form as he before had promised . . . himself therefor read the scroll of resignation, in manner and form followeth. . . .

Now forthwith in our presence and others he subscribed the same, and after delivered it unto the Archbishop of Canterbury, saying that . . . he would that the Duke of Lancaster there present should be his successor. . . .

Upon the morrow after, being Tuesday, and the last day of September, all the lords, spiritual and temporal, with the

Commons of the said parliament, assembled at Westminster where, in the presence of them, the Archbishop of York and the Bishop of Hereford, according to the King's request, showed unto them the voluntary renouncing of the King, with the favor also which he bare to his cousin of Lancaster to have him his successor. And moreover showed them the schedule or bill of renouncement, signed in King Richard's own hand, which they caused to be read first in Latin, as it was written, and after in English. This done, the question was first asked of the Lords, if they would admit and allow that renouncement: the which, when it was of them granted and confirmed, the like question was asked of the Commons, and of them in like manner confirmed. After this, it was then declared, that notwithstanding the foresaid renouncing, so by the Lords admitted and confirmed, it was necessary, in avoiding of all suspicions and surmises of evil-disposed persons, to have in writing and registered the manifold crimes and defaults before done by King Richard, to the end that they might first be openly declared to the people, and after to remain of record amongst other of the King's records forever.

All this was done accordingly. . . . Then forsomuch as the lords of the parliament had well considered the voluntary resignation of King Richard and that it was behooveful and, as they thought, necessary for the weal of the realm to proceed unto the sentence of his deposing.

Immediately as the sentence was in this wise passed, and that by reason thereof the realm stood void without head or governor for the time, the Duke of Lancaster, rising from the place where before he sat, and standing where all those in the house might behold him, in reverend manner made a sign of the cross on his forehead and likewise on his breast.

[*Bolingbroke claims the crown and the Archbishop of Canterbury preaches on the text "Vir dominabitur in populo," saying that*] Instead of a child willfully doing his lust and pleasure without reason, now shall a man be lord and ruler, that is replenished with sapience and reason, and shall govern the people by skillful doom, setting apart all willfulness and pleasure of himself.

[*Bolingbroke is crowned on the feast of Edward the Con-*

fessor. Richard hoped to escape with his life by handing to his successor all his goods and wealth.] But whatsoever was promised, he was deceived therein. For shortly after his resignation, he was conveyed to the castle of Leeds in Kent, and from thence to Pomfret, where he departed out of this miserable life (as after you shall hear). He was seemly of shape and favor, and of nature good enough, if the wickedness and naughty demeanor of such as were about him had not altered it.

[*Holinshed moralizes on Richard's fate.*] His chance verily was greatly infortunate.... He was prodigal, ambitious, and much given to the pleasure of the body. He kept the greatest port, and maintained the most plentiful house that ever any king in England did either before his time or since. For there resorted daily to his court above ten thousand persons that had meat and drink allowed them.... And this vanity was not only used at court in those days, but also other people abroad in the towns and countries had their garments cut far otherwise than had been accustomed before his days ... and every day there was devising of new fashions, to the great hindrance and decay of the commonwealth.... Furthermore, there reigned abundantly the filthy sin of lechery and fornication, with abominable adultery, specially in the King, but most chiefly in the prelacy.... But if I may boldly say what I think: he was a prince the most unthankfully used of his subjects, of any one of whom ye shall lightly read. For although (through the frailty of youth) he demeaned himself more dissolutely than seemed convenient for his royal estate, and made choice of such councilors as were not favored by the people, whereby he was the less favored himself: yet in no king's days were the commons in greater wealth, if they could have perceived their happy state, neither in any other time were the nobles and gentlemen more cherished, nor churchmen less wronged. But such was their ingratitude towards their bountiful and loving sovereign that those whom he had chiefly advanced were readiest to control him; for that they might not rule all things at their will, and remove from him such as they misliked, and place in their rooms whom they thought good, and that rather by strong hand than by gentle and courteous means, which stirred such malice betwixt him and them, till at length it could not be assuaged without peril of destruction to them both.

The Duke of Gloucester, chief instrument of this mischief, to what end he came ye have heard. And although the Duke of Hereford took upon him to revenge his death, yet wanted he moderation and loyalty in his doings, for the which both he himself and his lineal race were scourged afterwards, as a due punishment unto rebellious subjects. . . . What unnaturalness, or rather, what tigerlike cruelty was this . . . wolvishly to lie in wait for the distressed creature's life, and ravenously to thirst after his blood, the spilling whereof should have touched his conscience so, as that death ought rather to have been adventured for his safety, than so savagely to have sought his life after the loss of his royalty. . . .

Thus much ado there was in this parliament, specially about them that were thought to be guilty of the Duke of Gloucester's death, and of the condemning of the other lords adjudged traitors in the foresaid late parliament holden in the said one and twentieth year of King Richard's reign. Sir [William] Bagot, knight, then prisoner in the Tower, disclosed many secrets unto the which he was privy; and being brought on a day to the bar, a bill was read in English which he had made, containing certain evil practices of King Richard; and further what great affection the same King bare to the Duke of Aumerle, insomuch that he heard him say, that if he should renounce the government of the kingdom, he wished to leave it to the said Duke, as to the most able man for wisdom and manhood of all other: for though he could like better of the Duke of Hereford, yet he said that he knew if he were once King, he would prove an extreme enemy and cruel tyrant to the church.

It was further contained in that bill, that as the same Bagot rode on a day behind the Duke of Norfolk in the Savoy street toward Westminster, the Duke asked him what he knew of the manner of the Duke of Gloucester his death, and he answered that he knew nothing at all: but the people (quoth he) do say that you have murdered him. Whereunto the Duke sware great oaths that it was untrue, and that he had saved his life, contrary to the will of the King and certain other lords, by the space of three weeks and more; affirming withal, that he was never in all his lifetime more afraid of death than he was at his coming home from Calais at that time to the King's presence, by reason he had not put the Duke to death. And then (said he) the King appointed one of his own servants, and certain other that were servants to other lords to go with him to see the said Duke of Gloucester put to death, swearing that as he should answer afore God, it was never his mind that he should have died in the fort, but only for fear of the King, and saving of his own life. Nevertheless, there was no man in the realm to whom King Richard was so much beholden as to the Duke of Aumerle: for he was the man that to fulfill his mind had set him in hand with all that was done against the said Duke and the other lords. . . . There was also contained in the said bill that Bagot had heard the Duke of Aumerle say that he had rather than twenty thousand pounds that the Duke of Hereford were dead, not for any fear he had of him, but for the trouble and mischief that he was like to procure within the realm.

After that the bill had been read and heard, the Duke of Aumerle rose up and said, that as touching the points contained in the bill concerning him, they were utterly false and untrue, which he would prove with his body in what manner soever it should be thought requisite.

On the Saturday next ensuing, Sir William Bagot and the said John Hall were brought both to the bar, and Bagot was examined of certain points and sent again to prison. The Lord Fitzwater herewith rose up, and said to the King, that where the Duke of Aumerle excuseth himself of the Duke of Gloucester's death, I say (quoth he) that he was the very cause of his death, and so he appealed him of treason, offering by throwing down his hood as a gage to prove it with his body. There were twenty other lords also that threw down their hoods, as pledges to prove the like matter against the Duke of Aumerle. The Duke of Aumerle threw down his hood to try it against the Lord Fitzwater, as against him that lied falsely in that he had charged him with, by that his appeal. These gages were delivered to the Constable and Marshal of England and the parties put under arrest.

The Duke of Surrey stood up also against the Lord Fitzwater, avouching that where he had said that the appellants were causers of the Duke of Gloucester's death, it was false, for they were constrained to sue the same appeal, in like manner as the said Lord Fitzwater was compelled to give judgment against the Duke of Gloucester and the Earl of Arundel; so that the suing of the appeal was done by constraint, and if he said contrary he lied: and therewith he threw down his hood. The Lord Fitzwater answered hereunto that he was not present in the parliament house when judgment was given against them, and all the lords bare witness thereof. Moreover, where it was alleged that the Duke of Aumerle should send two of his servants to Calais to murder the Duke of Gloucester, the said Duke of Aumerle said that if the Duke of Norfolk affirm it he lied falsely, and that he would prove with his body, throwing down another hood which he had borrowed. The same was likewise delivered to the Constable and Marshal of England, and the King licensed the Duke of Norfolk to return, that he might arraign his appeal. . . .

On Wednesday following, request was made by the Commons, that sith King Richard had resigned, and was lawfully deposed from his royal dignity, he might have judgment decreed against him, so as the realm were not troubled by him, and that the causes of his deposing might be published through the realm for satisfying of the people: which demand was granted. [4.1.114] Whereupon the Bishop of Carlisle, a man both learned, wise, and stout of stomach, boldly showed forth his opinion concerning that demand, affirming that there was none amongst them worthy or meet to give judgment upon so noble a prince as King Richard was, whom they had taken for their sovereign and liege lord by the space of two and twenty years and more; "And I assure you" (said he) "there is not so rank a traitor, nor so errant a thief, nor yet so cruel a murderer apprehended or detained in prison for his offense, but he shall be brought before the justice to hear his judgment; and will ye proceed to the judgment of an anointed king, hearing neither his answer nor excuse? I say that the Duke of Lancaster, whom ye call king, hath more trespassed to King Richard and his realm, than King Richard hath done either to him or us; for it is manifest and well known that the Duke was banished the realm by King Richard and his council, and by the judgment of his own father, for the space of ten years, for what cause ye know, and yet without license of King Richard he is returned again into the realm, and (that is worse) hath taken upon him the name, title, and pre-eminence of King. And therefore I say, that you have done manifest wrong to proceed in anything against King Richard, without calling him openly to his answer and defense." As soon as the bishop had ended his tale, he was attached by the Earl Marshal and committed to ward in the Abbey of Saint Albans.

[*Aumerle, Surrey, and Exeter are deprived of their titles of Dukes.*]

[4.1] This year Thomas Mowbray, Duke of Norfolk, died in exile at Venice. . . . [2.2] The same year deceased the Duchess of Gloucester, through sorrow (as was thought) which she conceived for the loss of her son and heir the Lord Humphrey, who being sent for forth of Ireland . . . was taken with the pestilence, and died by the way. . . . [4.1.320–33] But now to speak of the conspiracy which was contrived by the Abbot of Westminster as chief instrument thereof. Ye shall understand that this Abbot (as it is reported) upon a time heard King Henry say, when he was but Earl of Derby and young of years, that princes had too little, and religious men too much. He therefore doubting now lest, if the King continued long in the estate, he would remove the great beam that then grieved his eyes and pricked his conscience, became an instrument to search out the minds of the nobility and to bring them to an assembly and council, where they might consult and commen together how to bring that to effect which they earnestly wished and desired: that was, the destruction of King Henry and the restoring of King Richard. For there were divers lords that showed themselves outwardly to favor King Henry, where they secretly wished and sought his confusion. The Abbot, after he had felt the minds of sundry of them, called to his house on a day in the term time all such lords and other

persons which he either knew or thought to be as affec-
tioned to King Richard, so envious to the prosperity of King
Henry, whose names were, John Holland, Earl of Huntington (late Duke of Exeter), Thomas Holland, Earl of Kent
(late Duke of Surrey), Edward, Earl of Rutland (late Duke
of Aumerle) son to the Duke of York, John Montacute, Earl
of Salisbury, Hugh, Lord Spenser (late Earl of Gloucester),
John, the Bishop of Carlisle, Sir Thomas Blunt, and Maudelen, a priest, one of King Richard's chapel.

The Abbot highly feasted these lords, his special friends,
and when they had well dined, they withdrew into a secret
chamber, where they sat down in council, and after much
talk and conference had about the bringing of their purpose
to pass concerning the destruction of King Henry, at length
by the advice of the Earl of Huntington, it was devised that
they should take upon them a solemn jousts to be enter-
prised between him and twenty on his part, and the Earl of
Salisbury and twenty with him at Oxford; to the which triumph King Henry should be desired, and when he should
be most busily marking the martial pastime, he suddenly
should be slain and destroyed, and so by that means King
Richard, who as yet lived, might be restored to liberty, and
have his former estate and dignity. It was further appointed,
who should assemble the people, the number and persons
which should accomplish and put in execution their devised
enterprise. Hereupon was an indenture sextipartite made,
sealed with their seals, and signed with their hands, in the
which each stood bound to other, to do their whole endeavor
for the accomplishing of the purposed exploit. Moreover,
they sware on the holy evangelists to be true and secret each
to other, even to the hour and point of death.

When all things were thus appointed, the Earl of Huntington came to the King unto Windsor, earnestly requiring
him that he would vouchsafe to be at Oxenford on the day
appointed of their jousts, both to behold the same, and to
be the discoverer and indifferent judge (if any ambiguity
should rise) of their courageous acts and doings. The King,
being thus instantly required of his brother-in-law, and
nothing less imagining than that which was pretended, gently granted to fulfill his request. Which thing obtained, all

the lords of the conspiracy departed home to their houses, as they noised it, to set armorers on work about the trimming of their armor against the jousts, and to prepare all other furniture and things ready, as to such an high and solemn triumph appertained. The Earl of Huntington came to his house and raised men on every side, and prepared horse and harness for his compassed purpose, and when he had all things ready, he departed towards Oxenford, and at his coming thither he found all his mates and confederates there, well appointed for their purpose, except the Earl of Rutland, by whose folly their practiced conspiracy was brought to light and disclosed to King Henry.

[5.2,3] For this Earl of Rutland, departing before from Westminster to see his father, the Duke of York, as he sat at dinner, had his counterpane of the indenture of the confederacy in his bosom. The father, espying it, would needs see what it was, and though the son humbly denied to show it, the father, being more earnest to see it, by force took it out of his bosom; and perceiving the contents thereof, in a great rage caused his horses to be saddled out of hand, and spitefully reproving his son of treason, for whom he was become surety and mainpernour for his good abearing in open parliament, he incontinently mounted on horseback to ride towards Windsor to the King, to declare unto him the malicious intent of his complices. The Earl of Rutland, seeing in what danger he stood, took his horse and rode another way to Windsor in post, so that he got thither before his father, and when he was alighted at the castle gate, he caused the gates to be shut, saying that he must needs deliver the keys to the King. When he came before the King's presence, he kneeled down on his knees, beseeching him of mercy and forgiveness, and declaring the whole matter unto him in order as everything had passed, obtained pardon. Therewith came his father, and being let in, delivered the indenture which he had taken from his son unto the King, who thereby perceiving his son's words to be true, changed his purpose for his going to Oxenford. . . .

The conspirators being at Oxenford at length perceived by the lack of the Earl of Rutland that their enterprise was revealed to the King, and thereupon determined now openly with spear and shield to bring to pass which before they covertly attempted, and so they adorned Maudelen, a man most resembling King Richard, in royal and princely vesture, and named him to be King Richard, affirming that by favor of his keepers he was escaped out of prison.

[*The conspirators, arriving at Windsor, find Henry gone. They retire before his army and arrive at Cirencester.*]

In the night season the bailiff of the town with four score archers set on the house where the Earl of Kent and the other lay, which house was manfully assaulted and strongly defended in great space. The Earl of Huntington being in another inn with the Lord Spenser set fire on divers houses in the town, thinking that the assailants would leave the assault and rescue their goods, which thing they nothing regarded. The host lying without, hearing noise, and seeing this fire in the town, thought verily that King Henry had been come thither with his puissance, and thereupon fled without measure, every man making shift to save himself. . . .

The Earl of Huntington . . . seeing no hope of comfort, fled into Essex. The other lords which were left fighting in the town of Cirencester were wounded to death and taken, and their heads stricken off and sent to London. . . .

[*The Earl of Huntington and others are captured and beheaded.*] [5.6] Shortly after, the Abbot of Westminster, in whose house the conspiracy was begun (as it is said) going between his monastery and mansion, for thought fell into a sudden palsy, and shortly after, without speech, ended his life.

The Bishop of Carlisle dieth through fear, or rather through grief of mine, to see the wicked prosper, as he took it.

The Bishop of Carlisle was impeached and condemned of the same conspiracy; but the King, of his merciful clemency, pardoned him of that offense, although he died shortly after, more through fear than force of sickness, as some have written.

[5.4,5] One writer, which seemeth to have great knowledge of King Richard's doings, saith that King Henry, sitting on a day at his table, sore sighing, said: "Have I no faithful friend which will deliver me of him, whose life will be my death, and whose death will be the preservation of my life?" This saying was much noted of them which were present, and especially of one called Sir Piers of Exton. This knight incontinently departed from the court with eight strong persons in his company, and came to Pomfret, commanding the esquire, that was accustomed to sew and take the assay before King Richard, to do so no more, saying: "Let him eat now, for he shall not long eat." King Richard sat down to dinner, and was served without courtesy or assay: whereupon, much marveling at the sudden change, he demanded of the esquire why he did not his duty. "Sir" (said he) "I am otherwise commanded by Sir Piers of Exton, which is newly come from King Henry." When King Richard heard that word, he took his carving knife in his hand, and strake the esquire on the head, saying: "The devil take Henry of Lancaster and thee together!" And with that word, Sir Piers entered the chamber, well armed, with eight tall men likewise armed, every of them having a bill in his hand.

King Richard, perceiving this, put the table from him, and stepping to the foremost man, wrung the bill out of his hands, and so valiantly defended himself, that he slew four of those that came to assail him. Sir Piers, being half dismayed herewith, leaped into the chair where King Richard was wont to sit, while the other four persons fought with him, and chased him about the chamber. And in conclusion, as King Richard traversed his ground, from one side of the chamber to another, and coming by the chair where Sir Piers stood, he was felled with a stroke of a poleax which Sir Piers gave him upon the head, and therewith rid him out of life, without giving him respite once to call to God for mercy of his past offenses. It is said that Sir Piers of Exton, after he had thus slain him, wept right bitterly, as one stricken with the prick of a guilty conscience, for murdering him whom he had so long time obeyed as King.

After he was thus dead, his body was imbalmed, and cered, and covered with lead, all save the face, to the intent that all men might see him, and perceive that he was departed from this life: for as the corpse was conveyed from Pomfret to London, in all the towns and places where those that had the conveyance of it did stay with it all night, they caused *Dirige* to be sung in the evening and mass of *Requiem* in the morning; and as well after the one service as the other, his face discovered was showed to all that coveted to behold it.

Thus was the corpse first brought to the Tower, and after through the city to the cathedral church of Saint Paul, barefaced, where it lay three days together that all men might behold it. There was a solemn obsequy done for him both at Paul's, and after at Westminster, at which time both at *Dirige* overnight, and in the morning at the mass of *Requiem,* the King and the citizens of London were present. . . .

[1413] In this fourteenth and last year of King Henry's reign, a council was holden in the White Friars in London, at the which, among other things, order was taken for ships and galleys to be made ready and all other things necessary to be provided for a voyage which he meant to make into the Holy Land, there to recover the city of Jerusalem from the Infidels.

Commentaries

WALTER PATER

Shakespeare's English Kings

One gracious prerogative, certainly, Shakespeare's English kings possess: they are a very eloquent company, and Richard is the most sweet-tongued of them all. In no other play perhaps is there such a flush of those gay, fresh, variegated flowers of speech—color and figure, not lightly attached to, but fused into, the very phrase itself—which Shakespeare cannot help dispensing to his characters, as in this "play of the Deposing of King Richard the Second," an exquisite poet if he is nothing else, from first to last, in light and gloom alike, able to see all things poetically, to give a poetic turn to his conduct of them, and refreshing with his golden language the tritest aspects of that ironic contrast between the pretensions of a king and the actual necessities of his destiny. What a garden of words! With him, blank verse, infinitely graceful, deliberate, musical in inflection, becomes indeed a true "verse royal," that rhyming lapse, which to the Shakespearean ear, at least in youth, came as the last touch of refinement on it, being here doubly appropriate. His eloquence blends with that fatal beauty, of which he was so frankly aware, so amiable to his friends, to his wife, of the effects of which on the people his enemies were so much afraid, on which Shakespeare himself dwells so attentively as the "royal blood" comes and goes in the face with his rapid changes of temper. As happens with sensitive

From *Appreciations* (1889).

natures, it attunes him to a congruous suavity of manners, by which anger itself became flattering: it blends with his merely youthful hopefulness and high spirits, his sympathetic love for gay people, things, apparel—"his cote of gold and stone, valued at thirty thousand marks," the novel Italian fashions he preferred, as also with those real amiabilities that made people forget the darker touches of his character, but never tire of the pathetic rehearsal of his fall, the meekness of which would have seemed merely abject in a less graceful performer.

Yet it is only fair to say that in the painstaking "revival" of *King Richard the Second*, by the late Charles Kean, those who were very young thirty years ago were afforded much more than Shakespeare's play could ever have been before— the very person of the king based on the stately old portrait in Westminster Abbey, "the earliest extant contemporary likeness of any English sovereign," the grace, the winning pathos, the sympathetic voice of the player, the tasteful archaeology confronting vulgar modern London with a scenic reproduction, for once really agreeable, of the London of Chaucer. In the hands of Kean the play became like an exquisite performance on the violin.

The long agony of one so gaily painted by nature's self, from his "tragic abdication" till the hour in which he

Sluiced out his innocent soul thro' streams of blood,

was for playwrights a subject ready to hand, and became early the theme of a popular drama, of which some have fancied surviving favorite fragments in the rhymed parts of Shakespeare's work.

The king Richard of Yngland
Was in his flowris then regnand:
But his flowris efter sone
Fadyt, and ware all undone:

says the old chronicle. Strangely enough, Shakespeare supposes him an overconfident believer in that divine right of

kings, of which people in Shakespeare's time were coming to hear so much; a general right, sealed to him (so
Richard is made to think) as an ineradicable personal gift
by the touch—stream rather, over head and breast and
shoulders—of the "holy oil" of his consecration at Westminster; not however, through some oversight, the genuine
balm used at the coronation of his successor, given, according to legend, by the Blessed Virgin to Saint Thomas
of Canterbury. Richard himself found that, it was said,
among other forgotten treasures, at the crisis of his changing fortunes, and vainly sought reconsecration therewith—
understood, wistfully, that it was reserved for his happier
rival. And yet his coronation, by the pageantry, the ampli-
tude, the learned care, of its order, so lengthy that the king,
then only eleven years of age, and fasting, as a communi-
cant at the ceremony, was carried away in a faint, fixed the
type under which it has ever since continued. And nowhere
is there so emphatic a reiteration as in *Richard the Second*
of the sentiment which those singular rites were calculated
to produce.

> Not all the water in the rough rude sea
> Can wash the balm off from an anointed king,

as supplementing another, almost supernatural, right. "Edward's seven sons," of whom Richard's father was one,

> Were as seven phials of his sacred blood.

But this, too, in the hands of Shakespeare, becomes for him,
like any other of those fantastic, ineffectual, easily discredi-
ted, personal graces, as capricious in its operation on men's
wills as merely physical beauty, kindling himself to eloquence indeed, but only giving double pathos to insults
which "barbarism itself" might have pitied—the dust in his
face, as he returns, through the streets of London, a prisoner
in the train of his victorious enemy.

> How soon my sorrow hath destroyed my face!

he cries, in that most poetic invention of the mirror scene, which does but reinforce again that physical charm which all confessed. The sense of "divine right'" in kings is found to act not so much as a secret of power over others, as of infatuation to themselves. And of all those personal gifts the one which alone never altogether fails him is just that royal utterance, his appreciation of the poetry of his own hapless lot, an eloquent self-pity, infecting others in spite of themselves, till they too become irresistibly eloquent about him.

In the Roman Pontifical, of which the order of Coronation is really a part, there is no form for the inverse process, no rite of "degradation," such as that by which an offending priest or bishop may be deprived, if not of the essential quality of "orders," yet, one by one, of its outward dignities. It is as if Shakespeare had had in mind some such inverted rite, like those old ecclesiastical or military ones, by which human hardness, or human justice, adds the last touch of unkindness to the execution of its sentences, in the scene where Richard "deposes" himself, as in some long, agonizing ceremony, reflectively drawn out, with an extraordinary refinement of intelligence and variety of piteous appeal, but also with a felicity of poetic invention, which puts these pages into a very select class, with the finest "vermeil and ivory" work of Chatterton or Keats.

> Fetch hither Richard that in common view
> He may surrender!

And Richard more than concurs: he throws himself into the part, realizes a type, falls gracefully as on the world's stage. Why is he sent for?

> To do that office of thine own good will
> Which tired majesty did make thee offer.—
> Now mark me! how I will undo myself.

"Hath Bolingbroke deposed thine intellect?" the Queen asks him, on his way to the Tower:

> Hath Bolingbroke
> Deposed thine intellect? hath he been in thy heart?

And in truth, but for that adventitious poetic gold, it would be only "plume-plucked Richard."

> I find myself a traitor with the rest,
> For I have given here my soul's consent
> To undeck the pompous body of a king.

He is duly reminded, indeed, how

> That which in mean men we entitle patience
> Is pale cold cowardice in noble breasts.

Yet at least within the poetic bounds of Shakespeare's play, through Shakespeare's bountiful gifts, his desire seems fulfilled.

> O! that I were as great
> As is my grief.

And his grief becomes nothing less than a central expression of all that in the revolutions of Fortune's wheel goes *down* in the world.

No! Shakespeare's kings are not, nor are meant to be, great men: rather, little or quite ordinary humanity, thrust upon greatness, with those pathetic results, the natural self-pity of the weak heightened in them into irresistible appeal to others as the net result of their royal prerogative. One after another, they seem to lie composed in Shakespeare's embalming pages, with just that touch of nature about them, making the whole world akin, which has infused into their tombs at Westminster a rare poetic grace. It is that irony of kingship, the sense that it is in its happiness child's play, in its sorrows, after all, but children's grief, which gives its finer accent to all the changeful feeling of these wonderful speeches: the great meekness of the graceful, wild creature, tamed at last.

Give Richard leave to live till Richard die!

his somewhat abject fear of death, turning to acquiescence
at moments of extreme weariness:

My large kingdom for a little grave!
A little, little grave, an obscure grave!

his religious appeal in the last reserve, with its bold reference to the judgment of Pilate, as he thinks once more of his
"anointing."

And as happens with children he attains contentment finally in the merely passive recognition of superior strength,
in the naturalness of the result of the great battle as a matter
of course, and experiences something of the royal prerogative of poetry to obscure, or at least to attune and soften
men's griefs. As in some sweet anthem of Handel, the sufferer, who put finger to the organ under the utmost pressure
of mental conflict, extracts a kind of peace at last from the
mere skill with which he sets his distress to music.

Beshrew thee, Cousin, that didst lead me forth
Of that sweet way I was in to despair!

"With Cain go wander through the shades of night!"
cries the new king to the gaoler Exton, dissimulating his
share in the murder he is thought to have suggested; and
in truth there is something of the murdered Abel about
Shakespeare's Richard. The fact seems to be that he died
of "waste and a broken heart": it was by way of proof that
his end had been a natural one that, stifling a real fear of the
face, the face of Richard, on men's minds, with the added
pleading now of all dead faces, Henry exposed the corpse
to general view; and Shakespeare, in bringing it on the
stage, in the last scene of his play, does but follow out the
motive with which he has emphasized Richard's physical
beauty all through it—that "most beauteous inn," as the
Queen says quaintly, meeting him on the way to death—
residence, then soon to be deserted, of that wayward, fren-

zied, but withal so affectionate soul. Though the body did
not go to Westminster immediately, his tomb,

> That small model of the barren earth
> Which serves as paste and cover to our bones,

the effigy clasping the hand of his youthful consort, was already prepared there, with "rich gilding and ornaments,"
monument of poetic regret, for Queen Anne of Bohemia,
not of course the "Queen" of Shakespeare, who however
seems to have transferred to this second wife something of
Richard's wildly proclaimed affection for the first. In this
way, through the connecting link of that sacred spot, our
thoughts once more associate Richard's two fallacious pre-
rogatives, his personal beauty and his "anointing."

According to Johnson, *Richard the Second* is one of those
plays which Shakespeare has "apparently revised"; and how
doubly delightful Shakespeare is where he seems to have revised! "Would that he had blotted a thousand"—a thousand
hasty phrases, we may venture once more to say with his
earlier critic, now that the tiresome German superstition has
passed away which challenged us to a dogmatic faith in the
plenary verbal inspiration of every one of Shakespeare's
clowns. Like some melodiously contending anthem of Handel's, I said, of Richard's meek "undoing" of himself in the
mirror-scene; and, in fact, the play of *Richard the Second*
does, like a musical composition, possess a certain concentration of all its parts, a simple continuity, an evenness in
execution, which are rare in the great dramatist. With *Romeo
and Juliet*, that perfect symphony (symphony of three independent poetic forms set in a grander one which it is the
merit of German criticism to have detected), it belongs to a
small group of plays, where, by happy birth and consistent
evolution, dramatic form approaches to something like the
unity of a lyrical ballad, a lyric, a song, a single strain of
music. Which sort of poetry we are to account the highest, is
perhaps a barren question. Yet if, in art generally, unity of
impression is a note of what is perfect, then lyric poetry,
which in spite of complex structure often preserves the
unity of a single passionate ejaculation, would rank higher

than dramatic poetry, where, especially to the reader, as distinguished from the spectator assisting at a theatrical performance, there must always be a sense of the effort necessary to keep the various parts from flying asunder, a sense of imperfect continuity, such as the older criticism vainly sought to obviate by the rule of the dramatic "unities." It follows that a play attains artistic perfection just in proportion as it approaches that unity of lyrical effect, as if a song or ballad were still lying at the root of it, all the various expression of the conflict of character and circumstance falling at last into the compass of a single melody, or musical theme. As, historically, the earliest classic drama arose out of the chorus, from which this or that person, this or that episode, detached itself, so, into the unity of a choric song the perfect drama ever tends to return, its intellectual scope deepened, complicated, enlarged, but still with an unmistakable singleness, or identity, in its impression on the mind. Just there, in that vivid single impression left on the mind when all is over, not in any mechanical limitation of time and place, is the secret of the "unities"—the true imaginative unity—of the drama.

RICHARD D. ALTICK

Symphonic Imagery in *Richard II*

Critics on occasion have remarked the peculiar unity of
tone which distinguishes *Richard II* from most of Shakespeare's other plays. Walter Pater wrote that, like a musical
composition, it possesses "a certain concentration of all its
parts, a simple continuity, an evenness in execution, which
are rare in the great dramatist. . . . It belongs to a small
group of plays, where, by happy birth and consistent evolution, dramatic form approaches to something like the unity
of a lyrical ballad, a lyric, a song, a single strain of music."
And J. Dover Wilson, in his edition of the play, has observed that "*Richard II* possesses a unity of tone and feeling
greater than that attained in many of his greater plays, a
unity found, I think, to the same degree elsewhere only in
Twelfth Night, *Antony and Cleopatra*, and *The Tempest*."
How can we account for that impression of harmony, of
oneness, which we receive when we read the play or listen
to its lines spoken upon the stage? The secret, it seems to
me, lies in an aspect of Shakespeare's genius which has oftener been condemned than praised. Critics and casual readers alike have groaned over the fine-drawn ingenuity of the
Shakespearean quibble, which, as Dr. Johnson maintained,
was "the fatal Cleopatra for which he lost the world, and
was content to lose it." But it is essentially the same habit
of the creative imagination—a highly sensitized associational gift—that produces iterative symbolism and imagery.
Simple wordplay results from the poet's awareness of the
diverse meanings of words, of which, however, he makes no

From *PMLA* LXII, 1947. Reprinted, with some alterations in the footnotes, by
permission of the author and The Modern Language Association of America.

better use than to demonstrate his own cleverness and to tickle for a moment the wit of the audience. These exhibitions of verbal agility are simply decorations scattered upon the surface of the poetic fabric; they can be ripped out without loss. But suppose that to the poet's associational sensitivity is added a further awareness of the multitudinous emotional overtones of words. When he puts this faculty to use he is no longer merely playing a game; instead, words have become the shells in which ideas and symbols are enclosed. Suppose, furthermore, that instead of being the occupation of a few fleeting lines of the text, certain words of multifold meanings are played upon throughout the five acts, recurring time after time like leitmotivs in music. And suppose finally that this process of repetition is applied especially to words of sensuous significance, words that evoke vivid responses in the imagination. When these things happen to certain words—when they cease to be mere vehicles for a brief indulgence of verbal fancy and, taking on a burden of serious meaning, become thematic material—the poet has crossed the borderline that separates wordplay from iterative imagery. Language has become the willing servant of structure, and what was on other occasions only a source of exuberant but undisciplined wit now is converted to the higher purpose of poetic unity.

That, briefly, is what happens in *Richard II*. The familiar wordplays of the earlier Shakespearean dramas persist: John of Gaunt puns endlessly upon his own name. But in this drama a word is not commonly taken up, rapidly revolved, so that all its various facets of meaning flash out, and then discarded. Instead, certain words are played upon throughout the drama. Far from being decorations, "gay, fresh, variegated flowers of speech," as Pater called them, they are woven deeply into the thought-web of the play. Each word-theme symbolizes one or another of the fundamental ideas of the story, and every time it reappears it perceptibly deepens and enriches those meanings and at the same time charges the atmosphere with emotional significance.

The most remarkable thing about these leitmotivs is the way in which they are constantly mingling and coalescing, two or three of them joining to form a single new figure, very much in the manner in which "hooked images," as Professor Lowes called them, were formed in the subconscious mind of Coleridge. This repeated criss-crossing of familiar images[1] makes of the whole text one vast arabesque of language, just as a dozen lines of *Love's Labour's Lost* form a miniature arabesque when the poet's quibbling mood is upon him. And since each image motif represents one of the dominant ideas of the play (heredity, patriotism, sycophancy, etc.) the coalescing of these images again and again emphasizes the complex relationship between the ideas themselves, so that the reader is kept ever aware that all that happens in *Richard II* results inevitably from the interaction of many elements.

It is pointless to try to explain by further generalizations this subtle and exceedingly intricate weaving together of metaphor and symbol—this glorified wordplay, if you will—which is the key to the total poetic effect of *Richard II*. All I can do is to draw from the fabric, one by one, the strands that compose it, and to suggest in some manner the magical way in which they interact and by association and actual fusion reciprocally deepen their meaning.

Miss Spurgeon has pointed out how in *Antony and Cleopatra* the cosmic grandeur of the theme is constantly emphasized by the repetition of the word *world*. In a similar manner the symbolism of *Richard II* is dominated by the related words *earth*, *land*, and *ground*. In no other play of Shakespeare is the complex of ideas represented by these words so tirelessly dwelt upon.[2] The words are but three in

[1] Throughout this paper I use the words *image* and *imagery* in their most inclusive sense of metaphorical as well as "picture-making" but nonfigurative language.

[2] In *Richard II* the three words occur a total of 71 times; in *King John*, the nearest rival, 46. —I should note at this point that my identification of all the word- and image-themes to be discussed in this essay is based upon statistical study. A given word or group of related words is called a "theme" (a) if Bartlett's *Concordance* shows a definite numerical preponderance for *Richard II* or (b) if the word or group of words is so closely related to one of the fundamental ideas of the play that it is of greater importance than the comparative numerical frequency would imply. I have not included any arithmetic in this paper because all such tabulations obviously must be subjective to some degree. No two persons, doing the same counting for the same purpose, would arrive at precisely the same numerical results. But I am confident that independent tabulation would enable anyone to arrive at my general conclusions. Statistics here, as in all such critical exercises, are merely grounds upon which to base a judgment that must eventually be a subjective one.

number, and superficially they seem roughly synonymous; but they have many intellectual ramifications, which become more and more meaningful as the play progresses and the words are used first for one thing and then for another. As our experience of the words increases, their connotation steadily deepens. In addition to their obvious meaning in a particular context they come to stand for something larger and more undefinable—a mingling of everything they have represented earlier.

Above all, *earth* is the symbol of the English nation. It is used by Shakespeare to connote those same values which we find in the equivalent synecdoche of *soil,* as in "native soil." It sums up all the feeling inherent in the sense of pride in nation—of jealousy when the country is threatened by foreign incursion, of bitter anger when its health has been destroyed by mismanagement or greed. "This earth of majesty," John of Gaunt calls England in his famous speech, ". . . This blessed plot, this earth, this realm, this England" (2.1.41,50). And a few lines farther on: "This land of such dear souls, this dear dear land . . ." (57). Having once appeared, so early in the play, in such lustrous context, the words *earth* and *land* forever after have richer significance. Whenever they recur, they are more meaningful, more powerful. Thus Richard's elaborate speech upon his arrival in Wales—

> As a long-parted mother with her child
> Plays fondly with her tears and smiles in meeting,
> So weeping, smiling, greet I thee, my earth,
> And do thee favors with my royal hands.
>
> . . . .
>
> Mock not my senseless conjuration, lords:
> This earth shall have a feeling, and these stones
> Prove armèd soldiers, ere her native king
> Shall falter under foul rebellion's arms   (3.2.8–11, 23–26)

—undoubtedly gains in emotional splendor (as well as dramatic irony) by its reminiscences of John of Gaunt's earlier language. The two men between them make the English earth the chief verbal theme of the play.

Richard, we have just seen, speaks pridefully of "*my* earth." To him, ownership of the land is the most tangible and positive symbol of his rightful kingship. He bids Northumberland tell Bolingbroke that "every stride he makes upon my land/ Is dangerous treason" (3.3.91–92), and as he lies dying from the stroke of Exton's sword his last thought is for his land: "Exton, thy fierce hand/ Hath with the King's blood stained the King's own land" (5.5.109–10). It is only natural, then, that *land* should be the key word in the discussion of England's sorry condition. Symbol of Englishmen's nationalistic pride and of the wealth of kings, it becomes symbol also of Englishmen's shame and kings' disgrace:

> Why, cousin, wert thou regent of the world,
> It were a shame to let this land by lease;
> But for thy world enjoying but this land
> Is it not more than shame to shame it so?
> Landlord of England art thou now, not king.   (2.1.109–13)

Northumberland's sad allusion to "this declining land" (240), York's to "this woeful land" (2.2.99) and Richard's to "this revolting land" (3.3.162) carry on this motif.

But *earth*, while it emblematizes the foundation of kingly pride and power, is also a familiar symbol of the vanity of human life and of what, in the Middle Ages, was a fascinating illustration of that vanity—the fall of kings. "Men," Mowbray sighs, "are but gilded loam or painted clay" (1.1.179); and Richard, luxuriating in self-pity, often remembers it; to earth he will return.

> Ah, Richard! [says Salisbury] With the eyes of heavy mind
> I see thy glory like a shooting star
> Fall to the base earth from the firmament.   (2.4.18–20)

The earth, Richard knows, is accustomed to receive the knees of courtiers: "Fair cousin," he tells Bolingbroke after he has given away his kingdom for the sheer joy of listening to himself do so, "you debase your princely knee/ To make the base earth proud with kissing it" (3.3.188–89). And the idea of the ground as the resting place for suppliant knees, and therefore the antithesis of kingly elevation, is repeated thrice in the two scenes dealing with Aumerle's conspiracy.[3]

The irony of this association of *earth* with both kingly glory and abasement is deepened by another role the word has in this earth-preoccupied play. For after death, earth receives its own; and in *Richard II* the common notion of the grave has new meaning, because the ubiquitous symbol of *earth* embraces it too. By the beginning of the third act, *earth* has lost its earlier joyful connotation to Richard, and this king, whose feverish imagination no amount of woe can cool, eagerly picks up a hint from Scroop:

> *Scroop.* Those whom you curse
> Have felt the worst of death's destroying wound
> And lie full low, graved in the hollow ground.
>
> . . . .
>
> *Richard.* Let's talk of graves, of worms, and epitaphs,
> Make dust our paper, and with rainy eyes
> Write sorrow on the bosom of the earth.
> Let's choose executors and talk of wills;
> And yet not so, for what can we bequeath
> Save our deposèd bodies to the ground?
> Our lands, our lives, and all are Bolingbroke's,
> And nothing can we call our own but death,
> And that small model of the barren earth
> Which serves as paste and cover to our bones.

---

[3] The much admired little passage about the roan Barbary takes on added poignancy when the other overtones of *ground* are remembered:
King Richard. Rode he on Barbary? Tell me, gentle friend,
   How went he under him?
Groom. So proudly as if he disdain'd the ground.
                                                    (5.5.81–83)

> For God's sake, let us sit upon the ground
> And tell sad stories of the death of kings.
>
> (3.2.138–140, 145–56)

And later, in another ecstasy of self-pity, he conjures up an elaborate image of making some pretty match with shedding tears:

> As thus, to drop them still upon one place,
> Till they have fretted us a pair of graves
> Within the Earth.   (3.3.165–67)

The same association occurs in the speeches of the other characters. Surrey, casting his gage at Fitzwater's feet, envisions his father's skull lying quietly in earth (4.1.66–69); a moment or two later the Bishop of Carlisle brings news that the banished Mowbray, having fought for Jesu Christ in glorious Christian field, "at Venice gave/ His body to that pleasant country's earth" (97–98); and in the same scene Richard, having handed over his crown to the usurper, exclaims,

> Long may'st thou live in Richard's seat to sit,
> And soon lie Richard in an earthy pit!   (217–18)

A final theme in the symphonic pattern dominated by the symbol of earth is that of the untended garden. Miss Spurgeon has adequately emphasized the importance of this iterated image in the history plays, and, as she points out, it reaches its climax in *Richard II*, particularly in the allegorical scene of the Queen's garden. In Shakespeare's imagination the misdeeds of Richard and his followers constituted an overwhelming indignity to the precious English earth— to a nation which, in happier days, had been a sea-wall'd garden. And thus the play is filled with references to ripeness and the seasons, to planting and cropping and plucking and reaping, to furrows and plowing, and caterpillars and withered bay trees and thorns and flowers.[4]

---

[4] We must not, of course, take *garden* too literally. Shakespeare obviously intended the term in its wider metaphorical sense of fields and orchards.

Among the host of garden images in the play, one especially is unforgettable because of the insistence with which Shakespeare thrice echoes it. It is the terrible metaphor of the English garden being drenched by showers of blood.

> I'll use the advantage of my power,
> And lay the summer's dust with showers of blood
> Rained from the wounds of slaughtered Englishmen.
>
> (3.3.41–43)

threatens Bolingbroke as he approaches Flint castle; and when the King himself appears upon the walls, he casts the figure back in Bolingbroke's face:

> But ere the crown he looks for live in peace
> Ten thousand bloody crowns of mothers' sons
> Shall ill become the flower of England's face,
> Change the complexion of her maid-pale peace
> To scarlet indignation, and bedew
> Her pastor's grass with faithful English blood.   (94–99)

The Bishop of Carlisle takes up the theme:

> And if you crown him, let me prophesy
> The blood of English shall manure the ground,
> And future ages groan for this foul act.   (4.1.136–38)

And the new King—amply justifying Professor Van Doren's remark that not only are most of the characters in this play poets, but they copy one another on occasion—echoes it:

> Lords, I protest, my soul is full of woe,
> That blood should sprinkle me to make me grow.   (5.6.45–46)

This extraordinary series of four images is one of the many examples of the manner in which the principal symbols of *Richard II* so often chime together, bringing the ideas they represent into momentary conjunction and thus compounding those single emotional strains into new and revealing harmonies. In this case the "showers of blood" metaphor provides a recurrent nexus between the pervasive symbol of earth and another, equally pervasive, symbol: that of blood.

Both Professor Bradley and Miss Spurgeon have pointed out the splendid horror which Shakespeare achieves in *Macbeth* by his repeated allusions to blood. Curiously enough, the word *blood*, together with such related words as *bloody* and *bleed*, occurs much less frequently in *Macbeth* than it does in most of the history plays. What gives the word the tremendous force it undoubtedly possesses in *Macbeth* is not the frequency with which it is spoken, but rather the intrinsic magnificence of the passages in which it appears and the fact that in this play it has but one significance—the literal one. In the history plays, however, the word *blood* plays two major roles. Often it has the same meaning it has in *Macbeth*, for these too are plays in which men's minds often turn toward the sword:

> . . . our kingdom's earth should not be soiled
> With that dear blood which it hath fosterèd.   (1.3.125–26)

says Richard in one more instinctive (and punning!) association of blood and earth. But *blood* in the history plays also stands figuratively for inheritance, descent, familial pride; and this is the chief motivating theme of the play—the right of a monarch of unquestionably legitimate blood to his throne. The two significances constantly interplay, giving the single word a new multiple connotation wherever it appears. The finest instance of this merging of ideas is in the Duchess of Gloucester's outburst to John of Gaunt. Here we have an elaborate contrapuntal metaphor, the basis of which is a figure derived from the familiar medieval genealogical symbol of the Tree of Jesse, and which is completed by a second figure of the seven vials of blood. The imposition of the figure involving the word *blood* (in its literal and therefore most vivid use) upon another figure which for centuries embodied the concept of family descent thus welds together with extraordinary tightness the word and its symbolic significance. The occurrence of *blood* in other senses on the borders of the metaphor (in the first and next-to-last lines of the passage) helps to focus attention upon the process occurring in the metaphor itself.

> Hath love in thy old blood no living fire?
> Edward's seven sons, whereof thyself art one,
> Were as seven vials of his sacred blood,
> Or seven fair branches springing from one root.
> Some of those seven are dried by nature's course,
> Some of those branches by the Destinies cut;
> But Thomas, my dear lord, my life, my Gloucester,
> One vial full of Edward's sacred blood,
> One flourishing branch of his most royal root,
> Is cracked, and all the precious liquor spilt,
> Is hacked down, and his summer leaves all faded
> By Envy's hand and Murder's bloody axe.
> Ah! Gaunt, his blood was thine. (1.2.10–22)

Because it has this multiple function, the word *blood* in this play loses much of the concentrated vividness and application it has in *Macbeth*, where it means but one unmistakable thing; but its ambiguity here gives it a new sort of power. If it is less effective as imagery, it does serve to underscore the basic idea of the play, that violation of the laws of blood descent leads but to the spilling of precious English blood. That is the meaning of the word as it pulses from beginning to end, marking the emotional rhythm of the play.

In *Richard II*, furthermore, the word has an additional unique use, one which involves an especially striking symbol. It has often been remarked how Shakespeare, seizing upon a hint in his sources, plays upon Richard's abnormal tendency to blanch and blush. In the imagery thus called forth, *blood* has a prominent part. How, demands the haughty king of John of Gaunt, dare thou

> with thy frozen admonition
Make pale our cheek, chasing the royal blood
With fury from his native residence.   (2.1.117–19)

And when the King hears the news of the Welshmen's defection, Aumerle steadies his quaking body:

> Comfort, my liege, why looks your Grace so pale?

> *Richard.* But now the blood of twenty thousand men
>   Did triumph in my face, and they are fled;
>   And till so much blood thither come again,
>   Have I not reason to look pale and dead?   (3.2.75–79)

This idiosyncrasy of the King is made the more vivid because the imagery of the play constantly refers to pallor, even in contexts far removed from him. The Welsh captain reports that "the pale-faced moon looks bloody on the earth" (2.4.10). In another speech, the words *pale* and *blood*, though not associated in a single image, occur so close to each other that it is tempting to suspect an habitual association in Shakespeare's mind:

> Pale trembling coward, there I throw my gage,
> Disclaiming here the kindred of the King,
> And lay aside my high blood's royalty.   (1.1.69–71)

And as we have already seen, the King prophesied that "ten thousand bloody crowns of mothers' sons/ Shall . . . change the complexion of [England's] maid-pale peace" (3.3.95–97). Elsewhere Bolingbroke speaks of "pale beggar-fear" (1.1.189); the Duchess of Gloucester accuses John of Gaunt of "pale cold cowardice" (1.2.34); and York describes how the returned exile and his army fright England's "pale-faced villages" with war (2.3.93).

The idea of pallor and blushing is linked in turn with what

is perhaps the most famous image-motif of the play, that of Richard (or the fact of his kingship) emblematized by the sun. More attention probably has been paid to the sun-king theme than it is worth, for although it occurs in two very familiar passages, it contributes far less to the harmonic unity of the play than do a number of other symbol strains. In any event, the conjunction of the sun image with that of blushing provides one more evidence of the closeness with which the poetic themes of the play are knit together. In the first of the sun-king speeches, Richard compares himself, at the length to which he is addicted, with "the searching eye of heaven" (3.2.37). Finally, after some ten lines of analogy:

> So when this thief, this traitor, Bolingbroke,
> Who all this while hath reveled in the night
> Whilst we were wand'ring with the Antipodes,
> Shall see us rising in our throne, the east,
> His treasons will sit blushing in his face.   (47–51)

And Bolingbroke in a later scene does him the sincere flattery of imitation:

> See, see, King Richard doth himself appear,
> As doth the blushing discontented sun
> From out the fiery portal of the East.   (3.3.61–63)

Another occurrence of the sun image provides a link with the pervasive motif of tears. Salisbury, having envisioned Richard's glory falling to the base earth from the firmament, continues:

> Thy sun sets weeping in the lowly west,
> Witnessing storms to come, woe, and unrest.   (2.4.21–22)

In no other history play is the idea of tears and weeping so insistently presented.[5] It is this element which enforces most strongly our impression of Richard as a weakling, a monarch essentially feminine in nature, who has no conception of stoic endurance or resignation but a strong predilection for grief. This is why the play seems so strangely devoid of the heroic; the King and Queen are too much devoted to luxuriating in their misery, and the other characters find a morbid delight in at least alluding to unmanly tears. Characteristically, Richard's first question to Aumerle, when the latter returns from bidding farewell to Bolingbroke, is, "What store of parting tears were shed?" (1.4.5). Bushy, discussing with the Queen her premonitions of disaster, speaks at length of "Sorrow's eye, glazèd with blinding tears" (2.2.16). Richard greets the fair soil of England with mingled smiles and tears; and from that point on, his talk is full of "rainy eyes" (3.2.146) and of making "foul weather with despisèd tears" (3.3.160). He counsels York,

> Uncle, give me your hands; nay, dry your eyes;
> Tears show their love, but want their remedies.   (200–1)

In the garden scene the Queen, rejecting her lady's offer to sing, sadly tells her:

>   'Tis well that thou hast cause;
> But thou should'st please me better would'st thou weep.

> *Lady.* I could weep, madam, would it do you good.

> *Queen.* And I could sing, would weeping do me good,
>   And never borrow any tear of thee.   (3.4.19–23)

And echoing that dialogue, the gardener, at the close of the scene, looks after her and says:

> Here did she fall a tear; here in this place
> I'll set a bank of rue, sour herb of grace;

---

[5] There are many more references to tears and weeping in *Titus Andronicus*, but the obvious inferiority of the poetry and the crudity of characterization make their presence far less remarkable.

Rue, even for ruth here shortly shall be seen,
In the remembrance of a weeping queen.   (104–7)

The theme reaches a climax in the deposition scene, in which the agonized King, handing his crown to Bolingbroke, sees himself as the lower of the two buckets in Fortune's well:

. . . full of tears am I,
Drinking my griefs, whilst you mount up on high. (4.1.187–88)

And a few lines later he merges the almost ubiquitous motif of tears with another constant theme of the play: "With mine own tears I wash away my balm" (206). Of the frequent association of the anointing of kings, blood, and the act of washing, I shall speak a little later.

Professor Van Doren, in his sensitive essay on *Richard II*, eloquently stresses the importance of the word *tongue* in the play. *Tongue*, he says, is the key word of the piece. I should prefer to give that distinction to *earth*; but there is no denying the effectiveness of Shakespeare's tireless repetition of the idea of speech, not only by the single word *tongue* but also by such allied words as *mouth*, *speech*, and *word*. A few minutes' study of Bartlett's *Concordance* will show that *Richard II* is unique in this insistence upon the concept of speech; that the word *tongue* occurs here oftener than in any other play is but one indication.

This group of associated words heavily underscores two leading ideas in the play. In the first place, it draws constant attention to the propensity for verbalizing (as Shakespeare would not have called it!) which is Richard's fatal weakness. He cannot bring himself to live in a world of hard actuality; the universe to him is real only as it is presented in packages of fine words. Aumerle tries almost roughly to recall him from his weaving of sweet, melancholy sounds to a realization of the crucial situation confronting him, but he rouses himself only momentarily and then relapses into a complacent enjoyment of the sound of

his own tongue. It is of this trait that we are constantly reminded as all the characters regularly use periphrases
when they must speak of what they or others have said. By
making the physical act of speech, the sheer fact of language, so conspicuous, they call attention to its illusory
nature—to the vast difference between what the semanti-
cists call the intensional and extensional universes. That
words are mere conventional sounds molded by the
tongue, and reality is something else again, is constantly
on the minds of all the characters. The initial dispute between Mowbray and Bolingbroke is "the bitter clamor of
two eager tongues" (1.1.49); Mowbray threatens to cram
his antagonist's lie "through the false passage of thy
throat" (125); and later, in a fine cadenza, he conceives of
his eternal banishment in terms of the engaoling of his
tongue, whose "use is to me no more/ Than an unstringèd
viol or a harp," and concludes:

> What is thy sentence then but speechless death,
> Which robs my tongue from breathing native breath?
> (1.3.161–62, 172–73)

Bolingbroke, for his part, marvels over the power of a single
word to change the lives of men:

> How long a time lies in one little word.
> Four lagging winters and four wanton springs
> End in a word—such is the breath of kings.   (212–14)

Gaunt too is preoccupied with tongues and speech; and
when Aumerle returns from his farewell with Bolingbroke,
from tears the image theme swiftly turns to tongues:

> *Richard.* What said our cousin when you parted with him?
>
> *Aumerle.* "Farewell."
>   And, for my heart disdainèd that my tongue
>   Should so profane the word, that taught me craft

To counterfeit oppression of such grief
That words seemed buried in my sorrow's grave.
Marry, would the word "Farewell" have length'ned
    hours
And added years to his short banishment,
He should have had a volume of farewells.   (1.4.10–18)

And we have but reached the end of Act 1; the remainder of the play is equally preoccupied with the unsubstantiality of human language.[6]

But the unremitting stress laid upon tongues and words in this play serves another important end: it reminds us that Richard's fall is due not only to his preference for his own words rather than for deeds, but also to his blind predilection for comfortable flattery rather than sound advice. Words not only hypnotize, suspend the sense of reality: they can sting and corrupt. And so the tongues of *Richard II* symbolize also the honeyed but poisonous speech of the sycophants who surround him. "No," replies York to Gaunt's suggestion that his dying words might yet undeaf Richard's ear,

. . . it is stopped with other flattering sounds,
As praises—of whose taste the wise are fond—
Lascivious meters, to whose venom sound
The open ear of youth doth always listen.   (2.1.17–20)

The venom to which York refers and the snake which produces it form another theme of the imagery of this play. The snake-venom motif closely links the idea of the garden on the one hand (for what grossly untended garden would be without its snakes?) and the idea of the tongue on the

---

[6] Another way in which Shakespeare adds to the constant tragic sense of unsubstantiality in this play—the confusion of appearance and reality—is the repeated use of the adjective *hollow*, especially in connection with death: "our hollow parting" (1.4.9), the "hollow womb" of the grave (2.1.83), "the hollow eyes of death" (270), a grave set in "the hollow ground" (3.2.140), "the hollow crown" in which Death keeps his court (160).

other. All three meet in the latter part of Richard's speech in 3.2:

> But let thy spiders, that suck up thy venom,
> And heavy-gaited toads lie in their way,
> Doing annoyance to the treacherous feet
> Which with usurping steps do trample thee;
> Yield stinging nettles to mine enemies;
> And when they from thy bosom pluck a flower,
> Guard it, I pray thee, with a lurking adder
> Whose double tongue may with a mortal touch
> Throw death upon thy sovereign's enemies.   (14–22)

And the double association occurs again in the garden scene, when the Queen demands of the gardener,

> Thou, old Adam's likeness, set to dress this garden,
> How dares thy harsh rude tongue sound this unpleasing news?
> What Eve, what serpent, hath suggested thee
> To make a second fall of cursèd man?   (3.4.73–76)

Mowbray elsewhere speaks of "slander's venomed spear" (1.1.171), and to Richard, the flatterers who have deserted him are, naturally enough, "villains, vipers, damned without redemption! . . . Snakes, in my heart-blood warmed, that sting my heart!" (3.2.129–31).

Although England's sorry state is most often figured in the references to the untended garden and the snakes that infest it, the situation is emphasized time and again by at least four other recurrent themes, some of which refer as well to the personal guilt of Richard. One such theme—anticipating a similar motif in *Hamlet*—involves repeated references to physical illness and injury. Richard in seeking to smooth over the quarrel between Mowbray and Bolingbroke says:

> Let's purge this choler without letting blood;
> This we prescribe, though no physician;
> Deep malice makes too deep incision.   (1.1.153–55)

There are repeated allusions to the swelling caused by infection. Richard in the same scene speaks of "the swelling difference of your settled hate" (201), and much later, after he has been deposed, he predicts to Northumberland that

> The time shall not be many hours of age
> More than it is, ere foul sin, gathering head,
> Shall break into corruption.   (5.1.57–59)

Thus too there are vivid mentions of the remedy for such festering:

> Fell Sorrow's tooth doth never rankle more
> Than when he bites, but lanceth not the sore.   (1.3.301–2)

> This fest'red joint cut off, the rest rest sound.   (5.3.84)

Plague, *pestilence*, and *infection* are words frequently in the mouths of the characters of this play. Aumerle, during the furious gage-casting of 4.1, cries, "May my hands rot off" if he does not seize Percy's gage (49); and elsewhere York, speaking to the unhappy Queen, says of the King,

> Now comes the sick hour that his surfeit made;
> Now shall he try his friends that flatter'd him.   (2.2.84–85)

Indeed, the imagery which deals with bodily injury directly associates the wretchedness of the monarch and his country with the tongues of the sycophants. A verbal juxtaposition of *tongue* and *wound* occurs early in the play: "Ere my tongue/ Shall wound my honor with such feeble wrong" (1.1.190–91). Gaunt carries the association one step farther when he explicitly connects Richard's and England's illness with the presence of gross flatterers in the King's retinue:

Thy deathbed is no lesser than thy land,
Wherein thou liest in reputation sick;
And thou, too careless patient as thou art,
Commit'st thy anointed body to the cure
Of those physicians that first wounded thee.
A thousand flatterers sit within thy crown,
Whose compass is no bigger than thy head. (2.1.95–101)

And Richard himself completes the circuit between the tongue-wound association and his personal grief: "He does me double wrong/ That wounds me with the flatteries of his tongue" (3.2.215–16).

Again, the evil that besets England is frequently symbolized as a dark blot upon fair parchment—an image which occurs oftener in this play than in any other. The suggestion for the image undoubtedly came from contemplation of the deeds and leases by which the king had farmed out the royal demesnes; as John of Gaunt said, England "is now bound in with shame,/ With inky blots and rotten parchment bonds" (2.1.63–64). The image recurs several times. "No, Bolingbroke," says Mowbray in 1.3, "if ever I were traitor,/ My name be blotted from the book of life" (200–1). Richard sighs through blanched lips, "Time hath set a blot upon my pride" (3.2.81) and later speaks of the record of Northumberland's offenses as including

one heinous article,
Containing the deposing of a king
And cracking the strong warrant of an oath,
Marked with a blot, damned in the book of heaven.
(4.1.232–35)

Carlisle and Aumerle in a duet harmonize the image with the two other motifs of gardening and generation:

Carlisle. The woe's to come; the children yet unborn
   Shall feel this day as sharp to them as thorn.

> *Aumerle.* You holy clergymen, is there no plot
> To rid the realm of this pernicious blot?   (321–24)

Aumerle's conspiracy which stems from this conversation is itself spoken of by Bolingbroke in Aumerle's own terms: "Thy abundant goodness shall excuse/ This deadly blot in thy digressing son" (5.3.64–65). The vividness of the image is increased by the presence elsewhere of allusions to books and writing: "He should have had a volume of farewells" (1.4.18); "The purple testament of bleeding war" (3.3.93);

> Let's talk of graves, of worms, and epitaphs;
> Make dust our paper, and with rainy eyes
> Write sorrow on the bosom of the earth.   (3.2.145–47)

(an interesting example of double association of imagery—tears, earth-grave, and writing); and in the deposition scene, when Richard calls for a mirror:

> I'll read enough,
> When I do see the very book indeed,
> Where all my sins are writ, and that's myself.   (4.1.272–74)

The blot image has a very direct relationship with another class of figures by which Shakespeare symbolizes guilt or evil: that of a stain which must be washed away. This image is most commonly associated with *Macbeth*, because of the extraordinary vividness with which it is used there. But the theme is much more insistent in *Richard II*. Twice it is associated, as in *Macbeth*, with blood:

> Yet, to wash your blood
> From off my hands, here in the view of men
> I will unfold some causes of your deaths.   (3.1.5–7)

> I'll make a voyage to the Holy Land,
> To wash this blood off from my guilty hand.   (5.6.49–50)

Elsewhere the association is with the story of the cru-
cifixion, in a repetition of which Richard fancies he is the
sufferer:

> Nay, all of you that stand and look upon me,
> Whilst that my wretchedness doth bait myself,
> Though some of you, with Pilate, wash your hands,
> Showing an outward pity: yet you Pilates
> Have here delivered me to my sour cross,
> And water cannot wash away your sin.   (4.1.236–41)

But in this play the absolution of guilt requires not merely
the symbolic cleansing of bloody hands; it entails the washing-
off of the sacred ointment of royalty—the ultimate expia-
tion of kingly sin. The full measure of Richard's fall is
epitomized in two further occurrences of the metaphor, the
first spoken when he is in the full flush of arrogant confi-
dence, the second when nemesis has overtaken him:

> Not all the water in the rough rude sea
> Can wash the balm off from an anointed king.   (3.2.54–55)

> With mine own tears I wash away my balm,
> With mine own hands I give away my crown.   (4.1.206–7)

Whatever the exact context of the image of washing, one
suggestion certainly is present whenever it appears: a suggestion of momentous change—the deposition of a monarch, the cleansing of a guilt-laden soul.

But the most unusual of all the symbols of unpleasantness
which occur in *Richard II* is the use of the adjective *sour*,
together with the repeated contrast of sweetness and sour-
ness. A reader of the play understandably passes over the
frequent use of *sweet* as a conventional epithet used both of
persons and of things. But the word, however commonplace
the specific phrases in which it occurs, has a role in the poetic design which decidedly is not commonplace, for it acts
as a foil for the very unaccustomed use of its antonym.

There is nothing less remarkable in Shakespeare than such phrases as "sweet Richard," "your sweet majesty," "sweet York, sweet husband," even such passages as this:

> And yet your fair discourse hath been as sugar,
> Making the hard way sweet and delectable.   (2.3.6–7)

But what is remarkable is the manner in which, in this play alone, mention of *sweet* so often invites mention of *sour*: "Things sweet to taste prove in digestion sour" (1.3.235); "Speak sweetly, man, although thy looks be sour" (3.2.193); "how sour sweet music is!" (5.5.42);

> Sweet love, I see, changing his property,
> Turns to the sourest and most deadly hate.   (3.2.135–36)

In addition to this repeated collocation of *sweet* and *sour*, the text of *Richard II* is notable for a persistent use, unmatched in any other play, of *sour* alone, as an adjective or verb:

> Not Gloucester's death, nor Hereford's banishment,
> Nor Gaunt's rebukes, nor England's private wrongs,
> . . . .
> Have ever made me sour my patient cheek.   (2.1.165–66, 169)

"I'll set a bank of rue, sour herb of grace" (3.4.105: this in significant collocation with the motif of tears, as the next is joined with the motif of washing)—"yet you Pilates/ Have here delivered me to my sour cross" (4.1.239–40);

> The grand conspirator, Abbot of Westminster,
> With clog of conscience and sour melancholy
> Hath yielded up his body to the grave.   (5.6.19–21)

The occurrence of *sour* thus lends unmistakable irony to every occurrence of *sweet*, however unimportant the latter may be in itself. Even at a distance of a few lines, mention of one quality seems to invite mention of the other, as if Shakespeare could never forget that the sour is as frequent in life as the sweet:

Duchess. The word is short, but not so short as sweet:
No word like "pardon" for kings' mouths so meet.

York. Speak it in French, King; say *"Pardonne moy."*

Duchess. Dost thou teach pardon pardon to destroy?
Ah, my sour husband, my hardhearted lord!
That sets the word itself against the word.   (5.3.116–21)

This contrapuntal use of *sweet* and *sour* is one of the most revealing instances of the artistry by which the poetry of *Richard II* is unified.[7]

Two more image themes, one of major importance, the other less conspicuous, remain to be mentioned. For one of them, we must return to the Tree of Jesse passage (1.2.10–22) quoted above. This passage is the fountainhead of one of the chief themes of the play—the idea of legitimate succession, of hereditary kingship. We have already noticed how, largely as a result of this early elaborate metaphor, the close identification of the word *blood* with the idea of family descent deepens the symbolic significance of that word as it recurs through the play. In addition, as Miss Spurgeon has pointed out, in *Richard II* there are many other cognate images derived from the idea of birth and generation, and of inheritance from father to son. The Tree

---

[7] The *sweet-sour* contrast occurs five times in *Richard II*; no more than twice in any other play.—Compare a similar juxtaposition in three of the sonnets:

Such civil war is in my love and hate
That I an accessary needs must be
To that sweet thief which sourly robs from me.   (No. 35)

O absence, what a torment wouldst thou prove
Were it not thy sour leisure gave sweet leave
To entertain the time with thoughts of love.   (No. 39)

of Jesse metaphor (whose importance Miss Spurgeon failed to note) is followed in the next scene by one involving the symbol of earth and thus suggesting the vital relationship between generation and patriotism:

> Then, England's ground, farewell; sweet soil, adieu;
> My mother and my nurse that bears me yet!   (1.3.305–6)

In John of Gaunt's dying speech, earth and generation again appear, significantly, in conjunction:

> This blessed plot, this earth, this realm, this England,
> This nurse, this teeming womb of royal kings.   (2.1.50–51)

In her scene with Bagot and Bushy, the Queen dwells constantly on the idea of birth:

> Some unborn sorrow, ripe in Fortune's womb,
> Is coming towards me.
>
> . . . .
>
>   Conceit is still derived
> From some forefather grief; mine is not so,
> For nothing hath begot my something grief.
>
> . . . .

> For sweetest things turn sourest by their deeds.   (No. 94)

It is interesting to note that in the same two groups of sonnets in which the *sweet-sour* collocation occurs can be found another word whose use is noteworthy in *Richard II*:

> And dost him grace when clouds do blot the heaven (No. 28)

> So shall those blots that do with me remain,
> Without thy help by me be borne alone   (No. 36)

> But what's so blessed-fair that fears no blot?   (No. 92)

> Where beauty's veil doth cover every blot   (No. 95)

If we accept the hypothesis that at a given period in his life Shakespeare habitually thought of certain abstract ideas in terms of particular metaphors, there is a good case for dating these sonnets at the time of *Richard II*. Conventional though the sweet-sour and blot ideas may be, it is plain that Shakespeare had them constantly in mind when writing *Richard II*; they are a hallmark of the style of the play. Their occurrence in these sonnets is possibly significant.

So, Green, thou art the midwife to my woe,
And Bolingbroke, my sorrow's dismal heir.
Now hath my soul brought forth her prodigy,
And I, a gasping new-delivered mother,
Have woe to woe, sorrow to sorrow, joined.

                                    (2.2.10–11, 34–36, 62–66)

Richard's last soliloquy begins with the same sort of elaborated conceit:

My brain I'll prove the female to my soul,
My soul the father; and these two beget
A generation of still-breeding thoughts,
And these same thoughts people this little world,
In humors like the people of this world,
For no thought is contented.   (5.5.6–11)

And throughout the play, as Miss Spurgeon notes, "the idea of inheritance from father to son . . . increases the feeling of the inevitable and the foreordained, as also of the unlimited consequences of action."

The word *crown* as the symbol of kingship is of course common throughout the history plays. In *Richard II*, however, the vividness of the image and the relevance of its symbolism to the grand theme of the play are heightened by several instances in which its metaphorical function goes beyond that of a simple, conventional metonymy:

A thousand flatterers sit within thy crown,
Whose compass is no bigger than thy head.   (2.1.100–1)

                for within the hollow crown
That rounds the mortal temples of a king
Keeps Death his court.   (3.2.160–62)

But ere the crown he looks for live in peace
Ten thousand bloody crowns of mothers' sons
Shall ill become the flower of England's face. (3.3.94–96)

Now is this golden crown like a deep well
That owes two buckets, filling one another,
The emptier ever dancing in the air,
The other down, unseen, and full of water.   (4.1.183–86)

In addition, the actual image of the crown is made more splendid by the occurrence, in the play's poetic fabric, of several images referring to jewels:

A jewel in a ten-times-barred-up chest
Is a bold spirit in a loyal breast.   (1.1.180–81)

Gaunt. The sullen passage of thy weary steps
    Esteem as foil wherein thou art to set
    The precious jewel of thy home return.

Bolingbroke. Nay, rather, every tedious stride I make
    Will but remember me what a deal of world
    I wander from the jewels that I love.   (1.3.264–69)

And again: "I'll give my jewels for a set of beads" (3.3.146), "This precious stone set in the silver sea" (2.1.46), and "Love to Richard/ Is a strange brooch in this all-hating world" (5.5.65–66).

Keeping in mind the leading metaphors and verbal motifs which I have reviewed—*earth-ground-land*, *blood*, pallor, garden, sun, tears, *Tongue-speech-word*, *snake-venom*, physical injury and illness, *blot*, washing, *sweet-sour*, generation, and jewel-crown—it is profitable to reread the whole play, noting especially how widely the various themes are distributed, and how frequently their strands cross to form new images. There is no extended passage of the text which is not tied in with the rest of the play by the occurrence of one or more of the familiar symbols. However, the images are not scattered with uniform evenness. As in *The Merchant of Venice*, metaphorical language tends to be concentrated at the emotional climaxes of *Richard II*. At certain crucial points in the action, a large number of the unifying image-threads appear almost simultaneously, so that our minds are virtually flooded with many diverse yet closely related ideas. The first part of 2.1 (the prophecy of Gaunt) offers a good instance of this rapid cumulation of symbols and the resultant heightening of emotional effect. The whole passage should be read as Shakespeare wrote it; here I list simply the phrases that reveal the various image themes, omitting a number which glance obliquely at the themes but are not directly connected with them:

line		
5	the tongues of dying men	
7	words	
8	words	
12	the setting sun	
13	As the last taste of sweets is sweetest last	
14	Writ in remembrance	
17	flattering sounds	
19	Lascivious meters, to whose venom sound	
23	Limps	
41	This earth of majesty	
44	infection	
45	breed	
46	This precious stone	
49	less happier lands	
50	this earth	
51	This nurse, this teeming womb of royal kings	
52	breed . . . birth	
57	land . . . land	
64	With inky blots, and rotten parchment bonds	
83	hollow womb	
95	land	
96	sick [followed by extended metaphor]	
100	thy crown	
103	thy land	
104–05	thy grandsire . . . his son's son . . . his sons	

110–13	this land . . . this land . . . Landlord
116	ague
118	pale . . . blood
122	This tongue
126	blood
131	blood
134	To crop at once a too-long-withered flower
136	words
141	words
149	His tongue
153	The ripest fruit first falls
157	Which live like venom, where no venom else

Thus in the first 157 lines of the scene we meet no less than twelve of the motifs of the play.

In another sort of harmonization, Shakespeare strikes a long chord containing a number of the image strains and then in the following minutes of the play echoes them separately. The "Dear earth, I do salute thee with my hand" speech at the beginning of 3.2 interweaves at least six themes which shortly are unraveled into individual strands. The idea of the garden which is the framework for the whole speech (6–26) recurs in the line "To ear the land that hath some hope to grow" (212). The repeated references to weeping in the initial speech ("I weep for joy" . . "with her tears" . . . "weeping") are echoed in "as if the world were all dissolved to tears" (108) and "rainy eyes" (146). Richard's "Nor with thy sweets comfort his ravenous sense" (13) is recalled in Scroop's "Sweet love . . . changing his property,/ Turns to the sourest and most deadly hate" (135–36) and in Richard's "Speak sweetly, man, although thy looks be sour" (193) and "that sweet way I was in to despair" (205). The lurking adder and the venom which the spiders suck up (20, 14) find their sequel in Richard's later "vipers . . . snakes . . . that sting my heart" (129–31). The double tongue (21) is succeeded by "Discomfort guides my tongue" (65), "my care-tuned tongue" (92), the tongue that "hath but a heavier tale to say" (197), and the one whose flatteries wound the King at the end of the scene (216). The initial reference to wounding ("Though rebels wound thee with their horses' hoofs" [7]) is succeeded by "death's destroying wound" (139); and the same general motif of bodily hurt is carried out by "this ague fit of fear is overblown" (190), which links the disease-theme to that of the garden. Finally, the frequent use of *earth* in Richard's first speech (6, 10, 12, 24) prepares the ear for the five-times-repeated occurrence of the idea (earth . . . ground . . . lands . . . earth . . . ground) in the "Let's talk of graves, of worms, and epitaphs" speech (145–77). This progressive analysis of the components of the original chord of images is accompanied by a succession of other images not included in the chord: an extended sun metaphor (36–50), a reference to washing (54–55), the most famous instance of the pallor-blood motif (76–81), two references to the crown (59, 115), and two allusions to writing (81, 146–47). And thus the mind is crowded with a richly overlapping series of images.

Another example of the close arraying of image patterns (without the initial chord) occurs in 3.3.84–99:

> Yet know, my master, God omnipotent,
> Is mustering in his clouds on our behalf
> Armies of pestilence, and they shall strike   (illness)
> Your children yet unborn and unbegot   (generation)
> That lift your vassal hands against my head,
> And threat the glory of my precious crown.   (crown)
> Tell Bolingbroke—for yon methinks he stands—
> That every stride he makes upon my land   (earth)
> Is dangerous treason. He is come to open
> The purple testament of bleeding war;   (books, blood)
> But ere the crown he looks for live in peace   (crown)
> Ten thousand bloody crowns of mothers' sons
>   (blood, crown, generation)
> Shall ill become the flower of England's face,   (garden)
> Change the complexion of her maid-pale peace   (pallor)
> To scarlet indignation, and bedew
> Her pastor's grass with faithful English blood.   (blood)

Curiously, the deposition scene, though it is rich enough in individual appearances of the familiar themes, does not mesh them so closely as one might expect.

A final aspect of the use of iterative imagery in *Richard II* is the manner in which a particularly important passage is prepared for by the interweaving into the poetry, long in advance, of inconspicuous but repeated hints of the imagery which is to dominate that passage. The method is exactly analogous to that by which in a symphony a melody appears, at first tentatively, indeed almost unnoticed, first in one choir of the orchestra, then another, until ultimately it comes to its reward as the theme of a climactic section. In such a manner is the audience prepared, although unconsciously, for Richard's last grandiose speech. One takes little note of the first timid appearance of a reference to beggary or bankruptcy in Bolingbroke's "Or with pale beggar-fear impeach my height" (1.1.189). But in the second act the motif recurs:

> Be York the next that must be bankrout so!
> Though death be poor, it ends a mortal woe.   (2.1.151–52)

and a hundred lines later the idea is repeated: "The King's grown bankrout like a broken man" (257). The haunting dread of destitution, then, however obliquely alluded to, is a recurrent theme, and adds its small but perceptible share to the whole atmosphere of impending disaster. It forms the burden of two plaints by Richard midway in the play:

> Let's choose executors and talk of wills:
> And yet not so, for what can we bequeath
> Save our deposèd bodies to the ground?
> Our lands, our lives, and all are Bolingbroke's.   (3.2.148–51)

> I'll give my jewels for a set of beads;
> My gorgeous palace for a hermitage;
> My gay apparel for an almsman's gown;
> My figured goblets for a dish of wood;
> My scepter for a palmer's walking-staff;

My subjects for a pair of carvèd saints;
And my large kingdom for a little grave.   (3.3.146–52)

But the time is not ripe for the climactic utterance of this
motif. It disappears, to return for a moment in a verbal hint
in the deposition scene:

Let it command a mirror hither straight,
That it may show me what a face I have,
Since it is bankrout of his majesty.   (4.1.264–66)

Being so great, I have no need to beg.   (308)

The Duchess of York momentarily takes up the motif: "A
beggar begs that never begged before" (5.3.77), and Bolingbroke replies:

Our scene is alt'red from a serious thing,
And now changed to "The Beggar and the King."   (78–79)

And now finally comes the climax toward which these fleeting references have been pointing: a climax which illumi-
nates the purpose and direction of the earlier talk about
beggary and bankruptcy:

Thoughts tending to content flatter themselves
That they are not the first of fortune's slaves,
Nor shall not be the last, like seely beggars
Who sitting in the stocks refuge their shame,
That many have, and others must, sit there;
And in this thought they find a kind of ease,
Bearing their own misfortunes on the back
Of such as have before endured the like.
Thus play I in one person many people,
And none contented; sometimes am I king,
Then treasons make me wish myself a beggar,

And so I am. Then crushing penury
Persuades me I was better when a king.   (5.5.23–35)

A similar process can be traced in the repetition of the word *face*, which, besides being obviously connected with the idea of Richard's personal comeliness, underscores the hovering sense the play contains of the illusory quality of life, of the deceptions that men accept as if they were reality. The word occurs casually, unremarkably, often without metaphorical intent; but its frequent appearance not only reinforces, however subtly, a dominant idea of the play, but also points toward a notable climax. "Mowbray's face" (1.1.195) . . . "Nor never look upon each other's face" (1.3.185) . . . "the northeast wind/ Which then blew bitterly against our faces" (1.4.6–7) . . . "His face thou hast, for even so looked he" (2.1.176) . . . "Frighting her pale-faced villages with war" (2.3.93) . . . "The pale-faced moon looks bloody on the earth" (2.4.10) . . . "His treasons will sit blushing in his face" (3.2.51) . . . "But now the blood of twenty thousand men/ Did triumph in my face" (76–77) . . .

Ten thousand bloody crowns of mothers' sons
Shall ill become the flower of England's face.   (3.3.95–96)

Meanwhile Bushy has introduced the corollary idea of shadow:

Each substance of a grief hath twenty shadows,
Which shows like grief itself, but is not so;   (2.2.14–15)

Which looked on as it is, is nought but shadows
Of what it is not.   (23–24)

The related themes merge as, in retrospect, it is plain they were destined to do, in the deposition scene:

> Was this face the face
> That every day under his household roof
> Did keep ten thousand men? Was this the face
> That, like the sun, did make beholders wink?
> Was this the face that faced so many follies,
> And was at last outfaced by Bolingbroke?
> A brittle glory shineth in this face,
> As brittle as the glory is the face,
> For there it is, cracked in a hundred shivers.
> Mark, silent king, the moral of this sport:
> How soon my sorrow hath destroyed my face.
>
> *Bolingbroke.* The shadow of your sorrow hath destroyed
>   The shadow of your face.
>
> *Richard.*   Say that again.
>   "The shadow of my sorrow"? Ha, let's see.   (4.1.280–93)

And thus from beginning to end *Richard II* is, in a double sense of which Shakespeare would have approved, a play on words. As countless writers have affirmed, it is entirely fitting that this should be so. King Richard, a poet *manqué*, loved words more dearly than he did his kingdom, and his tragedy is made the more moving by the style, half rhetorical, half lyrical, in which it is told. Splendid words, colorful metaphors, pregnant poetic symbols in this drama possess their own peculiar irony.

But the language of *Richard II*, regarded from the viewpoint I have adopted in this paper, has another significance, entirely apart from its appropriateness to theme. It suggests the existence of a vital relationship between two leading characteristics of Shakespeare's poetic style: the uncontrolled indulgence of verbal wit in the earlier plays and the use of great image-themes in the plays of his maturity. As I suggested in the beginning, wordplay and iterative imagery are but two different manifestations of a single faculty in the creative imagination—an exceedingly well-developed sense of association. In *Richard II* we see the crucial intermediate stage in the development, or perhaps more accurately the utilization, of Shakespeare's singular associative gift. In such passages as John of Gaunt's speech upon his name, we are reminded of the plays which preceded this from Shakespeare's pen. But, except on certain occasions when they contribute to the characterization of the poet-king, the brief coruscations of verbal wit which marked the earlier plays are less evident than formerly. On the other hand, when we stand back and view the play as a whole, its separate movements bound so closely together by image themes, we are enabled to anticipate the future development of Shakespeare's art. The technique that is emerging in *Richard II* is the technique that eventually will have its part in producing the poetry of *Lear* and *Macbeth* and *Othello*. Here we have the method: the tricks of repetition, of cumulative emotional effect, of interweaving and reciprocal coloration. What is yet to come is the full mastery of the artistic possibilities of such a technique. True, thanks to its tightly interwoven imagery *Richard II* has a poetic unity that is unsurpassed in any of the great tragedies; so far as structure is concerned, Shakespeare has levied from iterative language about all the aid that it will give. The great improvement will come in another region. Taken individually, in *Richard II* Shakespeare's images lack the qualities which they will possess in the later plays. They are, many of them, too conventional for our tastes; they are marred by diffuseness; they bear too many lingering traces of Shakespeare's affection for words for words' sake. The ultimate condensation, the compression of a universe of meaning into a single bold metaphor, remains to be achieved. But in the best imagery of *Richard II*, especially in those passages which combine several themes into a richly complex pattern of meaning, we receive abundant assurance that Shakespeare will be equal to his task. The process of welding language and thought into a single entity is well begun.

DEREK TRAVERSI

From Shakespeare from *Richard II* to *Henry V*

From the moment of Richard's descent, "like glistering Phaethon," into the "base court" his fate is substantially sealed. The last part of the play confirms his fall, investing it with the tragic quality that surrounds the misfortunes of an anointed king, and consummates the ruthless process of his rival's rise to power. After the short scene (3.4), conveying the Queen's meeting with her Gardeners, which clearly answers to a certain "symbolic" design, using an elaborately prolonged metaphor to underline the relationship between Richard's tragedy and the disorder of his realm, the return to the main action (4.1) is marked by a further access of realism, the fitting accompaniment of the new power. The quarrel between the lords, occasioned by Bagot's accusation of Aumerle for his part in Gloucester's death, is both elaborate in expression and detached, realistic in presentation. Aumerle, in spite of his defiance, is aware of weakness; the lords who turn against him, invoking "truth" and "honor," already have an eye to their future good. On either side, the expression is overpitched, strained as though conscious of its own falsity; the ringing rhetoric—in which an echo, as it were, of the opening scenes can still be detected—turns into shabby interchange of snarl and countersnarl which only Bolingbroke is detached enough to watch without illusion. When he intervenes, with a pacifying gesture to insinuate Mowbray's return, it is left to Carlisle to evoke the values implied in his former rival's crusading venture and—at the same time—

From *Shakespeare from Richard II to Henry V* by Derek Traversi (Stanford, Calif.: Stanford University Press, 1957; London: Hollis & Carter, Ltd., 1958). Reprinted by permission of Hollis & Carter, Ltd.

to announce the crusader's death. The counterpart of his announcement, valid in the present, is York's proclamation of Bolingbroke as king, briefly accepted by the latter with his "In God's name, I'll ascend the regal throne" (113).

The proclamation is immediately followed, in accordance with the main design, by Carlisle's assertion of Richard's divine right, and by his prophecy which looks forward to a future of civil war:

> And if you crown him, let me prophesy
> The blood of English shall manure the ground,
> And future ages groan for this foul act;
> Peace shall go sleep with Turks and infidels,
> And, in this seat of peace, tumultuous wars
> Shall kin with kin, and kind with kind, confound;
> Disorder, horror, fear, and mutiny
> Shall here inhabit, and this land be called
> The field of Golgotha and dead men's skulls.   (136–44)

The speech presents a community of style with the patriotic utterances of Gaunt, and the culminating reference to Golgotha will shortly be echoed by Richard himself. Its careful elaboration is intended to stand out against the blunt realism of Bolingbroke, here triumphant in the very process of creating for itself the cause of future tragedy. That realism, meanwhile, takes control in Northumberland's sharp comment,

> Well have you argued, sir; and for your pains
> Of capital treason we arrest you here.   (150–51)

which Henry caps by summoning Richard himself and by pointing openly to the political ground of his whole proceeding:

> Fetch hither Richard, that in common view
> He may surrender; *so we shall proceed*
> *Without suspicion.*   (155–57)

Finally, Henry's realistic estimate of his position is made clear in his sharp admonition to the arrested lords:

    Little are we beholding to your love,
    And little looked for at your helping hands.   (160–61)

From the first moment, the new king is shrewdly aware of the unsure foundations upon which his power rests.

    The entry of Richard, stressing the note of treachery supremely associated, not for the first time, with the evocation of Judas, is characteristically poised between pathos and emptiness. His situation is genuinely pathetic, and the emotion stands out, up to a point, against the cold purposefulness that surrounds him; yet it is impossible not to feel that the comparison of the crown to a deep well in which two buckets alternately rise and fall is too shallow to carry the weight of feeling which the speaker desires to lay upon it. It is no accident that Richard's elaborate renunciation of rights already surrendered is set against his rival's plain insistence on the end in view:

    I thought you had been willing to resign.

  . . . .

    Are you contented to resign the crown?   (189, 199)

In Richard's attitude, complex and contradictory by comparison, the germs of many later Shakespearean developments can be discerned. Pathetic and yet too self-conscious to be entirely tragic, sincere and yet engaged in acting his own sincerity, possessed of true feeling and elaborately artificial in expressing it, Richard is the distant predecessor of more than one hero of the mature tragedies, who suffer in acute self-consciousness and whose tragedy expresses itself in terms that clearly point to the presence of the weakness that has been, in part, its cause.

    The utterances of the deposed king turn, indeed, not merely on natural grief, but on a sense of vanity—*nothingness*—which the very artificiality of its expression confirms and, paradoxically, deepens:

    Ay, no; no, ay: for I must *nothing* be.

  . . . .

    Make me, that *nothing* have, with *nothing* grieved,

And thou with all pleased, that hast all achieved.
Long may'st thou live in Richard's seat to sit,
And soon lie Richard in an earthy pit.   (200, 215–18)

We must feel here that the word nearest to the speaker's
heart is, after all his elaborations, *nothing*, and that his mood
issues in an intense craving for death; but the nothingness—
it must be added—is also reflected, in the last analysis, in
Bolingbroke's absorbing pursuit of power. Richard's attitude to political responsibility is, of course, extreme, in a
sense self-indulgent; but it is also relevant, and not least
to the usurper who is now, with little but devices of policy
in his mind, replacing him on the throne. *Nothing, nothing*:
in the long run any relevant political conception will have
to face the challenge implied in that word, and confirmed
by the behavior shown in this play. As we read these elaborate expressions of feeling, we realize that the intricate
rhetorical devices of the earlier plays and of Shakespeare's
contemporaries are in the process of being turned, definitely
though still without complete consciousness, into an instrument for the simultaneous expression of different aspects of
reality.

The accusation of Richard by Northumberland, which now
follows, emphasizes the royal tragedy rather than the personal disaster. Having abdicated, he has drawn upon himself
sympathy; isolated and helpless, he appears less as the self-
indulgent monarch than as the victim of a betrayal which his
failings cannot excuse. To his final, exhausted "What more
remains?" there corresponds, however, not pity, but the re-
morseless persecution of the accusation against him:

                No more, but that you read
These accusations, and these grievous crimes,   (221–22)

followed by an admission that the real end of this proceeding is to justify the usurper in the eyes of the world:

    That by confessing them, the souls of men
    May deem that you are worthily deposed.   (225–26)

Surrounded by this ruthless calculation, Richard's weakness becomes subsidiary to his tragedy as king deposed; his reply to Northumberland raises to a fresh level of poignancy the Christian reference which, more especially from now on, runs as a principal thread of feeling through the tragedy:

> Nay, all of you that stand and look upon me,
> Whilst that my wretchedness doth bait myself,
> Though some of you, with Pilate, wash your hands,
> Showing an outward pity: yet you Pilates
> Have here delivered me to my sour cross,
> And water cannot wash away your sin.   (236–41)

Our reaction to this is necessarily double. Richard is still exhibiting his emotions, playing with feelings the seriousness of which we cannot, in view of his weakness and consequent responsibility for his state, fully accept; and yet the betrayal, based on the calculation that everywhere surrounds him, is indefensible and its effect deepened by the fact that it is a king whom his subjects, sworn to loyalty, are deserting.

Richard himself is not without insight in his misfortunes. When he says, in reply to Northumberland's pitiless "My lord, dispatch, read o'er these articles,"

> Mine eyes are full of tears, I cannot see:
> And yet salt water blinds them not so much,
> But they can see a sort of traitors here.   (243–45)

the play with images cannot cover the fact that a truth is being expressed. It is the tragedy of betrayal, as well as that of fallen royalty, that is being enacted round his person; and the treachery, moreover, is doubly personal because Richard, by his past irresponsibility, has betrayed himself before he was in turn betrayed:

> Nay, if I turn mine eyes upon myself,
> I find myself a traitor with the rest.   (246–47)

Richard has betrayed the office which he has unworthily
held, and the betrayal has bred treachery around him. Bolingbroke, in due course, will prove to be similarly divided between the political virtues that are his to a degree never
possessed by Richard, and a desire for power which is omi-
nously shared by the court of time-serving and ambitious
lords who accompany his rise to authority. The conception,
in all its possible variety, is only sketched and faintly indicated here; but the whole series of following plays will be
largely occupied with exploring it.

Beneath the conventionality of Richard's expression at this
stage lies, indeed, a genuine effort to define his relation to the
tragic course of events. This culminates in his request for a
looking glass, in which once more artificiality, conscious self-
exhibition, and true self-exploration are typically blended.
Henry, now secure master of the situation, contemptuously
accedes to the latest emotional trick of his victim, whilst
Northumberland, as ever, ruthlessly presses the charge:

Read o'er this paper while the glass doth come,   (268)

and stresses the political motive behind his disapproval of
his master's careless concession:

The Commons will not then be satisfied.   (271)

When the mirror is at last brought, Richard contemplates his
features with a kind of tragic self-analysis. This opens, as he
breaks the glass, in a typically artificial statement: "How
soon my sorrow hath destroyed my face" (290); but the
comment offered by Bolingbroke points to a deeper contrast
between shadow and reality, which is not without tragic
content:

The shadow of your sorrow hath destroyed
The shadow of your face.   (291–92)

This in turn produces from Richard, beyond the play on the
related concepts of "shadow," "sun," and "substance," an
indication of the deeper roots of his tragedy:

> Say that again.
> "The shadow of my sorrow"? Ha, let's see.
> 'Tis very true, my grief lies all within,
> And these external manners of laments
> Are merely shadows to the unseen grief
> That swells with silence in the tortured soul.
> There lies the substance. (292–98)

One can trace in Shakespeare a process by which literary artifice, expanding in complexity and psychological correspondence, becomes an instrument of self-analysis; and the person of Richard, as revealed here, represents an important stage in this process. The outer forms of grief are "shadows" of the "substance" within, in Richard as they will later be in Hamlet; between the tragic content of the two characters there is, of course, no comparison, but a process of development may possibly be traced by which the literary artifice of the one is transformed into the true complexity of the other. Once more, the later plays in the series will throw light upon the nature of this transformation. For the moment, Richard's expression of tragedy leads to the final breakdown which accompanies his request for "leave to go"

> Whither you will, so I were from your sights, (314)

in which the measureless bitterness of his situation is simply expressed.

By the opening of the last act, the central dramatic contrast has been fully developed, and the result, as the action moves towards its foreseen conclusion, is a certain drop in tension. To Richard in his decline, the felicity he formerly enjoyed appears as a "dream" from which he has now awakened to "the truth of what we are":

> A king of beasts indeed: if aught but beasts,
> I had been still a happy king of men. (5.1.35–36)

These meditations are interrupted once more by the entry of stern reality, in the form of Northumberland, who arrives to

convey the deposed king to Pomfret. Richard's reaction,
prophetic in tone, is linked with the later development of the
series:

> The time shall not be many hours of age
> More than it is, ere foul sin, gathering head,
> Shall break into corruption. Thou shalt think,
> Though he divide the realm and give thee half,
> It is too little, helping him to all;
> He shall think that thou which knowest the way
> To plant unrightful kings, wilt know again,
> Being ne'er so little urged another way,
> To pluck him headlong from the usurped throne.   (57–65)

Here, at last, Richard penetrates to a vision of the pitiless
nature of political processes in the world of "beasts" to which
he has become, too late, alive. The action in *Henry IV*—the
counterplay of intrigue between powers haunted by past
guilt in the form of a trustless present—is here foreshad-
owed. Henry, having taught his associates to overthrow a
king, will always fear that the lesson may be turned against
himself; and his friends, in turn, will at once anticipate the
consequences against themselves of this fear, and crave to
extend the power which they have so precariously won. After this prophecy which Northumberland grimly accepts—
"My guilt be on my head, and there an end" (69)—the final
parting of Richard and his queen is a thin, artificial affair
which leads us, however, further along the road of the foreseen tragedy.

The following scene, in the Duke of York's palace, points
equally to the inevitable conclusion. York's account of the
contrasted entries into London of Bolingbroke and Richard
stresses, on the one hand, the former's politic submission to
the populace—

> he, from the one side to the other turning,
> Bareheaded, lower than his proud steed's neck,
> Bespake them thus: "I thank you, countrymen"   (5.2.18–20)

—and, on the other, the desertion of Richard, on whose "*sa-*

cred head" dust was thrown, and in the reference to whose "gentle sorrow," "grief and patience," we may perhaps see that echo of the Christian passion which, whilst never applicable to the person of the victim, seems none the less present in Shakespeare's treatment of the betrayed king. The suggestion has already been implied in Richard's own references to Judas; but as his tragedy moves from the realm of sentiment toward a dreadful reality, so does it gather emotional force. We are moving into a harsh world of political realities, in which conscience and human feeling have small place: the world to which York refers when he says:

> But heaven hath a hand in these events,
> To whose high will we bound our calm contents.
> To Bolingbroke are we sworn subjects now.   (37–39)

The mood is one of fatalism rather than of acceptance, of subjection to events rather than of a true concordance with them; but whether the issues which "heaven" will bring to birth are propitious or otherwise, time alone will show. Meanwhile, the first sign of the new order, developed in a spirit that recalls the conscious formalism of the *Henry VI* plays, is York's readiness to impeach his son for treason to his new master. Sweeping aside his wife's plea, and apparently unmoved by the prospect of being left heirless, he is ready to sacrifice his own blood for a usurper who has only used him as an instrument and who will from now on distrust him as a possible rival. Fear is the mainspring of his action, as it is a sign of the new order; it is as though Richard's recent prophecy were already on the way to becoming reality.

The reappearance of the new king (5.3), with his suggestion that his son is a "plague" hanging over him in punishment for sin, also introduces a theme prominent in later plays. It is not, however, developed, nor is the mention of the "sparks of better hope" also seen by his father in Hal's behavior. The cynicism of the dissolute prince's attitude to the Oxford jousts is, as Percy describes it, not without meaning:

> His answer was, he would unto the stews,
> And from the commonest creature pluck a glove,
> And wear it as a favor, and with that
> He would unhorse the lustiest challenger.   (16–19)

This, perhaps, is more significant than may appear. The Prince's reaction is at once an assertion of his own degradation, and a sardonic comment on the decorative but empty tournament world which the events of this play have so effectively shattered. Besides the obvious show of dissolution in Henry's son, the report implies a repudiation of verbal dignities in a world in which the most venerable concepts— including that of "honor" itself—are becoming subject to compromise: a world of chivalry already in decay under Richard and finally killed by his rival's accession. The Prince will, in due course, make the best of the new order of unprejudiced realism, more limited and less artificial than its predecessor, into which he is born; his activities, in the next play, in the taverns and streets of London will testify at once to the baseness around him, in which he participates, and to the greater breadth and firmness, when compared with Richard and even with Hotspur, of his contacts with life.

All this, however, belongs to the future, and the main action is conducted, in the meantime, on a perfunctory level, as in the following contest between York and his duchess for his son's life. On this, indeed, Henry seems to say the last word with his brief:

> Our scene is alt'red from a serious thing,
> And now changed to "The Beggar and the King,"   (78–79)

where the incredible theatrical effect is surely placed. The whole of this part of the play suggests that the author's interest in his creation, temporarily exhausted after the presentation of contrasted orders and personalities, was now flagging.

Richard's last long speech (5.5) returns to, and in some sense sums up, the personal tragedy now being wound up against the growing somberness and disintegration of which he has been at once the cause and the victim. Like so much else in this play, it gives a peculiar impression of convention shading almost imperceptibly into a sustained attempt at self-analysis and the expression of true feeling. The opening parallel,

> I have been studying how I may compare
> This prison where I live unto the world, (1–2)

is thoroughly artificial; the rhythm falls to an accustomed beat, and the succession of ideas is rather mechanical than revealing. The reference to the Christian axioms, which follows, though it has parallels in the play, is scarcely less abstract; the general impression is of aphoristic wisdom using familiar illustrations—the prisoner in the stocks, the actor on the stage—to point an attitude which strikes us less as a tragic reflection than as an academic exercise in poetic pessimism. Only as the speech moves to its climax is a deeper note attained, a more felt reference to a universal human situation touched upon, when Richard returns to the idea of *nothing* which has been so persistently present as a background, expressed and implied, to his thoughts:

> whate'er I be,
> Nor I, nor any man that but man is,
> With nothing shall be pleased, till he be eased
> With being nothing. (38–41)

Here, at least, in the balance of "any man that but man is," followed by the echo of "pleased" and "eased," and the opposition of "nothing" to "nothing," is a serious attempt to make expression respond to feeling, in something like a tragic statement about life. It is noteworthy, moreover, that this increase in depth is immediately followed, most improbably in terms of realism, by the playing of "music," in what we may consider a first dim indication of one of the mature Shakespearean symbols. The harmony, suitably contradictory in its effects, like the speaker's thoughts—

> How sour sweet music is
> When time is broke, and no proportion kept; (42–43)

resolves itself, in an attempt at more subtle analysis, into a
complicated parallel:

> here have I the daintiness of ear
> To check time broke in a disordered string,
> But for the concord of my state and time,
> Had not an ear to hear my true time broke.   (45–48)

Beneath the artificial balance of the phrasing, the speaker
is at least attempting to make a valid statement of his condition, and in the observation which follows—"I wasted
time, and now doth Time waste me" (49)—he almost suc-
ceeds. Even the elaborate expression has a certain justifica-
tion in terms of character, as the utterance of one who has
habitually *acted* on his royal stage, observed, as it were, the
effect of his attitudes with an eye to public effect and personal gratification:

> Thus play I in one person many people,
> And none contented.   (31–32)

The devices of this speech, to be fully convincing, would
need to be filled out with personal experience to a degree
never here attained; but, imperfect as it is, the meditation
does foreshadow later developments in the presentation of
the tragic hero. Certainly, the murder which follows is, by
comparison, no more than a pedestrian piece of melodra-
matic writing. Perhaps Richard's last individual word is
spoken in the bitter comment to the Groom on the value of
human titles and honors: "The cheapest of us is ten groats
too dear" (68). This is at once legitimate comment and the
confirmation of a character, the evaluation of an inhuman
political situation and the expression of a king who has always tended to find in an effective show of cynicism a
refuge from the collapse of his self-indulgent sentiments.

The final scene (5.6) rounds off the play in a mood of
foreboding and the anticipation of thwarted purposes. Already it is clear that Bolingbroke's crime, tacitly admitted as
such, will bring neither personal nor political peace. The

"latest news," announced by his own mouth, is that the "rebels"—not now his own supporters, but those who have in turn risen against his usurped power—have "consumed with fire" the town of Cirencester. On all sides, executions respond to renewed civil strife; the heads of numerous "traitors"—so called by him who has just ceased to be such—are on their way to London, and the spiritual power, henceforth to be increasingly involved in political intrigues, is curtailed by the death of the Abbot of Westminster and by the banishment of Carlisle, in whom Henry himself recognizes the presence of virtue:

> High sparks of honor in thee have I seen. (29)

Upon this catalogue of mischance and cross-purposes the murderers of Richard enter with his body, not to be commended for their "deed of slander," but yet to pin bluntly upon their master the guilt to which he himself admits:

> *Exton.* From your own mouth, my lord, did I this deed.

> *Bolingbroke.* They love not poison that do poison need,
>   Nor do I thee; though I did wish him dead,
>   I hate the murderer, love him murderèd. (37–40)

Beneath the careful balance of the phrasing, the presence of "the guilt of conscience" is firmly asserted in the new king, and his last words announce the intention, which will accompany him as an unfulfilled aspiration to his death, to redeem this "guilt" by a spiritual enterprise in "the Holy Land." This aspiration, the failure to fulfill it, and its transformation into a more limited political purpose, are the themes of the plays to follow.

S. SCHOENBAUM

Richard II and the Realities of Power

The most celebrated revival of *Richard II* was that
mounted by the Lord Chamberlain's men at the Globe Theatre on Saturday, February 7, 1601. The circumstances are
described by Augustine Phillips, the actor who bore Shakespeare such affectionate regard that he bequeathed to him a
thirty-shilling piece of gold. According to Phillips, some
half-dozen men of position in the land—including the Per-
cies (Sir Charles and Sir Jocelyn) and Lord Monteagle—
had approached the players, offering them a reward of forty
shillings "to have the play of the deposyng and kyllyng of
Kyng Rychard the second to be played the Saterday next."[1]
The actors hesitated, "holdyng that play to be so old and so
long out of vse as they shold have small or no Company at
yt," but in the end they consented. The purpose of the revival, as we all know, was to further sedition. At noon that
Saturday the conspirators met for dinner, and afterward re-
paired to the playhouse, where they applauded the downfall
and murder of a king. "So earnest hee was," Francis Bacon
said of one, Sir Gilly Meyrick, "to satisfie his eyes with the
sight of that tragedie which hee thought soone after his lord
should bring from the stage to the state, but that God turned
it vpon their owne heads." Meyrick was steward to the Earl
of Essex. On Sunday the attempted coup took place. Shakespeare's troupe collected their two pounds. Essex and others
were tried and executed. On the eve of the Earl's beheading,
the Lord Chamberlain's men acted before the Queen at

This is the second half of an article reprinted from *Shakespeare Survey* 28
(1975) by permission of Cambridge University Press and the author.
[1] E. K. Chambers, *William Shakespeare* (II.27) conveniently prints extracts
from the principal documents.

Whitehall. We do not know which play; presumably not *Richard II*.

Most authorities agree that the performance bespoken by the conspirators was of Shakespeare's *Richard II*. It is not unusual to find this information given as a fact. We do well, however, to recognize that we are dealing not with a fact but an inference. Neither Phillips nor anyone else interviewed at the time mentions Shakespeare's name in connection with the event. Prosecutor Coke muddies the waters slightly when he speaks of "the story of Henry IV being set forth in a play," but as Bolingbroke becomes king before the end of *Richard II*, that is accountable. There is, of course, no reason why there should not have been other plays on this interesting theme which, like the one seen by Forman, failed to achieve print: and the designation of the one acted on February 7 as "old" opens up the whole vista of Elizabethan theatrical history. But the company in this instance was Shakespeare's, Phillips's description suits Shakespeare's *Richard II*, and no alternative possibility presents itself for consideration. So in what follows I shall assume the "old" *Richard II* wheeled out for the Essex *putsch* was by Shakespeare, while not claiming more than that this is a plausible assumption.

To do so disposes of one problem only to raise another. Why *Richard II*? After all, the play hardly comes across as an inflammatory tract in favour of deposition and regicide. Richard in his sufferings is too sympathetic, and ultimately (at Pomfret Castle) heroic, while Bolingbroke in his triumph is too ambiguous. It seems an odd choice to rouse the rabble. Scholarly unease is understandable. "I do not know the answer to the riddle," Lily B. Campbell confesses, and to Irving Ribner "Shakespeare's relation to the Essex rebellion remains a puzzling problem which has yet to be satisfactorily settled."[2]

This may be so, but we do well to bear in mind that the revival in fact failed to kindle seditious sparks; if such was the conspirators' intention, it was one of many miscalculations.

[2] L. B. Campbell, *Shakespeare's "Histories": Mirrors of Elizabethan Policy* (1947), pp. 211–12; Ribner, *English History Play* (1965), p. 155n.

More likely, perhaps, that they were thinking of themselves rather than of the multitude, and sought by reviving a play about a successful deposition to buoy up their own spirits on the eve of the desperate adventure.

Yet might there not be another dimension, perilous to ignore and even more perilous to face? Many critics have fancied Shakespeare as moving about comfortably in the corridors of power, playfully taking the mickey out of the Sir Walter Raleigh set in *Love's Labor's Lost*, concocting a suitable wedding entertainment for the dowager Countess of Southampton with *A Midsummer Night's Dream*, or advising King James on the respective merits of mercy and justice in *Measure for Measure*. The list might be extended, and there are recent additions. Such speculations, showing Shakespeare hobnobbing with the mighty, represent what might be described as the Richard Ryan syndrome in Shakespeare studies. In his *Dramatic Table Talk* (in 1825), Ryan recorded the anecdote of Queen Elizabeth trying to catch Shakespeare's eye while he was acting at the playhouse, and resorting to the timeworn female ruse of dropping her glove; her favorite (we are told) picked it up and presented it to her, but not without first declaiming, "And though now bent on this high embassy,/Yet *stoop* we to take up our Cousin's glove!" It is not what one would describe as a very probable story. The Ryan syndrome is nevertheless very prominent in Shakespeare studies; it has enlisted some choice spirits, and has illuminated the contexts for the plays if not always the plays themselves. Now Professor Richard Levin in several essays has been casting a cold eye on the whole phenomenon, to which he gives the term "occasionalism." Sceptical reappraisal along these lines is long overdue, and we do well to pay heed to Professor Levin's home truths.

But what of *Richard II*, which was used in Shakespeare's own day as a move in a power struggle? Here the connection is direct, not fancied. Might not Richard's reign (in the dramatist's conception) stand in an analogical relation to Elizabeth's reign, and animadvert obliquely—as censorship enforced—on actual persons and events? Of course the trouble with oblique commentaries is that they are oblique;

we may miss what is there and find what is not. To his *Dictionary of National Biography* biographer the content of the Elizabethan historian John Hayward's *Life and Reign of King Henry IV* looks innocent enough of veiled allusiveness, and even a contemporary, Chamberlain, wondered what all the fuss was about.

Such considerations serve only to whet pursuit, and the trail, in truth, is not an utter blank. "I am Richard II, know ye not that?" the Queen declared in Lambarde's presence, and she was not the first to make the comparison. As early as 1578 Sir Francis Knollys complained to Elizabeth's secretary that the Queen persisted in misliking safe counsel— in such circumstances "who woll not rather shrynkingly . . . play the partes of King Richard the Second's men, than to enter into the odious office of crossing of her Majesties' wylle?" (To be one of Richard's men is to be a sycophant; there are other such references.) Knollys was related to the Queen, and also the grandfather of the Earl of Essex. The latter traced his descent from Anne, daughter of Thomas of Woodstock, the Duke of Gloucester, sixth son of Edward III— the same Thomas of Woodstock who had his life snuffed out at Calais by Richard's command. And were not Elizabeth's hands, like Richard's, stained with "guilt of kindred blood"? "The slaying of kindred here (i.e. in *Richard II*) . . . was probably intended to remind Elizabethans of the execution of Mary, Queen of Scots." This suggestion was made almost half a century ago, by Evelyn May Albright, in what remains the most elaborate investigation of the Richard-Elizabeth analogy in relation to the play put on for the Essex conspiracy.[3] Miss Albright further notes that complaints about the influence of favorites, about oppressive taxes, and about the exaction of benevolences—all made in Shakespeare's *Richard II*—find their parallels in agitation about Elizabeth's government. There is even a passing reference to "the prevention of poor Bolingbroke/About his marriage"; and we all know how Elizabeth meddled in marriages. From

[3] Evelyn May Albright, "Shakespeare's *Richard II* and the Essex Conspiracy," *PMLA* XLII (1927): 686–720. Her essay drew a rejoinder from Ray Heffner, *PMLA* XLV (1930): 754–80. Undaunted, she replied in *PMLA* XLVI (1931): 694–719.

such hints it is but an easy leap to interpreting York's speech in Act 2, Scene 1—the speech about the consequences of Richard's seizure of "The royalties and rights of banish'd Hereford"—as "a warning to Elizabeth" concerning "a popular favorite whom she is treating badly, and whose family also have been unfairly dealt with." And who might that favorite be other than Essex?

This is heady stuff for which some evidence, besides the detection of covert allusions in Shakespeare's text, would be welcome. Such evidence has been offered in the form of Hayward's history of Henry IV, to which I have already referred. His book was published with a brief Latin dedication to Essex, in which the latter is extolled as the expectancy and rose of the fair state. Hayward's title is a misnomer, presumably prudential, for his history deals mostly with Richard's reign, not Henry's. That the work deliberately exploited the Elizabeth-Richard analogy was widely believed at the time; we hear of this "seditious pamphlet" and "treasonable book." "He selecteth a storie 200 yere old," noted Sir Edward Coke, "and publisheth it this last yere; intending the application of it to this tyme."[4]

Elizabeth, outraged, wanted Hayward executed, and were it not for Bacon's discreet intervention, he probably would have been. As it was, not until after Elizabeth's death was Hayward released from prison to assemble the prayers and meditations of the enlarged *Sanctuary of a Troubled Soul.* Shakespeare and his fellows do not seem to have got into any trouble at all, which is odd if he was up to mischief similar to that for which Hayward was tried. Never mind; perhaps some neutral party, high up, intervened to get Shakespeare off the hook. Such a party has lately been suggested in the person of the Keeper of the Rolls; the same William Lambarde to whom Elizabeth made her famous protestation.[5]

What remains is to demonstrate that Hayward's *Henry IV*

---

[4] Margaret Dowling prints Coke's notes on Hayward's *Henry IV* in an important article, "Sir John Hayward's Troubles over his *Life of Henry IV*," *The Library*, 4th ser., XI (1931): 212–24. For the passage cited, see p. 213.
[5] W. Nicholas Knight, *Shakespeare's Hidden Life: Shakespeare at the Law 1585–1595* (1973), p. 144.

was one of Shakespeare's sources when he came to write *Richard II*. We are shown parallels as regards general ideas, groupings of ideas, echoes of words and phrases, the characterization of Bolingbroke, and a couple of specific episodes (Henry's repudiation of Piers of Exton, and Aumerle's supposed duplicity with Richard at Flint Castle). Some of these hold interest. There is a problem, however, and that is that Hayward's *Life and Reign of King Henry IV* was first published in 1599; three or four years after Shakespeare composed his play. Such a fact might ordinarily be deemed awkward, but there is a way around it, and that is to posit that the history circulated in manuscript for some years before being printed, and that Shakespeare saw and used it. Otherwise we might be tempted to account for the parallels as Hayward's borrowings from Shakespeare. There is nothing like a hypothetical manuscript to resolve an awkwardness of chronology. Only in this case the awkwardness remains, for Hayward is on record as saying that he had begun "to write this history about a year before it was published, but had intended it a dozen years before, although he acquainted no man therewith."[6] One might reckon that such a statement would successfully discourage enthusiasm for the theory of Hayward's influence on Shakespeare, but this would be to underestimate scholarly ingenuity. In the phrase *although he acquainted no man therewith*, maybe *therewith* refers to the interval but not to Hayward's materials? I think not. Yet Ribner, in what is the standard study of the English history play in Shakespeare's age, can suggest that there is "some possibility" that Shakespeare saw Hayward's *Henry IV* in manuscript—a manuscript that did not then exist.

Nor, although properly wary, does Ribner rule out the Albright thesis altogether. During the past year somebody has written that "Shakespeare's connection with the Essex affair was all too obvious through his praise of the Earl in *Henry V* and his authorship of the deposition scene in *Richard II*," and he goes on to speak of Shakespeare's "partisanship" for Essex.[7] It is one of many odd statements in a curious book. How many innocent spectators, standing at a play and caught

---

[6] Quoted by Albright, *PMLA* XLVI (1931): 695.
[7] Knight, *Shakespeare's Hidden Life*, p. 143.

up in the great issues of the drama, would pause to reflect on Essex's descent from Gloucester's line, or apply passing references to abuses of Richard's rule to the politics of the moment? I don't see Shakespeare as a seditious playwright involved, however peripherally, in a conspiracy against his monarch, any more than I see him as a darling of the Court, a sort of minister without portfolio, sagely advising his Queen, and later his King, on how to manage the affairs of state. I expect that he had his hands full writing his plays, acting in them and in those of others, and as "housekeeper" advising his troupe about affairs in which we know he had a stake.

This is not to say that he failed to interest himself in the world of policy and power. That world was all around him. He found it chronicled in Plutarch and the Tudor historians. Machiavelli analyzed it. Perhaps Shakespeare glimpsed it, as an observant bystander, when his company performed at Court, or were called upon to fulfill some ceremonial function, as when they attended upon the new Spanish ambassador and his train at Somerset House in August 1604. These opportunities he seized upon, not for political advantage by insinuating himself into the affairs of state, but imaginatively, for the purposes of his art, in which we find depicted the world of policy and power. Here, behind the scenes of public confrontation, as likely as not another drama—concealed or only obliquely revealed—is going on. In that drama the issues may be graver than those overtly bandied about. Such moments show Shakespeare's sophisticated grasp of the workings of *Realpolitik*. So it is in *Richard II*, especially in the big public scenes of the first act.

"I cannot believe," Yeats wrote, "that Shakespeare looked on his Richard II with any but sympathetic eyes, understanding indeed how ill-fitted he was to be King, at a certain moment of history, but understanding that he was lovable and full of capricious fancy. . . ."[8] "What explains his failure to oppose Bolingbroke at all, his sudden collapse, as soon as

---

[8] William Butler Yeats, "At Stratford-on-Avon," *Ideas of Good and Evil* in *Collected Works* (1908), p. 123.

the threat of deposition becomes real, into a state of sheer elegy, of pure poetry?" asks Mark Van Doren. "The answer is simple. Richard is a poet, not a king."⁹ These views have much in common: they are expressed by poets with an understandable sympathy for poetical characters. But of course in a blank-verse play the characters, unless they be peasants, usually speak in numbers. Mainly criticism emphasizes Richard's weakness. The position has been lately put by Robert Ornstein. "The first scene of *Richard II* intimates the King's shallowness and weakness. . . ." Or: "Precisely why Richard chooses to halt the joust between Bolingbroke and Mowbray at the very last moment we do not know; but we recognize the characteristic theatricality of the gesture: here is the weakling's pleasure in commanding (and humiliating) men stronger than himself."¹⁰ Ornstein makes other remarks to the same effect, and together these restate, with more than usual eloquence and sensitivity, a dominant consensus. Now, one should very warily go about differing from views with widespread (even if less than universal) acceptance, for they are quite likely to be correct. So it is with some diffidence that I suggest that in Act 1, in the council chamber at Windsor and at the lists in Coventry, Richard displays as much political acumen as weakness, that his behavior is not capricious but calculated, and that he does not fail but achieves a success necessarily limited by the realities of his situation.¹¹

It is no use trying to evaluate a man's strength or weakness without reference to the circumstances that determine the options he can exercise. Richard may prattle about Divine Right, but in his world power is wielded not divinely, but by men, those men in whose presence Richard goes through the rhetoric of public gestures. In the first scene Richard's maneuverability is limited by an episode from his

⁹ Mark Van Doren, *Shakespeare* (1939), p. 89.

¹⁰ Robert Ornstein, *Kingdom for a Stage* (1972), p. 110.

¹¹ A view of these scenes very similar to my own is taken by Moody E. Prior in *The Drama of Power* (1973). Prior's whole carefully considered discussion, which expresses what is still a minority view, should be read. In another recent contribution, *Shakespeare Survey* 27 (1974): 33–41, Lois Potter interestingly observes how in *Richard II* rhetorically elaborated language is associated with powerlessness, and brevity with strength: and how in the early scenes it is Richard (not Bolingbroke) who displays terseness.

past which has come back to haunt him. The past, whether
in the form of an untoward incident on the road to Thebes or
indiscreet conversations in the illusory privacy of the Oval
Office, has a way of doing just that to men of exalted sta-
tion. The problem for Richard, lovable poet and weakling, is
that he is responsible for the murder of his uncle Gloucester,
and everybody knows it. This fact Shakespeare chooses to
treat indirectly, as befits the evasions of power struggles.
Although Richard's embarrassment affects the conduct of
all the principals, they remain silent on this score; it is rather
as though the dramatist expected his audience to have made
mental notes of *Woodstock*. No outside source is required
once we get to Act 1, Scene 2, however, for there we have
Gaunt referring, in the presence of Gloucester's widow, to
correction lying "in those hands/Which made the fault that
we cannot correct" (4–5), and some lines later he declares:

> God's is the quarrel; for God's substitute,
> His deputy anointed in His sight,
> Hath caused his death,   (37–39)

This is plain enough about where the guilt resides, and
should enforce retrospective revaluation of the preceding
scene. It is extraordinary how many have failed to do so.

Well, in a way not so extraordinary. There is much to dis-
tract us at Windsor, and a little later at Coventry. The King
sits in state with his nobles, attendants come on in armor,
there are horses—or, as in the recent notable production by
the Royal Shakespeare Company, hobbyhorses—on which
much of the whole action takes place. Horses on the stage
are a great distraction. But however we look at it, and however these scenes are staged, the pageantry of the chivalric
tournament—for all the world like events depicted on a medieval tapestry—will leave a powerful impression.[12] Few
producers can resist the temptation to make the most of the
spectacle, and Shakespeare, dedicated professional that he

---

[12] The "medievalism" of *Richard II* can, however, be overstressed; Nicholas
Brooke is surely right when he suggests: "The politics of the play were clearly con-
temporaneous; the jousting was Elizabethan; and the figure of Richard is far more
significant to the play than a mere image of medieval man" (*Shakespeare's Early
Tragedies*, 1968, p. 109). Brooke has a number of acute things to say about the play.

was, has set it up that way. Nor does the declamatory mode, with its high-flown rhetoric of subterfuge, make matters easier.

Despite the rhetoric, Richard is understandably nervous. When Bolingbroke and Mowbray greet their sovereign with fulsome wishes for many happy days, indeed years, he reacts suspiciously: "We thank you both; yet one but flatters us. . . ." (1.1.25) He will not in fact be granted many happy days. In this scene Bolingbroke levels several charges against Mowbray, but the heart of the matter is the death of Gloucester, whose blood,

> like sacrificing Abel's, cries
> Even from the tongueless caverns of the earth
> To me for justice and rough chastisement.   (104–6)

Why to Bolingbroke in particular? As the Abel reference suggests, because he is Gloucester's kin. But Richard is equally Gloucester's nephew, and moreover the chief guardian of justice in the realm. Yet he isn't calling out for any chastisement, for reasons of which everyone present is aware.

Mowbray defends himself as best he can. "For Gloucester's death," he declares, "I slew him not, but, to my own disgrace,/Neglected my sworn duty in that case" (132–34). This is obscure, and deliberately so. What is he saying? He did not kill Gloucester with his own hands—"slew him not"—but had others do the dirty work for him? What was his neglect of sworn duty? His responsibility for a royal life, A. P. Rossiter suggests, citing *Woodstock*: "that allegiance/ Thou ow'st the offspring of King Edward's house," as Woodstock puts it to Mowbray's counterpart in the anonymous play. Or was Mowbray's neglect his delay in performing the King's command? His dilatoriness, according to Holinshed, gave Richard "no small displeasure."

Bolingbroke's challenge, ostensibly directed against Mowbray, equally levels at the King. Unsurprisingly, Richard would like to forget about the whole thing as soon as possible, and so he tries to reconcile challenger and challenged. But matters have passed beyond the point of no return, under the circumstances a commission to investigate

the charges is out of the question, and so the King sets
up the trial by combat. In Act 1, Scene 3, we go through the
full panoply of chivalric ceremony, until Richard casts his
warder down. There follows the council session with its ver-
dict of a ten-year exile for Bolingbroke and lifetime banishment for Mowbray. Cunningly, Richard makes these proud
men, seemingly so hopelessly at odds with one another,
swear never to patch up their differences,

> Nor never by advisèd purpose meet
> To plot, contrive, or complot any ill
> 'Gainst us, our state, our subjects, or our land.   (188–90)

Bolingbroke's sentence is then reduced by four years.

This episode has generally been viewed as demonstrating
Richard's vacillation and caprice: more prone to poetry than
rule, the irresolute King falteringly exercises his authority. I
believe, instead, that Richard brilliantly demonstrates his
political skill under conditions of grave disadvantage. At a
single stroke he manages to rid himself of two embarrass-
ments: his aggressive cousin Bolingbroke, who represents a
direct threat, and Mowbray, to whom he owes too much and
who has outlived his usefulness. Had the joust taken place,
and Bolingbroke triumphed, he would be still more dangerous. If, on the other hand, Mowbray came out on top, he
would have an even greater hold on his monarch; the continuing presence of such men is rarely coveted. But why is
Bolingbroke, less beloved, given the lighter sentence? One
senses Richard's need to placate his court. Gaunt in particular is uneasy, although (we learn) he has consented to the
King's plan during the council we have seen represented by
condensed stage time. In his book on *Shakespeare's Historical Plays* Sen Gupta suggests that it is out of pity for Gaunt,
"and not with an eye to the public . . . that King Richard
reduces Bolingbroke's banishment from ten years to six."[13]
But Richard has little room for pity in this steely scene, and
sentimental regard for Gaunt is later conspicuously absent

---

[13] S. C. Sen Gupta, *Shakespeare's Historical Plays* (1964), p. 116.

during the deathbed interview. The seeming clemency of the reduced sentence is a gesture of public magnanimity that costs Richard nothing—why worry about what will happen in six years?—but serves as a sop to Gaunt.

The King and his retinue depart; the scene closes. Later we see Richard in private conversation with his favorites. The masks are off. They mock "high Hereford," their speech contrasting with the fraudulent rhetoric of the public scenes that have preceded. The King can now be himself.

In this reading of Act 1 of *Richard II*, my aim has been to show that Shakespeare treats in a most sophisticated way the manipulation of power in a poker game where the stakes are exceedingly high. If Richard's triumph is short-lived, that is because he overplays his hand by confiscating Gaunt's estate immediately upon the Duke's death, a blunder that gives the wronged son a pretext for his return and direct confrontation with the King. It may be alleged that, even without his blunder, the King's maneuverings, however adroit, would have gained him only a temporary respite. Perhaps so, but that is speculation. It is, however, Richard's limitation that he never grasps the significance of Gloucester's death to his own tragedy.

The world with which I have been concerned—labyrinthine, remorselessly unsentimental, dangerous, and ego-centered—lurks everywhere in the Shakespeare canon. The power-seekers shrewdly ferret out the hidden points of vulnerability in their rivals, and work them over with the same impersonal cruelty as the prizefighter in the ring aiming his blows at his adversary's bleeding eye. They dissimulate. They develop sudden politic cravings for strawberries. They stage elaborate little theatricals in which, appropriately costumed, they themselves perform in a bid to manipulate opinion. A father, playing crafty-sick, withholds military support from his son, abandoning him to defeat and death on the battlefield. A commander gives up pursuit of the demoralized enemy because he is conscious that by outclassing his general he courts disfavor. A duke eloquently promotes a royal match in order to rule the Queen, and through her the King and the realm. A ragged multitude, headed by a peasant

with aristocratic pretensions, creates a savage spectacle in
the capital; the uprising seems spontaneous, but is in fact
manipulated from above by an ambitious peer in the expec-
tation that if his creature thrives he will "reap the harvest
which the rascal sowed." But the possible examples are almost limitless. No playwright in this period treats such
themes so often or with such complex variety.

Were I to choose an epigraph for my paper, it would be a
familiar one. "It is a strange desire, to seek power and to
lose liberty," Bacon wrote in his essay "Of Great Place": "or
to seek power over others and to lose power over a man's
self. The rising unto place is laborious; and by pains men
come to greater pains; and it is sometimes base; and by in-
dignities man comes to dignities. The standing is slippery,
and the regress is either a downfall, or at least an eclipse,
which is a melancholy thing." From Bacon we expect such
hard-won wisdom, but we are perhaps less prepared to find
it so pervasively present in gentle Shakespeare. I am conscious that by these remarks I am placing myself in a vul-
nerable position, as I am only too well aware that I have but
scratched the surface of a complex topic by treating it repre-
sentatively. Still, there may be something to be said for
adding another Shakespeare to the list. The psychoanalysts
have had a go at him; the Marxists too. Criticism has given
us (amongst others) Shakespeare the practical professional,
Shakespeare the theater poet, Shakespeare the mythmaker,
and Shakespeare the Christian gentleman. He also wandered
imaginatively in the corridors of power, and what he recorded of the behavior of men in those treacherous environs
enables us to speak of Shakespeare the politic realist.

GRAHAM HOLDERNESS

The Women

In one of the key scenes of the play, King Richard marks his departure from the stage by speaking, almost as an afterthought, to his Queen Isabel:

> *King Richard.* Come on, our queen, tomorrow must we part;
> Be merry, for our time of stay is short. (2.1.222–23)

A reader of the printed play text (as distinct from the spectator of a performance) could be forgiven for wondering, at least momentarily, where this queen came from. Only saying a brief sentence herself, she has not been spoken or even referred to in the course of the 150 or so lines during which she occupies the stage. It is actually necessary to look back to the stage direction which announces the arrival of the king (at line 68) to see that the queen enters with the king and a group of nobles. For the reader of the play (whose attention is necessarily focused on those characters who manifest their presence in speech), a self-effacing character, who is also ignored by everyone else in the room, simply does not exist. In a stage production, of course, things are different. The text calls for the queen to be physically, visibly present among the king's entourage, and her passive presence could actually be made quite significant. But when deciding what to do with the queen, actors and directors are left entirely to their own devices, reliant on the resources of their own imaginations; the verbal text itself has nothing whatsoever to say about the strange, virtually silent presence of Queen Isabel.

From Graham Holderness, *William Shakespeare: "Richard II"* (Penguin Critical Studies, 1989), pp. 75–85. Copyright © Graham Holderness, 1989. Used by permission of the publisher.

Act 2.1 involves eleven characters, only one of whom—the queen—is female. That disproportionate marginalization of the female population is typical of this play as a whole. Only five female characters, which includes the ladies attending Queen Isabel in the garden scene, appear in a cast of over thirty identified parts (not counting various supernumerary servants, attendants and soldiers, who are also overwhelmingly male). These are the Duchess of Gloucester, who appears only in 1.2 (her death is then reported in 2.2, line 97); the Duchess of York, who appears only in 5.2 and 3; and the queen, who appears in three scenes—2.2, 3.4, 5.1—in addition to her presence in 2.1.

Now a number of common-sense arguments naturally present themselves to suggest that there is really nothing remarkable in this. There is never more than a handful of female parts in any of Shakespeare's plays, a fact obviously connected with the Elizabethan practice of using boys to play the roles of women. *Richard II* is a history play, and Elizabethan history plays were drawn from historical writings which did not particularly emphasize the presence or agency of women in history: history was largely thought of as an account of the actions of men. Lastly, this particular historical drama deals with the kind of political and military crises which necessarily excluded women from active participation: political struggles, trials by combat, military campaigns. That exclusion of women from the decisive and determinant activities of a society is something we would naturally, from the perspective of modern ideas, decry. But it is a historical injustice for which we can hardly blame Shakespeare. In the historical story of the deposition of Richard II, the playwright found no remarkable or influential women, so that absence was duly and dutifully reflected in the play.

A moment's consideration will reveal that all these apparently "common-sense" arguments are extremely suspect. It is a fact that only a small number of female roles is to be found in Elizabethan plays. But the women characters who occupy those roles usually have a disproportionate influence within the world of the play: Viola, Rosalind, Portia, Cordelia, Desdemona, Lady Macbeth. It is often even the case that they show strengths and abilities, kinds of determination and resourcefulness, not displayed by their menfolk. As we witness Portia dominating and winning Antonio's trial in *The Merchant of Venice*, or Cordelia leading an army in *King Lear*, or Lady Macbeth returning to the murdered Duncan's chamber in *Macbeth*, we are unlikely to derive from Shakespeare's plays any simple notion of women as "the weaker sex." This is certainly not the case in *Richard II*, where the queen is a pathetic melancholy spectator of her husband's downfall.

As we have seen, the Elizabethan dramatist's relationship with his historical sources was not a passive and automatic subservience. Although the Tudor period saw the emergence of a modern conception of historical "fact" (Samuel Daniel, author of a long poem about the Wars of the Roses which Shakespeare seems to have used, carefully distinguished between authentic historical fact and imaginative fiction), all the history plays of this period mingle fact with interpretation, historical authenticity with imaginative elaboration. When Shakespeare dramatized other periods of history in which women are described as significant figures, he gave them even more prominent roles—Joan of Arc and Queen Margaret in the *Henry VI* plays are obvious examples. After *Richard II* Shakespeare started to interpolate fictional comic subplots into the "factual" material of the chronicle drama, thus providing more space for the participation of women. In the *Henry IV* plays, women like the Hostess and Doll Tearsheet have active and important (if distinctly "low-life") roles to play. So Shakespeare was quite free to make more of Queen Isabel than the historical sources themselves warranted. In fact he did, since the young woman who appears in the play to express her unfocused melancholy, to complain of her husband's declining fortunes, and to lament his tragic overthrow, has no real historical authority at all. Isabel was a child of ten when these events occurred. Her passive role in the play is then, we might say, historically appropriate; her dramatic characterization is all Shakespeare's invention.

The third argument from "common sense," that the particular historical character of this action excludes the active agency of women in a particularly decisive and intractable way, has rather more force. It is one thing to invent an interesting dramatic character for Isabel: but if women in the fourteenth century did not (outside chivalric romances) take part in chivalric combats, Shakespeare could hardly clap his queen in armor and let her fight the king's battles for him. Those active and enterprising heroines who appear in other Shakespeare plays seem to belong to an age when a formidable "queen" showed herself capable (in a sense) of fighting her own battles, such as that against the Spanish Armada. They appear naturally sympathetic to our own later age in which the principle of female equality, though hardly universally attained, is at least generally accepted. Mowbray's words, and Isabel's character, belong rather to that post-feudal society of the late fourteenth century in which, according to the dominant systems of belief, men were warriors and women were a protected species.

It seems to me possible that the marginalization of women in a play like *Richard II* is not simply the symptomatic expression of an unconscious misogyny, or a passive reflection of predetermined historical conditions. It is rather a historical reality that the play foregrounds, interrogates and criticizes. Women may not be much in evidence in the play, but femininity is. Let us take a closer look at the scene with which we began (2.1), the scene of Isabel's strangely absent presence. As I noted above, Isabel appears there in a scene populated otherwise entirely by men. The problems and issues debated in the scene are specifically "masculine" preserves: politics, war, economics, law, property. Throughout the scene what the characters say about their specific situation carries with it wider dimensions of reference, so that other groups of people are continually being alluded to and moving into temporary focus. Again, these are all groups of men. Young men, sick men, dying men, living men, flattering courtiers, lawyers, Englishmen ("this happy breed"), Frenchmen, Irishmen, fathers, grandfathers, brothers, sons, uncles, kings, knights, commons, nobles, ancestors, "men of war." It would be hard to imagine a world more thoroughly cleared of any sign of the female gender.

Yet if we look a little closer, vestigial traces of femininity begin to surface: the repressed returns. John of Gaunt sings the praises of that "happy breed of men" (45) who under the strong government of warrior kings like Edward III had excelled in the conquest of other nations. Englishmen are famous for their strength, their military successes, their masculinity. But to describe a category of men, however unimpeachably manly, as a "breed," is to draw attention to the fact that somehow they must have been "bred," and therefore that members of the female sex must have played something more than a marginal role in the process. Gaunt also talks about "birth" (52), though there he is perhaps talking less about the biological process by which children are delivered than about the male-dominated dynastic system of lineage. More distinctively revealing are his references to England as a "nurse" and as a "teeming womb of royal kings" (51), metaphors which draw attention to the specifically female capacities of gestation and suckling. As Gaunt's celebration of the achievements of the English aristocracy extends to include the Crusades, he actually finds space to mention a woman's name:

> *Gaunt.* . . . this teeming womb of royal kings,
>   Feared by their breed, and famous by their birth,
>   Renownèd for their deeds as far from home,
>   For Christian service and true chivalry,
>   As is the sepulcher in stubborn Jewry
>   Of the world's ransom, blessed Mary's son.   (51–56)

The allusion to the Virgin Mary is perhaps representative of Gaunt's view of women. Whatever cults of worship may attach to Mary, her primary significance is the fact that she gave birth to a remarkable man, Jesus. In Gaunt's feudal and aristocratic perspective, women appear as the passive vehicles by means of which the patriarchal seed is procreated, the patrilineal dynasty secured. Even the femininity of his metaphorical "England" is ultimately spurious, since that maternal symbol is so completely a construction of the kings and warriors who have served their country in loyalty, fidelity and truth. Nonetheless, however strenuous Gaunt's efforts to suppress the reality of the feminine, it continues to appear, if only in the interstices of his metaphorical language. You cannot really talk about nurses and wombs and birth and breeding without bringing into play a feminine dimension of meaning. Once that meaning occupies a space inside the imaginative universe of the play, it proves remarkably hard to expel.

We will now examine the part played in the drama by its three principal female characters. All three are present in the play not in their own right, or because they have any distinctive individual contribution to make to the play's action, but in terms of their relationships with men. They are all, primarily and even exclusively, wives and mothers. The Duchess of Gloucester is there to lament and preserve the memory of her murdered husband. The Duchess of York is there to plead, successfully, for the life of Aumerle her son. Queen Isabel has literally nothing to do in the play except to feel sadness and pity for her husband.

The Duchess of Gloucester, though restricted like Isabel to a melancholy choric role, is nonetheless a formidable portrait of female assertiveness, which is however ultimately deflected and turned to self-destructive grief and melancholy. The qualities she displays are those which in the gender-divided world of this play seem the peculiar prerogative of men. She is a fierce defender of the aristocratic royal family also celebrated by Gaunt and York; she asserts the responsibilities of aristocratic pride and status; she hungers for direct and immediate blood-revenge to appease the injuries to her family; and she advocates a military resistance to Richard's tyranny.

> *Duchess of Gloucester.* That which in mean men we entitle
>   patience
>   Is pale cold cowardice in noble breasts.
>   What shall I say? To safeguard thine own life
>   The best way is to venge my Gloucester's death. (1.2.33–36)

But the Duchess's very strength and courage are self-denying, self-annihilating, since the noble family she idealizes, the dynasty of Edward III, consists entirely of men. The role of women in the composition of this dynasty is silently effaced, and they have no place or position in the family tree. The royal "blood" that privileges and sacralizes the aristocratic family is a peculiarly masculine substance: it can either be spilt by murder, or redeemed by blood-revenge. Christian patience is scornfully dismissed as the natural subjection of the common, the "mean" man; for the aristocratic subject, *noblesse oblige*—nobility carries obligations—and principal among those duties is the responsibility for avenging the death of a murdered kinsman.

The duchess seeks to persuade Gaunt to take revenge against Richard but Gaunt is committed to preserving the security of the crown, however much he may disapprove of the particular king who wears it. The duchess's hopes of revenge focus therefore on the possibility of Bolingbroke's emerging victorious from the combat with Mowbray. If Bolingbroke were to kill Mowbray, then a kinsman of Gloucester's would have succeeded in killing his murderer, and in casting a guilty shadow over the instigator of the murder, Richard himself. Revenge would be satisfied, her dead husband's ghost appeased.

> *Duchess of Gloucester.* O! sit my husband's wrongs on Hereford's spear,
>   That it may enter butcher Mowbray's breast;
>   Or if misfortune miss the first career,
>   Be Mowbray's sins so heavy in his bosom,
>   That they may break his foaming courser's back
>   And throw the rider headlong in the lists,
>   A caitiff recreant to my cousin Hereford.   (47–53)

Such militant violence of language proves the duchess capable of that hot-blooded martial vigor defined by Mowbray in the opening scene as the peculiar prerogative of the male sex. For her, the wager of battle to be fought between Mowbray and Bolingbroke is not a legal process to determine guilt and innocence, not a litmus test for the detection of treachery. It is an opportunity for the prosecution of private revenge.

Despite her masculine imagery of chivalry, revenge and violence, the duchess is prevented by her sex from acting in person to promote any of these desired ends. She can only ask men to act for her. Her femininity is negated twice over, first in her espousal of masculine feelings and values that repress the female, and second in the social prohibitions restraining her from taking any personal role in the activities she deems essential if her personal honor—which is defined entirely in terms of the honor of the men to whom she is related—is to be effectively defended. Her energies of principle and pride thus frustrated, they turn inward with a damaging impact upon her vital self-esteem—"Grief boundeth where it falls" (58)—and produce the emptiness and inconsolable sorrow that destroy her—"Desolate, desolate will I hence and die" (73).

Sadness and melancholy are the natural fate of women in this play. Our introduction to Queen Isabel is to a mood of unfocused sadness, a grief without cause, which yet proves to be a prophetic monitor of imminent calamity. Isabel naturally uses the imagery of pregnancy and birth, but displaces such possibilities from her own body, envisaging the birth of nothing but misfortune:

> *Queen Isabel.* Some unborn sorrow ripe in Fortune's womb
>   Is coming towards me.   (2.2.10–11)

Silent in her husband's presence, when left alone on Richard's departure to Ireland the queen is released to self-expression. But her only experience is that of self-abnegation, since she is possessed by a vague melancholy which seems both a disproportionate response to her lord's absence, and an ominous foreboding of his impending tragedy. When Green brings the news of Bolingbroke's return from banishment, that phantom pregnancy is delivered of its burden of sorrow.

> *Queen Isabel.* So, Green, thou art the midwife to my woe,
>   And Bolingbroke, my sorrow's dismal heir;
>   Now hath my soul brought forth her prodigy,
>   And I, a gasping, new-delivered mother,
>   Have woe to woe, sorrow to sorrow, joined.   (62–66)

Isabel's "inward soul" (11 and 28) seems to contain nothing of her own, only grief for the absence or future suffering of another. To describe this experience of unfocused sorrow awaiting a cause to which it may be attached, the queen uses the imagery of pregnancy and birth. Isabel means that her prophetic sadness joins with her real sorrow to give her a double "woe"; but also that as a "mother" whose symbolic confinement delivers her of a tragic destiny, she also suffers twice—from the pain of childbirth, and from the pain of discovering her "child" to be the "prodigy" of Bolingbroke's usurpation. Isabel's language specifically draws attention to the way in which women in this play are condemned to suffering by the patriarchism of the aristocratic dynasty. Their only function in this masculine world is that of bearing sons for their powerful husbands; so that even in the successful achievement of their biological function, their own lives are negated. The more illustrious and legendary the lives of their husbands and sons, the more completely are they themselves eclipsed from the significant structure of the family. Isabel's lot is particularly hard, since she will not bear Richard's children (the historical Isabel was a child of ten when these events occurred): her "dismal heir" (63) is the succession of Bolingbroke. Deprived by fate of what is seen as the only kind of power women can possess—the capacity to reproduce powerful men—Isabel's life seems unspeakably and inconsolably sad. In place of the child she will not bear, the Gardener plants in elegiac remembrance of her sorrow a "bank of rue":

   Gardener. Rue even for ruth here shortly shall be seen,
      In the remembrance of a weeping queen.   (3.4.106–7)

In the queen's last scene (5.1), where she takes leave of the deposed king, Isabel laments Richard's fall, and in doing so she acknowledges the blossom of her own life to be "withered":

   Queen Isabel. But soft, but see, or rather do not see
      My fair rose wither.   (7–8)

Again, her function is quite literally marginal: to stand by the roadside to observe the "woeful pageant" of the king's disgrace. Here however Isabel makes her one display of strength, manifesting that potentiality for resistance already seen in the Duchess of Gloucester:

> *Queen Isabel.* The lion dying thrusteth forth his paw
> And wounds the earth, if nothing else, with rage
> To be o'erpowe'red, and wilt thou, pupil-like,
> Take the correction mildly, kiss the rod . . . ?   (29–32)

But whatever reserves of strength and defiance the woman has, she cannot act for herself. She can only ask men to act for her. Richard's response to this encouragement is to declare that he is, in effect, already dead, and the queen already ("Good sometimes queen" [37]) a widow.

The other main female character in the play, the Duchess of York, offers what is in effect a contrasting success story, precisely because she accepts and embraces the subjected and marginal role of women. Her significance is that she is mother to Aumerle, the close companion and supporter of Richard who joins the Abbot of Westminster's conspiracy against the life of Henry. She is a mother, now past the age of childbearing. The prospect of losing her son would rob her of her very existence, reduce her to the shadowy unreality of the childless Isabel:

> *Duchess of York.* Is not my teeming date drunk up with time?
> And wilt thou pluck my fair son from mine age?
> And rob me of a happy mother's name?   (5.2.91–93)

In her appeal to her husband to save their son, the duchess brings out the contradictions of this patriarchal maternity. Her suffering in childbirth to deliver Aumerle predisposes her to a pity her husband cannot feel:

> *Duchess of York.*   Hadst thou groaned for him
> As I have done, thou would'st be more pitiful.   (102–3)

Although she does not question the patriarchal principle that a woman's only proper profession is that of bearing sons, the duchess does at least suggest that femininity may have its own peculiar experiences and values, in some ways quite separate from the world of masculine ideology. But this potential affirmation of femininity is soon eclipsed, since in order to save Aumerle, the duchess has to plead with men, and to argue on their terms. She tries to persuade York that Aumerle resembles only him, not her or any of her relatives:

> *Duchess of York.* He is as like thee as a man may be,
>   Not like to me, or any of my kin.   (108–9)

To save her son the duchess is not only prepared to humiliate herself—"For ever will I walk upon my knees" (5.3.92)—but even to sacrifice the personal traces of her maternal inheritance: only as the exclusive property of his father will Aumerle appear to be worth saving. Though she resists her husband, who is determined to incriminate his son, the duchess can do so only by appealing to a greater, symbolic father, who represents the paternalistic principle of divinity ("God the father") in mortal form, the king: "A god on earth thou art" (135).

The play's representation of its female characters shows quite clearly that in this male-dominated society women are consistently marginalized and subjected to a passive social role. They are the instruments and vehicles of masculine power, possessing no effective or positive social identity of their own. This severe limitation on the active presence of women, which is so unusual in Shakespeare's plays, seems to me an aspect of the play's historical vision. This is the unenviable lot of women in a feudal, patriarchal and chivalric society. They may be romanticized as mothers or idealized as lovers, but in themselves they are nothing—they derive their significance only from their relationships with husbands, brothers, sons. It is not a representation of the natural lot of women, or a depiction of women as they existed in Shakespeare's England, where the most powerful member of society was after all, a woman, Queen Elizabeth.

The condition of female self-abnegation provokes a consistent and comprehensive response of pity and compassion, like the Gardener's planting, in elegiac remembrance of Isabel's sorrow, of a bank of the herb rue, symbol of sadness and regret. And when Bushy in 2.2 attempts to comfort and console the queen's nameless grief, he unwittingly discloses the strange and insubstantial existence allowed to women by the feudal and patriarchal society. In an elaborate conceit, Bushy argues that grief and sorrow multiply themselves into numerous "shadows," so that when observed from an angle, like perspective paintings, they appear greater than their real substance. The queen's sadness at her lord's departure is thus exaggerated into a disproportionate anxiety. But how then is the sufferer supposed to distinguish shadow from substance, reality from illusion? If Isabel looks correctly at the real conditions of her life, she will see ". . . nought but shadows / Of what it is not" (23–24). Thus we see the woman's life de-realized by the very pity that is offered as her consolation.

The play reveals quite clearly that in this kind of patriarchal society, dominated by powerful men and their concerns, women have a purely marginal function. It cannot convincingly be argued that the play simply presents that condition as natural and unremarkable, since the women in the play are the objects of a powerful sense of pity. Of course it is easier to offer pity than to secure justice. It could be argued that Shakespeare's own ideology is as patriarchal as John of Gaunt's, since the play cannot imagine women as anything other than the instruments of men and the bearers and protectors of male children: the saddest thing that can be said of a woman is that she has no children. Feminist critics would argue that this kind of pity is a more dangerous enemy to the cause of female emancipation than open injustice. Though it appears to have the interests of women at heart, it still cannot conceive of women as anything other than the passive instruments of masculine oppression or compassion.

This is really the point where the debate begins. My own conviction is that the play can be read as demonstrative of a deep-seated structural injustice in the way this society positions women. If we read the play historically, we can see that it goes further than the utterance of mere compassion for the unfulfilled lives of its female characters. It reveals quite clearly that as long as women are positioned in society in the way they are here, there can be no realization or fulfilment of female existence. Whether a woman has children or is denied them, whether her husband is successful or a failure, the woman's own life remains empty and sterile. In 5.3 Bolingbroke, now Henry IV, reveals for the first time that he has a son: the young Prince Henry, who will not appear in this play, but whose personal and political development will be the principal subject of the remaining plays in this historical sequence. There is nowhere in this play, or in any of the others, a specific reference to Prince Henry having a mother, Bolingbroke a wife. The child is his father's son.

KENNETH MUIR

Richard II on Stage and Screen

Richard II was first performed by the Lord Chamberlain's men, almost certainly in 1595, with the company's leading actor, Burbage, in the title role. The abdication scene, although omitted from the early quartos, was probably not cut in performance. Six years later (February 7, 1601), a performance of the play was subsidized by the Essex conspirators; as it was no longer in the repertory, Shakespeare's fellows, whatever their political sympathies, were at first reluctant. Essex himself was not present at this performance; but he had been to see the play on previous occasions, and the deposition of a monarch for misgovernment and favoritism was thought to be good for morale on the eve of the rebellion. The actors were interrogated, but not punished. The Bolingbroke usurpation was a sensitive political matter. John Hayward's prose history of Henry IV, with a fulsome dedication to Essex, was suppressed, the author being imprisoned. The Queen herself complained to Lambarde of the way in which the story was used and of the popularity of the play: "I am Richard II. Know ye not that?"

On September 30, 1607, occurred the first amateur performance. It was played by sailors aboard the *Dragon*, lying off Sierre Leone. Captain Keeling believed that amateur dramatics kept the sailors "from idleness and unlawful games or sleep."

After the Restoration in 1660, when the theaters were once again open, there was an adaptation of the play by Nahum Tate. As this coincided with the exclusion crisis (1680)—an attempt to prevent the accession of James II—it was banned after playing for only two days in 1681.

Another adaptation, by Lewis Theobald (1719), ran for at least two seasons. Theobald eliminated Richard's misgovernment by cutting the first two acts, but he salvaged Bolingbroke's speech on banishment and Gaunt's praise of England by giving both speeches to other characters. All his departures from history and from Shakespeare were dramatically inept.

It was not until 1738 that the authentic play was performed at Covent Garden. It was said that the voice of Delane, who played the King, "was too loudly extended for the despondency of grief." Garrick, the greatest actor of the later eighteenth century, toyed with the idea of producing the play, but he was dissuaded.

In the nineteenth century Macready performed the play in the provinces (1812–1815). Edmund Kean appeared in an adaptation by Richard Wroughton, at first in London (1815) and later in New York (1826). Hazlitt, in spite of his admiration for Kean's acting, complained that he had made the part "a character of passions, whereas it is a character of pathos." Moreover, Hazlitt complained, "There are only one or two electrical shocks given in it," and Kean depended on such bits, since he lacked "equal truth or purity of style." Crabb Robinson, who thought *Richard II* "a heavy and uninteresting play," believed that Kean's acting in the first three acts "has in it nothing worth notice" but in the remainder of the play he "exhibits the weak, passionate and eloquent monarch to great advantage."

Meanwhile, James William Wallack had acted in the part in Philadelphia, Boston, and New York (1819). There were revivals by Charles Kean in Philadelphia (1831) and by Junius Brutus Booth, the Elder, in Baltimore (1831–32). Edwin Booth, brother of John Wilkes Booth, played it in New York (1875, 1878) and Chicago, where he was shot at by a madman (1879). In London, meanwhile, there were revivals by Macready (1850–51) and Charles Kean. Macready was applauded but the play failed to attract. Charles Kean's revival (1857) had the advantage of a return to Shakespeare's text—despite savage cuts even in his own part—and the more dubious advantage of historical and archaeological accuracy. Whatever the cause, the production (especially praised for the elaborate spectacle of the deposed Richard's entry into London in Bolingbroke's train) ran for a record eighty-five nights. J. W. Cole, in his *Life . . . of Charles Kean* (1859), said: "The most exceptious critics have admitted that in this arduous delineation there was no mannerism, no imitation of any style, no exaggeration, nothing artificial or laboured." As a result the veritable historical Richard was displayed "warmed and coloured by the imagination of the poet, and called into re-animated existence by the kindred genius of the interpreter." The actor resembled Richard's portrait in Westminster Abbey. Pater spoke of "the grace, the warming pathos, the sympathetic voice of the player . . . In the hands of Kean the play became like an exquisite performance on the violin."

The next important performance was that of Frank Benson at Stratford-upon-Avon (1896), which he repeated several times during the next seventeen years. It was not universally admired. Kate Terry was particularly scornful. She said that "Benson's presence is undignified, he is too slight, too weakly in figure and face and his voice is exasperating. It lacks tone and sonority and inflection." Yet one of Benson's performances, at Manchester, was made famous by C. E. Montague's review, published in the *Manchester Guardian* in 1899. He argued that Shakespeare "meant to draw in Richard not only a rake and muff on a throne and falling off it but, in the same person, an exquisite poet; to show with one hand how kingdoms are lost and with the other how the creative imagination goes about its work." On the one hand, Richard had the "attributes of a feckless wastrel," on the other hand, he had the attributes of "a consummate artist." In the last three acts Richard exercises "his gift of exquisite responsiveness to the appeal made to his artistic sensibility by whatever life throws for the moment in his way." The same actor was seen by W. B. Yeats at Stratford in 1901, and the contrast he drew between the "poetic" Richard and the commonplace Bolingbroke and Prince Hal was doubtless influenced by Benson's performance. As Walter Raleigh remarked: "It is difficult to condemn Richard without taking sides against poetry." Yet Benson, interrogated by James Agate, confessed that Montague's interpretation was not one he had intended. (It may be added that all Shakespeare's tragic heroes have great poetry to speak, without being suspected of artistic sensibility.)

William Poel produced the play for the Elizabethan Stage Society in 1899 in the lecture room of London University in Burlington Gardens. Richard was beautifully played by Harley Granville-Barker, then aged twenty-two. Four years later Sir Herbert Beerbohm Tree gave a splendid, but absurdly ornate, production at His Majesty's Theatre. Reviewers varied in their opinions of Tree's Richard, some finding him moving, others finding him merely theatrical. Bolingbroke was played by Oscar Asche, who afterward drew the crowds in the spectacular *Chu Chin Chow*. The Tree production was revived in 1905 and 1910. Bernard Shaw was justifiably scathing. Tree, he said, was giving "at immense trouble and expense, and with extraordinary executive cunning, a great deal that Shakespeare had not asked for, and denying him something much simpler that he did ask for, and set great store by." Shaw gave examples of Tree's interpolations—Richard's pet dog licking Bolingbroke's hand, the "great white horse and the look of hunted terror with which Richard turned his head, as the crowd hooted him," whereas Shakespeare had described Richard's saint-like patience on this occasion.

After the First World War, *Richard II* became a popular play. It was frequently revived at the Old Vic, with a series of famous actors in the title role—Ernest Milton (1921), George Hayes (1925), John Gielgud (1929), and Maurice Evans (1934). My own first experience of a production was that in which George Hayes played the King, with Ion Swinley as a magnificent John of Gaunt. I had been assured at school that Richard was a contemptible character, only "manly" in his death scene; and Hayes, without whitewashing the faults of the hero, gave a very different impression. Hayes repeated his success at Stratford-on-Avon and, when the theater there burned down, on tour in America. Arthur Colby Sprague, in *Shakespeare's Histories*, memorably describes a Boston performance in 1930. The theater was packed, and the performance was a triumph. H. T. Parker, writing in the *Boston Evening Transcript*, declared that

"Shakespeare's verse has not been spoken so variously and vividly upon a Boston stage. It was characterized not cadenced. It was born of the instant in the play—not remembered and recited."

John Gielgud's performance at the Old Vic was the first in which he made his reputation, and one which he refined at the same theater in 1929, and which reached its perfection a few years later in his own production at the Queen's Theatre. Michael Redgrave played Bolingbroke, Leon Quartermaine was Gaunt, Peggy Ashcroft, the Queen. Gielgud, perhaps under Granville-Barker's influence, had realized the centrality of the poetry and the importance of ritual, as he pointed out in his Preface, reprinted in *Stage Directions*:

> *Richard II* is a ceremonial play . . . It is not until after his return from Ireland . . . that [the King's] inner character begins to be developed in a series of exquisite cadenzas and variations . . . The actor of Richard may then be allowed, like the solo violin in a concerto, to take certain liberties with his cadenzas, developing these intricacies legitimately in an almost unlimited variety of pace and detail.

Gielgud in this preface was describing his own production, and it explains his success in the part.

Maurice Evans played Richard at the Old Vic in 1934 and in New York in 1937. His performance was immensely successful—in America more successful than Gielgud's. Between 1937 and 1946 he played the part some four hundred times. Although James Agate greatly preferred Gielgud's performance, Evans's appealed more to an American audience than the more "poetic" interpretation so brilliantly exemplified by Gielgud.

In 1951, in a staging of the second historical tetralogy at Stratford-on-Avon, Michael Redgrave played Richard II and Hotspur. As the theme of the tetralogy was the way in which the misrule of the legitimate Richard and the usurpation of Bolingbroke led happily to the role of the legitimate and heroic King Henry V, Richard was deliberately made less sympathetic than in recent productions. Redgrave spoke in an affected manner, and appeared as "a dainty feline homosexual." He confessed in *In My Mind's Eye* that he had laid some emphasis on Richard's pettiness and hysteria in the first half of the play—"too much emphasis in fact, in my anxiety that the audience should get the point." But Redgrave's playing was considerably altered later in the run: he modified the effeminacy and gave (according to Richard Findlater) a wonderful performance. I agreed: There was also an excellent Bolingbroke by a consistently reliable actor, Harry Andrews.

John Neville played Richard at the Old Vic in 1954, a performance which, Robert Speaight claimed "grew impressively, adding emotion to melody in the later scenes where the one had at first been sacrificed to the other." When Neville repeated the performance in New York, two well-known critics gave different verdicts. Walter Kerr said that "it is the cold, shrewd, sometimes bitter realities of political life that take on the most vivid coloring." But Brooks Atkinson said that Neville "grows in stature as the King loses authority—a supercilious but winning dandy in early scenes, a crushed, though bitter and perceptive ruin at the end."

John Gielgud directed Paul Scofield as Richard at the Lyric Theatre, Hammersmith (1955), and wished he had played the part himself. He wore, said J. C. Trewin, "a mask of celestial composure in which two half-closed eyes glitter with unscrutable menace." Joan Littlewood's production at Stratford-upon-Avon, which offered "a Richard so effeminate, cruel, and strange as to seem insane from the outset" sounds even less inviting. It can hardly have been either of these which a critic in *The Times* called "a recent and rather insipid rendering of the C. E. Montague interpretation of the King as an artist in self pity." This, said the critic, was "at bottom a sentimental compromise by which we are discreetly spared the embarrassment of taking Richard the martyr quite as seriously as he takes himself." These remarks cleared the way for an appreciation of a production at the Birmingham Repertory Theatre by Douglas Seale (June 1955) in which Jack May "achieved an interpretation of great interest and high dramatic quality. Gone is the capricious and effeminate wastrel. In his place is a pale and passionate young King with the claws of a lion." Played like this, it was "a superb drama from first to last, and the protagonist is admirably supported."

There were performances of the play in 1962 at Stratford, Connecticut (in which the Richard resembled a sort of gangster), and at Stratford, Ontario, in 1964, directed by Stuart Burge, in which Richard's homosexual tendencies were clearly shown and in which use was made of "every possible bit of Christ symbolism."

In 1964 *Richard II* was staged at Stratford-on-Avon as part of the history cycle. David Warner was more successful as the saintly Henry VI than as the less than saintly Richard. He was, one critic said, "too sympathetic, too nice." My own criticism was rather that Warner was completely lacking in regal dignity or any consciousness of the divine right of kings. As in 1951 the performance of *Richard II* in a sequence of history plays led to some loss of individuality. In the same year there was a production at the Phoenix Theatre, Leicester, which won high praise. In 1968 a critic of the Stratford, Connecticut, production spoke of its use of Christian images that were not supported by the text.

There was an impressive production of the play given by the Prospect Theatre Company at the Edinburgh Festival in August 1969. It was directed by Richard Cottrell; and a companion production of Marlowe's *Edward II*, directed by Toby Robertson, gave Ian McKellen the opportunity of distinguishing the characters of the royal victims. Critics were almost unanimous in their praise of McKellen's performances, and one contrasted his full-blooded and risk-taking style with the more cautious methods then employed at the Stratford Memorial Theatre. Irving Wardle, the critic of *The Times*, brilliantly analyzing McKellen's success, suggested that the actor makes us feel that he has moved into "temperamental areas" that were new to him, and the audience "are able to share this ecstatic sense of self-discovery. By his power of imagination he succeeded in portraying the two kings." His Richard, Mr. Wardle continued, is "a study in ceremony which he takes in deadly sacramental earnest, making his first entry in the midst of a priest-like procession, palms upraised and face chastely impassive, consciously holding himself as a sacred vessel."

This first appearance contrasts with his behavior in the following scene, where he appears as "a profane dandy lounging among his parasites and dispensing cold little smiles and arrogant jokes through clenched teeth." In the abdication scene, some critics felt that McKellen went over the top with his "agonized yelps of animal pain." But in the second half of the play he substituted "sardonic bite and hysterical anger" for self-pity. In the dungeon the music "prompts him to a deranged ballet of flailing arms and thickened choking delivery." McKellen's performance showed how it was possible to reconcile three or four different conceptions of the part, and of the play as a whole. The production was revived at the Mermaid Theatre, and in 1970 at the Piccadilly.

At Stratford-on-Avon in 1971 Richard Pasco played the King. Richard David in his review in *Shakespeare Survey* 25 of the season's productions pointed to the difficulty of presenting the play when no one believes in the divine right of kings, and he thought that "the real authority, and the power to inspire devotion in others, which Shakespeare's Richard can show, even without the benefit of divinity, was whittled away." Nevertheless the confrontations between Richard and Bolingbroke "were strong, above all in the deposition scene."

If the production in which McKellen starred was a notable example of actor's theater—however much it owed to the director—the production by John Barton at Stratford-on-Avon in 1973 was clearly one in which the actors were very much subordinated to the director's decisions. Anne Barton, in the program note she wrote for the production, referred to Kantorowicz's *The King's Two Bodies*—one body, "flawless, abstract and immortal," the other "fallible, individual and subject to death and time." All Shakespeare's monarchs are flawed, but because one of their two bodies was unflawed, it was sinful to depose them. This idea can throw light on all Shakespeare's English Histories, but the use made of it in this production reduces the individuality of the characters. By making Richard Pasco and Ian Richardson alternate in the roles of Richard and Bolingbroke—the parts are allocated by the figure of Shakespeare at the beginning of the play—it is implied that their characters are similar and that they act as they do because of the positions in which they are placed. I feel that their differences are much more important than their resemblances. Barton thought it necessary to build up Bolingbroke's character by additions from *Henry IV*. All the characters were made as symbolic as possible. The Duchess of Gloucester was played as a ghost; Gaunt spoke his praise of England directly to the audience; the speech of the Welsh Captain (2.4) was spoken by a chorus of eight actors; Northumberland was stylized as a puppet master. Sometimes this method worked very well. By turning the gardeners into monks Barton cleverly evaded the inappropriateness of verse for mere rustics.

As Altick demonstrated in an article reprinted in this volume, there is a complex web of imagery and symbolism in the play, which a director should be aware of. But Barton, I think, went too far in underlining the imagery and symbolism. Sometimes, as when Richard the Sun King descends like Phaethon, the staging brought out both the sun imagery and the fall; and at the end of the play when the figure between the past and present Kings is revealed as Death, this is an apt visualization of a recurring image. But often the illustration of imagery was tasteless and absurd. A pot of earth at the front of the stage was supposed to remind us of the earth imagery; a visible snowman illustrated Richard's desire to be "a mockery King of snow"; and the Groom gave Richard a toy horse in the prison scene because of his inquiries about Barbary. The introduction of Bolingbroke disguised as the Groom had a startling but puzzling effect which quite destroyed the pathos of the original.

The production as a whole was full of ingenious touches and it was fascinating to watch. But what we were watching was not a powerful drama of fully realized characters in conflict, but rather Barton's variations on the same theme, with the characters as comparatively unimportant as they are in some recent writings on Shakespeare's plays.

In 1986 there was another production of the play at Stratford. Barry Kyle provided lavish scenic effects, and Jeremy

Irons was a poetic Richard, made excessively sympathetic by the depiction of his opponents as gangsters.

There seems to have been a certain interaction between criticism and performance. If Benson's performance was influenced by Walter Pater's criticism—the first real appreciation of the play—Benson inspired the criticism by C. E. Montague and Yeats, and Yeats influenced Masefield. These writers in turn influence the performances of Hayes and Gielgud, and Gielgud acknowledged the influence of Harley Granville-Barker, who had himself played the part before Gielgud was born. Later critics have reacted against such interpretations. Nicholas Brooke in *Shakespeare's Early Tragedies* declared that "the conception of Richard as a wilting poet" is belied by his deeds in the first act. Lois Potter, in *Shakespeare Survey* 27, remarked that Shakespeare also gives us intriguing glimpses of the other Richard: "sharp-tongued, self-mocking and quite unresigned." The former of these remarks was made after Jack May's performance, the second after McKellen's. We have seen that Barton's production owed something to Kantorowicz's ideas; and when Sam Schoenbaum argued that the play was concerned with the realities of power and that it enables us to speak of Shakespeare the politic realist, he may well have been influenced by recent productions as well as by his knowledge of the world of the sixteenth century.

Richard II has been well represented on film and television. Between 1950 and 1978 there have been one black-and-white film, featuring Maurice Evans (1954), and four television versions. It formed the first two parts of *An Age of Kings* (1960), screened by the BBC, Richard played by David Williams, Bolingbroke by Tom Fleming. Ten years later the BBC screened Richard Cottrell's production with Ian McKellen's great performance. In 1978 it formed part of the BBC complete screening of Shakespeare, with Derek Jacobi a fine Richard and John Gielgud a splendid Gaunt, but the production itself rather disappointing.

Bibliographic Note: In the above account I have concentrated on those performances I have had the chance of seeing in sixty years of playgoing; but for these, as well as for those I have not seen, I have consulted reviews. The variorum edition of the play (ed. M. W. Black, 1956) contains a useful list of productions. A chapter in *Shakespeare's Histories* by Arthur Colby Sprague (1964) gives the best account of productions of the play up till then. Stanley Wells gives a full, favorable account of Barton's production in *Royal Shakespeare* (1976); there are also interesting accounts of this production by Peter Thompson, in *Shakespeare Survey* 27 (1974) and by Robert Smallwood in *Shakespeare: An Illustrated Stage History*, eds. Jonathan Bate and Russell Jackson (1996). The BBC television production of 1978 is reviewed by Jack Jorgens in *Shakespeare Quarterly* 30 (1979), and is discussed by Susan Willis, in *The BBC Shakespeare Plays* (1991).

There are useful reviews each year in *Shakespeare Survey* and *Shakespeare Quarterly*, and the former was particularly useful for its survey of film and television performances (1986).

Suggested References

The number of possible references is vast and grows alarmingly. (The *Shakespeare Quarterly* devotes one issue each year to a list of the previous year's work, and *Shakespeare Survey*—an annual publication—includes a substantial review of biographical, critical, and textual studies, as well as a survey of performances.) The vast bibliography is best approached through James Harner, *The World Shakespeare Bibliography on CD-Rom: 1900–Present*. The first release, in 1996, included more than 12,000 annotated items from 1990–93, plus references to several thousand book reviews, productions, films, and audio recordings. The plan is to update the publication annually, moving forward one year and backward three years. Thus, the second issue (1997), with 24,700 entries, and another 35,000 or so references to reviews, newspaper pieces, and so on, covered 1987–94.

Though no works are indispensable, those listed below have been found especially helpful. The arrangement is as follows:

1. Shakespeare's Times
2. Shakespeare's Life
3. Shakespeare's Theater
4. Shakespeare on Stage and Screen
5. Miscellaneous Reference Works
6. Shakespeare's Plays: General Studies
7. The Comedies
8. The Romances
9. The Tragedies
10. The Histories
11. *Richard II*

The titles in the first five sections are accompanied by brief explanatory annotations.

1. Shakespeare's Times

Andrews, John F., ed. *William Shakespeare: His World, His Work, His Influence*, 3 vols. (1985). Sixty articles, dealing not only with such subjects as "The State," "The Church," "Law," "Science, Magic, and Folklore," but also with the plays and poems themselves and Shakespeare's influence (e.g., translations, films, reputation)

Byrne, Muriel St. Clare. *Elizabethan Life in Town and Country* (8th ed., 1970). Chapters on manners, beliefs, education, etc., with illustrations.

Dollimore, John, and Alan Sinfield, eds. *Political Shakespeare: New Essays in Cultural Materialism* (1985). Essays on such topics as the subordination of women and colonialism, presented in connection with some of Shakespeare's plays.

Greenblatt, Stephen. *Representing the English Renaissance* (1988). New Historicist essays, especially on connections between political and aesthetic matters, statecraft and stagecraft.

Joseph, B. L. *Shakespeare's Eden: the Commonwealth of England 1558–1629* (1971). An account of the social, political, economic, and cultural life of England.

Kernan, Alvin. *Shakespeare, the King's Playwright: Theater in the Stuart Court 1603–1613* (1995). The social setting and the politics of the court of James I, in relation to *Hamlet*, *Measure for Measure*, *Macbeth*, *King Lear*, *Antony and Cleopatra*, *Coriolanus*, and *The Tempest*.

Montrose, Louis. *The Purpose of Playing: Shakespeare and the Cultural Politics of the Elizabethan Theatre* (1996). A poststructuralist view, discussing the professional theater "within the ideological and material frameworks of Elizabethan culture and society," with an extended analysis of *A Midsummer Night's Dream*.

Mullaney, Steven. *The Place of the Stage: License, Play, and Power in Renaissance England* (1988). New Historicist analysis, arguing that popular drama became a cultural institution "only by . . . taking up a place on the margins of society."

Schoenbaum, S. *Shakespeare: The Globe and the World*

(1979). A readable, abundantly illustrated introductory book on the world of the Elizabethans.

Shakespeare's England, 2 vols. (1916). A large collection of scholarly essays on a wide variety of topics, e.g., astrology, costume, gardening, horsemanship, with special attention to Shakespeare's references to these topics.

2. Shakespeare's Life

Andrews, John F., ed. *William Shakespeare: His World, His Work, His Influence,* 3 vols. (1985). See the description above.

Bentley, Gerald E. *Shakespeare: A Biographical Handbook* (1961). The facts about Shakespeare, with virtually no conjecture intermingled.

Chambers, E. K. *William Shakespeare: A Study of Facts and Problems,* 2 vols. (1930). The fullest collection of data.

Fraser, Russell. *Young Shakespeare* (1988). A highly readable account that simultaneously considers Shakespeare's life and Shakespeare's art.

———. *Shakespeare: The Later Years* (1992).

Schoenbaum, S. *Shakespeare's Lives* (1970). A review of the evidence and an examination of many biographies, including those of Baconians and other heretics.

———. *William Shakespeare: A Compact Documentary Life* (1977). An abbreviated version, in a smaller format, of the next title. The compact version reproduces some fifty documents in reduced form. A readable presentation of all that the documents tell us about Shakespeare.

———. *William Shakespeare: A Documentary Life* (1975). A large-format book setting forth the biography with facsimiles of more than two hundred documents, and with transcriptions and commentaries.

3. Shakespeare's Theater

Astington, John H., ed. *The Development of Shakespeare's Theater* (1992). Eight specialized essays on theatrical companies, playing spaces, and performance.

Beckerman, Bernard. *Shakespeare at the Globe, 1599–1609* (1962). On the playhouse and on Elizabethan dramaturgy, acting, and staging.

Bentley, Gerald E. *The Profession of Dramatist in Shakespeare's Time* (1971). An account of the dramatist's status in the Elizabethan period.

———. *The Profession of Player in Shakespeare's Time, 1590–1642* (1984). An account of the status of members of London companies (sharers, hired men, apprentices, managers) and a discussion of conditions when they toured.

Berry, Herbert. *Shakespeare's Playhouses* (1987). Usefully emphasizes how little we know about the construction of Elizabethan theaters.

Brown, John Russell. *Shakespeare's Plays in Performance* (1966). A speculative and practical analysis relevant to all of the plays, but with emphasis on *The Merchant of Venice*, *Richard II*, *Hamlet*, *Romeo and Juliet*, and *Twelfth Night*.

———. *William Shakespeare: Writing for Performance* (1996). A discussion aimed at helping readers to develop theatrically conscious habits of reading.

Chambers, E. K. *The Elizabethan Stage*, 4 vols. (1945). A major reference work on theaters, theatrical companies, and staging at court.

Cook, Ann Jennalie. *The Privileged Playgoers of Shakespeare's London, 1576–1642* (1981). Sees Shakespeare's audience as wealthier, more middle-class, and more intellectual than Harbage (below) does.

Dessen, Alan C. *Elizabethan Drama and the Viewer's Eye* (1977). On how certain scenes may have looked to spectators in an Elizabethan theater.

Gurr, Andrew. *Playgoing in Shakespeare's London* (1987). Something of a middle ground between Cook (above) and Harbage (below).

———. *The Shakespearean Stage, 1579–1642* (2nd ed., 1980). On the acting companies, the actors, the playhouses, the stages, and the audiences.

Harbage, Alfred. *Shakespeare's Audience* (1941). A study of the size and nature of the theatrical public, emphasizing the representativeness of its working class and middle-class audience.

Hodges, C. Walter. *The Globe Restored* (1968). A conjectural restoration, with lucid drawings.

Hosley, Richard. "The Playhouses," in *The Revels History of Drama in English*, vol. 3, general editors Clifford Leech and T. W. Craik (1975). An essay of a hundred pages on the physical aspects of the playhouses.

Howard, Jane E. "Crossdressing, the Theatre, and Gender Struggle in Early Modern England," *Shakespeare Quarterly* 39 (1988): 418–40. Judicious comments on the effects of boys playing female roles.

Orrell, John. *The Human Stage: English Theatre Design, 1567–1640* (1988). Argues that the public, private, and court playhouses are less indebted to popular structures (e.g., innyards and bear-baiting pits) than to banqueting halls and to Renaissance conceptions of Roman amphitheaters.

Slater, Ann Pasternak. *Shakespeare the Director* (1982). An analysis of theatrical effects (e.g., kissing, kneeling) in stage directions and dialogue.

Styan, J. L. *Shakespeare's Stagecraft* (1967). An introduction to Shakespeare's visual and aural stagecraft, with chapters on such topics as acting conventions, stage groupings, and speech.

Thompson, Peter. *Shakespeare's Professional Career* (1992). An examination of patronage and related theatrical conditions.

———. *Shakespeare's Theatre* (1983). A discussion of how plays were staged in Shakespeare's time.

4. Shakespeare on Stage and Screen

Bate, Jonathan, and Russell Jackson, eds. *Shakespeare: An Illustrated Stage History* (1996). Highly readable essays on stage productions from the Renaissance to the present.

Berry, Ralph. *Changing Styles in Shakespeare* (1981). Discusses productions of six plays (*Coriolanus*, *Hamlet*, *Henry V*, *Measure for Measure*, *The Tempest*, and *Twelfth Night*) on the English stage, chiefly 1950–1980.

————. *On Directing Shakespeare: Interviews with Contemporary Directors* (1989). An enlarged edition of a book first published in 1977, this version includes the seven interviews from the early 1970s and adds five interviews conducted in 1988.

Brockbank, Philip, ed. *Players of Shakespeare: Essays in Shakespearean Performance* (1985). Comments by twelve actors, reporting their experiences with roles. See also the entry for Russell Jackson (below).

Bulman, J. C., and H. R. Coursen, eds. *Shakespeare on Television* (1988). An anthology of general and theoretical essays, essays on individual productions, and shorter reviews, with a bibliography and a videography listing cassettes that may be rented.

Coursen, H. P. *Watching Shakespeare on Television* (1993). Analyses not only of TV versions but also of films and videotapes of stage presentations that are shown on television.

Davies, Anthony, and Stanley Wells, eds. *Shakespeare and the Moving Image: The Plays on Film and Television* (1994). General essays (e.g., on the comedies) as well as essays devoted entirely to *Hamlet*, *King Lear*, and *Macbeth*.

Dawson, Anthony B. *Watching Shakespeare: A Playgoer's Guide* (1988). About half of the plays are discussed, chiefly in terms of decisions that actors and directors make in putting the works onto the stage.

Dessen, Alan. *Elizabethan Stage Conventions and Modern Interpretations* (1984). On interpreting conventions such as the representation of light and darkness and stage violence (duels, battles).

Donaldson, Peter. *Shakespearean Films/Shakespearean Directors* (1990). Postmodernist analyses, drawing on Freudianism, Feminism, Deconstruction, and Queer Theory.

Jackson, Russell, and Robert Smallwood, eds. *Players of Shakespeare 2: Further Essays in Shakespearean Performance by Players with the Royal Shakespeare Company* (1988). Fourteen actors discuss their roles in productions between 1982 and 1987.

————. *Players of Shakespeare 3: Further Essays in Shake-

spearean Performance by Players with the Royal Shakespeare Company (1993). Comments by thirteen performers.

Jorgens, Jack. *Shakespeare on Film* (1977). Fairly detailed studies of eighteen films, preceded by an introductory chapter addressing such issues as music, and whether to "open" the play by including scenes of landscape.

Kennedy, Dennis. *Looking at Shakespeare: A Visual History of Twentieth-Century Performance* (1993). Lucid descriptions (with 170 photographs) of European, British, and American performances.

Leiter, Samuel L. *Shakespeare Around the Globe: A Guide to Notable Postwar Revivals* (1986). For each play there are about two pages of introductory comments, then discussions (about five hundred words per production) of ten or so productions, and finally bibliographic references.

McMurty, Jo. *Shakespeare Films in the Classroom* (1994). Useful evaluations of the chief films most likely to be shown in undergraduate courses.

Rothwell, Kenneth, and Annabelle Henkin Melzer. *Shakespeare on Screen: An International Filmography and Videography* (1990). A reference guide to several hundred films and videos produced between 1899 and 1989, including spinoffs such as musicals and dance versions.

Sprague, Arthur Colby. *Shakespeare and the Actors* (1944). Detailed discussions of stage business (gestures, etc.) over the years.

Willis, Susan. *The BBC Shakespeare Plays: Making the Televised Canon* (1991). A history of the series, with interviews and production diaries for some plays.

5. Miscellaneous Reference Works

Abbott, E. A. *A Shakespearean Grammar* (new edition, 1877). An examination of differences between Elizabethan and modern grammar.

Allen, Michael J. B., and Kenneth Muir, eds. *Shakespeare's Plays in Quarto* (1981). One volume containing facsimiles of the plays issued in small format before they were collected in the First Folio of 1623.

Bevington, David. *Shakespeare* (1978). A short guide to hundreds of important writings on the subject.

Blake, Norman. *Shakespeare's Language: An Introduction* (1983). On vocabulary, parts of speech, and word order.

Bullough, Geoffrey. *Narrative and Dramatic Sources of Shakespeare*, 8 vols. (1957–75). A collection of many of the books Shakespeare drew on, with judicious comments.

Campbell, Oscar James, and Edward G. Quinn, eds. *The Reader's Encyclopedia of Shakespeare* (1966). Old, but still the most useful single reference work on Shakespeare.

Cercignani, Fausto. *Shakespeare's Works and Elizabethan Pronunciation* (1981). Considered the best work on the topic, but remains controversial.

Dent, R. W. *Shakespeare's Proverbial Language: An Index* (1981). An index of proverbs, with an introduction concerning a form Shakespeare frequently drew on.

Greg, W. W. *The Shakespeare First Folio* (1955). A detailed yet readable history of the first collection (1623) of Shakespeare's plays.

Harner, James. *The World Shakespeare Bibliography*. See headnote to Suggested References.

Hosley, Richard. *Shakespeare's Holinshed* (1968). Valuable presentation of one of Shakespeare's major sources.

Kökeritz, Helge. *Shakespeare's Names* (1959). A guide to pronouncing some 1,800 names appearing in Shakespeare.

———. *Shakespeare's Pronunciation* (1953). Contains much information about puns and rhymes, but see Cercignani (above).

Muir, Kenneth. *The Sources of Shakespeare's Plays* (1978). An account of Shakespeare's use of his reading. It covers all the plays, in chronological order.

Miriam Joseph, Sister. *Shakespeare's Use of the Arts of Language* (1947). A study of Shakespeare's use of rhetorical devices, reprinted in part as *Rhetoric in Shakespeare's Time* (1962).

The Norton Facsimile: The First Folio of Shakespeare's Plays (1968). A handsome and accurate facsimile of the first collection (1623) of Shakespeare's plays, with a valuable introduction by Charlton Hinman.

Onions, C. T. *A Shakespeare Glossary*, rev. and enlarged by

R. D. Eagleson (1986). Definitions of words (or senses of words) now obsolete.

Partridge, Eric. *Shakespeare's Bawdy*, rev. ed. (1955). Relatively brief dictionary of bawdy words; useful, but see Williams, below.

Shakespeare Quarterly. See headnote to Suggested References.

Shakespeare Survey. See headnote to Suggested References.

Spevack, Marvin. *The Harvard Concordance to Shakespeare* (1973). An index to Shakespeare's words.

Vickers, Brian. *Appropriating Shakespeare: Contemporary Critical Quarrels* (1993). A survey—chiefly hostile—of recent schools of criticism.

Wells, Stanley, ed. *Shakespeare: A Bibliographical Guide* (new edition, 1990). Nineteen chapters (some devoted to single plays, others devoted to groups of related plays) on recent scholarship on the life and all of the works.

Williams, Gordon. *A Dictionary of Sexual Language and Imagery in Shakespearean and Stuart Literature*, 3 vols. (1994). Extended discussions of words and passages; much fuller than Partridge, cited above.

6. Shakespeare's Plays: General Studies

Bamber, Linda. *Comic Women, Tragic Men: A Study of Gender and Genre in Shakespeare* (1982).

Barnet, Sylvan. *A Short Guide to Shakespeare* (1974).

Callaghan, Dympna, Lorraine Helms, and Jyotsna Singh. *The Weyward Sisters: Shakespeare and Feminist Politics* (1994).

Clemen, Wolfgang H. *The Development of Shakespeare's Imagery* (1951).

Cook, Ann Jennalie. *Making a Match: Courtship in Shakespeare and His Society* (1991).

Dollimore, Jonathan, and Alan Sinfield. *Political Shakespeare: New Essays in Cultural Materialism* (1985).

Dusinberre, Juliet. *Shakespeare and the Nature of Women* (1975).

Granville-Barker, Harley. *Prefaces to Shakespeare*, 2 vols. (1946–47; volume 1 contains essays on *Hamlet*, *King*

Lear, Merchant of Venice, Antony and Cleopatra, and *Cymbeline*; volume 2 contains essays on *Othello, Coriolanus, Julius Caesar, Romeo and Juliet, Love's Labor's Lost).*

————. *More Prefaces to Shakespeare* (1974; essays on *Twelfth Night, A Midsummer Night's Dream, The Winter's Tale, Macbeth*).

Harbage, Alfred. *William Shakespeare: A Reader's Guide* (1963).

Howard, Jean E. *Shakespeare's Art of Orchestration: Stage Technique and Audience Response* (1984).

Jones, Emrys. *Scenic Form in Shakespeare* (1971).

Lenz, Carolyn Ruth Swift, Gayle Greene, and Carol Thomas Neely, eds. *The Woman's Part: Feminist Criticism of Shakespeare* (1980).

Novy, Marianne. *Love's Argument: Gender Relations in Shakespeare* (1984).

Rose, Mark. *Shakespearean Design* (1972).

Scragg, Leah. *Discovering Shakespeare's Meaning* (1994).

————. *Shakespeare's "Mouldy Tales": Recurrent Plot Motifs in Shakespearean Drama* (1992).

Traub, Valerie. *Desire and Anxiety: Circulations of Sexuality in Shakespearean Drama* (1992).

Traversi, D. A. *An Approach to Shakespeare,* 2 vols. (3rd rev. ed, 1968–69).

Vickers, Brian. *The Artistry of Shakespeare's Prose* (1968).

Wells, Stanley. *Shakespeare: A Dramatic Life* (1994).

Wright, George T. *Shakespeare's Metrical Art* (1988).

7. The Comedies

Barber, C. L. *Shakespeare's Festive Comedy* (1959; discusses *Love's Labor's Lost, A Midsummer Night's Dream, The Merchant of Venice, As You Like It, Twelfth Night*).

Barton, Anne. *The Names of Comedy* (1990).

Berry, Ralph. *Shakespeare's Comedy: Explorations in Form* (1972).

Bradbury, Malcolm, and David Palmer, eds. *Shakespearean Comedy* (1972).

Bryant, J. A., Jr. *Shakespeare and the Uses of Comedy* (1986).

Carroll, William. *The Metamorphoses of Shakespearean Comedy* (1985).

Champion, Larry S. *The Evolution of Shakespeare's Comedy* (1970).

Evans, Bertrand. *Shakespeare's Comedies* (1960).

Frye, Northrop. *Shakespearean Comedy and Romance* (1965).

Leggatt, Alexander. *Shakespeare's Comedy of Love* (1974).

Miola, Robert S. *Shakespeare and Classical Comedy: The Influence of Plautus and Terence* (1994).

Nevo, Ruth. *Comic Transformations in Shakespeare* (1980).

Ornstein, Robert. *Shakespeare's Comedies: From Roman Farce to Romantic Mystery* (1986).

Richman, David. *Laughter, Pain, and Wonder: Shakespeare's Comedies and the Audience in the Theater* (1990).

Salingar, Leo. *Shakespeare and the Traditions of Comedy* (1974).

Slights, Camille Wells. *Shakespeare's Comic Commonwealths* (1993).

Waller, Gary, ed. *Shakespeare's Comedies* (1991).

Westlund, Joseph. *Shakespeare's Reparative Comedies: A Psychoanalytic View of the Middle Plays* (1984).

Williamson, Marilyn. *The Patriarchy of Shakespeare's Comedies* (1986).

8. The Romances (*Pericles, Cymbeline, The Winter's Tale, The Tempest, The Two Noble Kinsmen*)

Adams, Robert M. *Shakespeare: The Four Romances* (1989).

Felperin, Howard. *Shakespearean Romance* (1972).

Frye, Northrop. *A Natural Perspective: The Development of Shakespearean Comedy and Romance* (1965).

Mowat, Barbara. *The Dramaturgy of Shakespeare's Romances* (1976).

Warren, Roger. *Staging Shakespeare's Late Plays* (1990).

Young, David. *The Heart's Forest: A Study of Shakespeare's Pastoral Plays* (1972).

9. The Tragedies

Bradley, A. C. *Shakespearean Tragedy* (1904).

Brooke, Nicholas. *Shakespeare's Early Tragedies* (1968).

Champion, Larry. *Shakespeare's Tragic Perspective* (1976).

Drakakis, John, ed. *Shakespearean Tragedy* (1992).

Evans, Bertrand. *Shakespeare's Tragic Practice* (1979).

Everett, Barbara. *Young Hamlet: Essays on Shakespeare's Tragedies* (1989).

Foakes, R. A. *Hamlet versus Lear: Cultural Politics and Shakespeare's Art* (1993).

Frye, Northrop. *Fools of Time: Studies in Shakespearean Tragedy* (1967).

Harbage, Alfred, ed. *Shakespeare: The Tragedies* (1964).

Mack, Maynard. *Everybody's Shakespeare: Reflections Chiefly on the Tragedies* (1993).

McAlindon, T. *Shakespeare's Tragic Cosmos* (1991).

Miola, Robert S. *Shakespeare and Classical Tragedy: The Influence of Seneca* (1992).

———. *Shakespeare's Rome* (1983).

Nevo, Ruth. *Tragic Form in Shakespeare* (1972).

Rackin, Phyllis. *Shakespeare's Tragedies* (1978).

Rose, Mark, ed. *Shakespeare's Early Tragedies: A Collection of Critical Essays* (1995).

Rosen, William. *Shakespeare and the Craft of Tragedy* (1960).

Snyder, Susan. *The Comic Matrix of Shakespeare's Tragedies* (1979).

Wofford, Susanne. *Shakespeare's Late Tragedies: A Collection of Critical Essays* (1996).

Young, David. *The Action to the Word: Structure and Style in Shakespearean Tragedy* (1990).

———. *Shakespeare's Middle Tragedies: A Collection of Critical Essays* (1993).

10. The Histories

Blanpied, John W. *Time and the Artist in Shakespeare's English Histories* (1983).

Campbell, Lily B. *Shakespeare's "Histories": Mirrors of Elizabethan Policy* (1947).

Champion, Larry S. *Perspective in Shakespeare's English Histories* (1980).

Hodgdon, Barbara. *The End Crowns All: Closure and Contradiction in Shakespeare's History* (1991).

Holderness, Graham. *Shakespeare Recycled: The Making of Historical Drama* (1992).

———, ed. *Shakespeare's History Plays: "Richard II" to "Henry V"* (1992).

Leggatt, Alexander. *Shakespeare's Political Drama: The History Plays and the Roman Plays* (1988).

Ornstein, Robert. *A Kingdom for a Stage: The Achievement of Shakespeare's History Plays* (1972).

Rackin, Phyllis. *Stages of History: Shakespeare's English Chronicles* (1990).

Saccio, Peter. *Shakespeare's English Kings: History, Chronicle, and Drama* (1977).

Tillyard, E. M. W. *Shakespeare's History Plays* (1944).

Velz, John W., ed. *Shakespeare's English Histories: A Quest for Form and Genre* (1996).

11. *Richard II*

For material concerning the play on the stage, see especially the references cited on page 242 and in Section 4 of this list of Suggested References. For the play in the context of Shakespeare's other history plays, see Section 10. The volumes by Harold Bloom and Jeanne T. Newlin, listed below, are convenient collections of essays on the play.

Berger, Harry. *Imaginary Audition: Shakespeare on Stage and Page* (1989).

Bergeron, David. "*Richard II* and Carnival Politics." *Shakespeare Quarterly* 42 (1991): 33–44.

Bloom, Harold, ed. *William Shakespeare's "Richard II"* (1988).

Hamilton, Donna. "The State of Law in *Richard II.*" *Shakespeare Quarterly* 34 (1983): 5–17.

Holderness, Graham. *"Richard II"* (1989).

Moore, Jeanie Grant. "Queen of Sorrow, King of Grief: Reflections and Perspectives in *Richard II*." In *Another Country: Feminist Perspectives on Renaissance Drama*. Ed. Dorothea Kehler and Susan Baker (1991), pp. 19–35.

Newlin, Jeanne T., ed. *"Richard II": Critical Essays* (1984).

Roberts, Josephine A. *"Richard II": An Annotated Bibliography* (1988).